Economies of the World

EDITED BY

NITA WATTS

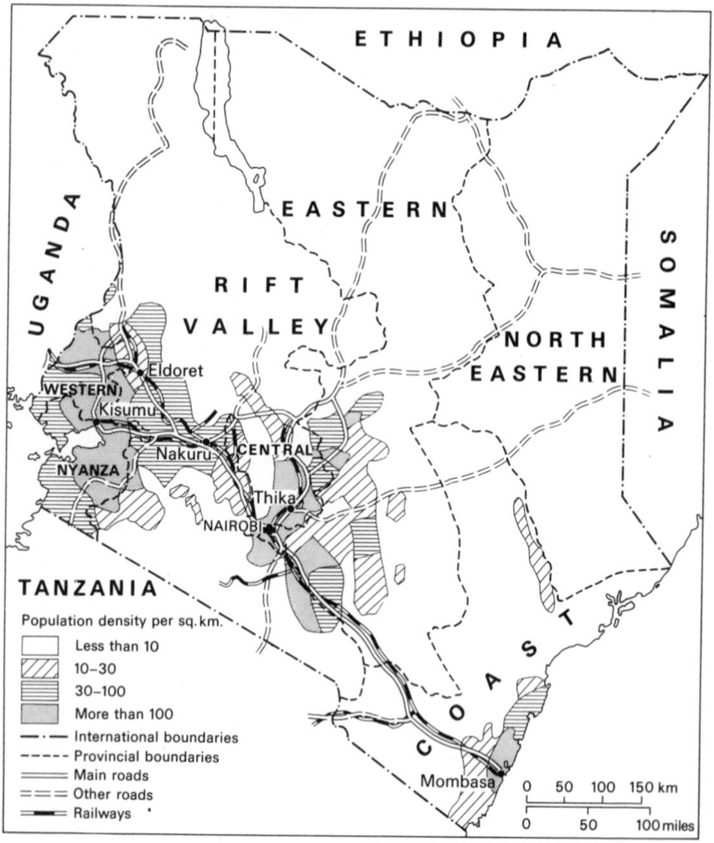

ETHIOPIA
UGANDA
EASTERN
RIFT VALLEY
NORTH EASTERN
SOMALIA
Eldoret
WESTERN
Kisumu
Nakuru
CENTRAL
NYANZA
Thika
NAIROBI
TANZANIA
COAST
Mombasa
Population density per sq.km.
Less than 10
10–30
30–100
More than 100
International boundaries
Provincial boundaries
Main roads
Other roads
Railways
0 50 100 150 km
0 50 100 miles

The Economy of Kenya

THE KENYATTA ERA

BY

ARTHUR HAZLEWOOD

OXFORD UNIVERSITY PRESS

1979

Oxford University Press, Walton Street, Oxford OX2 6DP

OXFORD LONDON GLASGOW
NEW YORK TORONTO MELBOURNE WELLINGTON
KUALA LUMPUR SINGAPORE JAKARTA HONG KONG TOKYO
DELHI BOMBAY CALCUTTA MADRAS KARACHI
NAIROBI DAR ES SALAAM CAPE TOWN

Published in the United States
by Oxford University Press, New York

British Library Cataloguing in Publication Data
Hazlewood, Arthur Dennis
The economy of Kenya. – (Economies of the world).
1. Kenya – Economic conditions
I. Title II. Series
330.9'676'204 HC517.K4 79–41098
ISBN 0–19–877101–0
ISBN 0–19–877102–9 Pbk

Set by Hope Services, Abingdon
and printed in Great Britain
at The University Press, Oxford
by Eric Buckley
Printer to the University

CONTENTS

LIST OF TABLES

INTRODUCTION

The first fifteen years of independent Kenya, like the years leading to Independence, were dominated in the public eye by the towering personality of Jomo Kenyatta. 'The Kenyatta Era', which came to an end in August, 1978, while this book was still unfinished, defines the period with which the book is primarily concerned. But it does more than that. It points to the importance of the President's influence on the 'pragmatic blend of laissez faire capitalism and African socialism which has characterized Kenyan economic policy'.[1]

The encouragement of the acquisitive spirit during the Kenyatta Era had its negative side. Jomo Kenyatta, the Founding Father of the Nation, 'will always be remembered . . . for his great contribution in liberating the nation from the colonial yoke'. But it is now being said that 'when Kenya became independent it acquired new problems – tribalism, nepotism, greed, bribery and corruption'. Opportunities were offered to, and eagerly seized by 'a few individuals who . . . [were] concerned only with accumulating as much wealth as possible'.[2] However, this view of the matter greatly exaggerates the novelty of the 'problems' and their ephemerality. Was there no 'tribalism' before independence? In reality, Jomo Kenyatta was not the father but a skilful tamer of the tiger of tribalism. It survived, and surely still survives, but its depredations were kept within bounds. The early months in office of President Moi were marked by a determined effort to eradicate the ills of the preceding years, and by 'a bonanza of populist decisions',[3] unfortunately at an inauspicious time for the economy and the public finances. But it would be unrealistic to expect that all could be put right over night, however great the efforts to that end, and that nepotism and corruption, which are hardly unique to Kenya, will entirely disappear. It is too easy, with hindsight, to attribute all ills to the past and, with optimism, to exaggerate the possibilities for change. And to acknowledge the ills of the Kenyatta Era, which became particularly apparent during its later years, is not to deny or dismiss the achievements of the period. Great advances were made in the welfare of ordinary people during the first fifteen years of independence, despite the impression that might be given by some writings on Kenya, and this book aims to give proper weight to them.

[1] World Bank, *Kenya: Into the Second Decade*, 1975, p.4.
[2] These quotations are all from the *Sunday Nation*, 31 December, 1978.
[3] *African Business*, March 1979.

A sizeable literature on the economy of Kenya has accumulated. Yet there seems to be no general survey, such as this book attempts, taking a balanced and undoctrinal view, obsessed neither with the latest fashion in economic dogma nor with the ubiquitous machinations of neo-colonialism.

I have drawn to some degree on earlier writings. The second chapter is based on a chapter in Gerald Holtham and Arthur Hazlewood, *Aid and Inequality in Kenya*, published in 1976, and one or two other passages are also taken from that work. I am grateful to my fellow author, to the Overseas Development Institute which sponsored the study, and to the publisher, Croom Helm, for allowing me to make use of that material. I am also grateful to the publisher and editor of the *Journal of Modern African Studies* for allowing me to use in Chapter 9 material first published in 1978 in my article 'Kenya: Income Distribution and Poverty – an Unfashionable View'. It is a pleasure to thank Susan Ousley of Pembroke College for efficient typing.

My greatest debt in the writing of this book is to the Kenyans and expatriates I have encountered during visits to Kenya over a period of twenty years, and particularly to those responsible for the excellent statistical and economic publications on which so much of the book is based. More specifically, I am indebted to the following for discussions and comments on drafts of the book: Tim Curtin, Haley Goris, Hiram Karani, Tony Killick, Muthoni Likimani, Tim Marchant, George Musoko, Duncan Ndegwa, Philip Ndegwa, Davidson Ngini, Marianne Ouma, Parmeet Singh, Lawrence Smith. I am similarly indebted to members of the staff of the British High Commission in Nairobi and of the East African Development Division. In Oxford I have received valuable comments from Teddy Jackson, Ken Mayhew and Nita Watts. None of these is, of course, in any way to be held responsible for the views expressed. I am grateful to the Ministry of Overseas Development for financing a visit to Kenya in September, 1978, from which the book greatly benefited, and to Professor Maitha and other members of the Department of Economics at the University of Nairobi to which I was attached during that visit. Finally, for enabling me over the years to work on subjects of my own choosing, I am indebted, as always, to Teddy Jackson, Director of the Institute of Economics and Statistics. The book was written when I was a Senior Research Officer at that Institute, before my election as Warden of Queen Elizabeth House, Oxford, and Director of the Oxford University Institute of Commonwealth Studies.

Despite the advice and help I have received, I have inevitably in so wide-ranging a study fallen into factual errors. For these I apologise in the hope that they are not too numerous and do not fundamentally distort the picture of the Kenya economy that I have attempted to paint.

CHAPTER 1

LAND AND PEOPLE

Kenya is a new country. The name, indeed, did not come into official use until 1920, when the former East Africa Protectorate was renamed. Modern Kenya, it has been said, was created by the railway. This view, highly anglo-centric as it is, contains the truth that it was with the building of the railway, with British Government funds, that the political delineation of the area which became the Republic of Kenya firmly began. Construction of the Uganda Railway, as it was then called, commenced from the East African coast at Mombasa in 1896, and reached its planned terminal on the shores of Lake Victoria in 1902. By 1899 the line had reached a point 300 miles inland at the approach to a high plateau over which it would have to pass on its way to the west. A railway camp at this point was the origin of the City of Nairobi, the capital of Kenya.

European travellers, traders, and missionaries had been introducing themselves into the interior of East Africa increasingly towards the end of the nineteenth century, and interest and activity had accumulated in Uganda. The primary concern in the building of the railway was to obtain access to Uganda. The region between the coast and the Lake was an obstacle, and a railway was the way to overcome it. The completion of the railway achieved this aim, and brought Uganda within days instead of months of the coast. But the construction was a costly enterprise, and there was no traffic to be obtained along the line of rail. The stimulus for the development of the area between the coast and the Lake, by the settlement of European farmers, had at least one of its origins in the financial problems of the railway. The railway made settlement feasible; and settlement would provide the traffic to make the railway pay. The year 1902 marks the beginning of a deliberate policy of European settlement.

Britain had declared a Protectorate over the East African territories under the suzerainty of the Sultan of Zanzibar in 1895. In 1902 the eastern province of Uganda, covering the area stretching from Lake Victoria to a few miles west of Nairobi, was transferred to the East Africa Protectorate. This transfer brought the whole of the railway, and the whole of the area considered suitable for European farming, under a single territorial administration, and the Protectorate acquired boundaries not radically different from those of present-day Kenya.

In 1920 the nominal sovereignty of the Sultan of Zanzibar was confined by Britain to a 10-mile-wide coastal strip, which was rented from the Sultan. The remainder of the Protectorate was formally annexed by Britain, and the country acquired the style of the Colony and Protectorate of Kenya.

The origin and meaning of the name Kenya is a matter of dispute. It is perhaps an anglicization of the Kamba name for Mount Kenya.[1] Whatever its origins, the name had sufficient authenticity for there to be no question of a change when Independence came on 12 December 1963.[2]

Kenya, with a land area of 225,000 square miles (equal to that of France), straddles the equator, which cuts across the country about 90 miles north of Nairobi. Kenya's boundaries are defined in the east by the Indian Ocean and Somalia, in the west by Lake Victoria and Uganda, in the south by Tanzania, and to the north by Ethiopia and Sudan. From the coast to the shores of Lake Victoria is a distance of some 450 miles. From the narrow coastal strip the land rises to the edge of the highlands, where Nairobi has an altitude of 5,500 feet. The highlands, which occupy the south-western quarter of Kenya, are a plateau mostly with an altitude of around 4,000 feet, but rising to as much as 10,000 feet, and deeply cut by the Great Rift Valley. North of Nairobi near the equator, is the 17,000-foot peak of Mount Kenya. The three-quarters of Kenya to the north and east of the highlands is mainly low plateau of around 2,000 feet in altitude.

Rainfall is heavy at the coast and in the highlands. Elsewhere rainfall is sparse and there are large areas of semi-desert. For land to be properly suited to grazing at least 20″ of rainfall is required, and for agriculture a rainfall of between 30″ and 40″ is necessary. Yet only one-third of Kenya receives a rainfall of more than 20″. The average for northern Kenya is under 10″, and much of the east receives less than 20″ on average. In contrast, large areas of the highlands have a rainfall of 40″ to 50″, and in places the average rises to over 60″. But the average does not tell the whole story. The rainfall, even in places where on average it is adequate for cultivation, is unreliable. There are wide variations around the average from year to year, and in some years the rains can fail. The uneven distribution of rainfall over the country, its overall inadequancy, and its unreliability are fundamental to the economy of Kenya.

In terms of population, Kenya is not a large country. It is estimated that in 1974 the population numbered just under 13 million. But the rate of growth of the population is among the world's fastest, and has been increasing. Advances in public health and standards of living have brought a rapid decline in death-rates, especially among children.

In the early years of this century the population probably totalled around 3 to 4 million, and may for a time have been declining. In 1948 it was still under 5½ million. Between then and 1962 population grew at an average annual rate of 3.2 per cent; between 1962 and 1969 the rate of growth was 3.4 per cent; and for the period 1969–74 it had increased to 3.5 per cent. The crude birth-rate at the time of the 1962 census was 48 per thousand, which may be compared with the world average of 36. Prognostications are unsafe. But on assumptions that allow for a decline in fertility, a population is forecast in the year 2000 of 28 million, which, if there were no decline in fertility would be 34 million.

It is not to be imagined that the whole of Kenya is densely populated. Far from it. The average population density is no more than 22 per square mile. But this average is totally misleading, because it takes no account of the fact that very large parts of Kenya, in the north and east in particular, are virtually uninhabited. The reason for the very unequal distribution of population over the country is that large areas have very low economic potential for agriculture or animal husbandry. Land classified as of high or medium potential comprises no more than one-fifth of the total and on this land the average population density is not 22 but 126 persons per square mile. Another figure which indicates the unequal distribution of the population, which is so striking a characteristic of Kenya, is that one-half of the population lives on 6 per cent of the land area. The nature of the population distribution is clearly seen on the map. There are three main population clusters, at the coast, in the central highlands, and around Lake Victoria.

Kenya is not a highly urbanized country, although as a consequence of migration from the rural areas the urban population is expanding at a rate of 7 per cent a year. In 1969 the population of forty-eight towns amounted to 1.1 million, or about 10 per cent of the total population; by 1974 the urban population had risen to 1.6 million, equal to 13 per cent of the total. Most of the places identified as urban centres are very small, and in 1966 there were only twenty-two centres of more than 5,000 people, accounting in all for a population of just under 1 million. There are only two large towns, and two of moderate size. The four between them contained 84 per cent of the total urban population at the time of the 1969 census, and Nairobi and Mombasa accounted for three-quarters of that figure.

Fast-growing populations are young populations, and in Kenya roughly half the total population is under 15 years of age.[3] The young and the old together leave only some 48 per cent of the total population in the working-age groups.[4]

The youthfulness of the population has, of course, serious implications for the provision of education. Although the provision of education in Kenya compares well with that in many other countries, it is still woefully inadequate in total, as well as in other ways. In 1974 some 40 per cent of the population was literate. The rapidly growing population of school age[5] would require the direction of enormous resources into education if it were to be universally provided.

At the present time Kenya has relatively few old people. Average longevity is no more than 49 years, compared with 71 years in Britain. The increasing number of old people together with the large proportion of the population below working age would impose a heavy burden on the productive population if medical improvements led to any substantial rise in longevity.

Non-African peoples have been of significance in the economic life of Kenya and in economic change during the twentieth century out of all proportion to their numbers. The distinctions between European, Asian, and African were fundamental to the economy of colonial Kenya, and they retain their importance today, even though the relationships between the groups have undergone enormous changes.

In colonial times Kenya was a country of European settlement, and of a type of settler that led one observer[6] to exclaim that 'It has the greatest proportion among its inhabitants, of ex-soldiers, generals, colonels, majors, of any country in the world. It contains a goodly number of names in Burke's Peerage – and some quite terrific specimens in the flesh.' But whatever its characteristics and social composition, in total the European population of Kenya was never larger than that of a small English town. In 1911 there were only 3,000 Europeans in the country, and in 1921, despite the post-war efforts to settle former officers, it had risen to only 10,000. After the second world war the number of Europeans climbed from 30,000 in 1948 to a peak of 61,000 in 1960, at a time when the African population was estimated to number nearly 8 million. Thereafter the European population declined, though not dramatically, to the 41,000 recorded in the 1969 census.[7]

Although the popular image in Britain of the Kenya European is perhaps that of the 'White Highlands' farmer, the European population always had a substantial urban element, which increased over time. In 1948, 58 per cent, and in 1969, 68 per cent of the European population lived in the towns.

The Asian population is even more urbanized, and much larger than – roughly three times – the European, and it continued to grow after the European population had begun to decrease. The estimates indicate a peak Asian population of 192,000 in 1967, and a decline thereafter to 139,000 by the time in the 1969 census.[8] In the census 92 per cent of the Asian population is shown as residing in towns.

These non-African 'tribes' are small in comparison with all but the smallest African tribes. The 1969 census identifies thirteen tribal groups which together accounted for 95 per cent of the Kenya African population, the remainder being composed of a number of smaller groups. Five tribes, each numbering more than 1 million people, accounted together for 71 per cent of the African population. The Masai, the symbol of Kenya in the tourist brochures, in contrast numbered 155,000.

The African population of Kenya is overwhelmingly rural. The African population of the towns is a mixture of tribes. In the countryside there are much more clearly defined tribal areas. Although there have been large shifts of population, even in quite recent years, the bulk of the population lives on what it – and others – regards as its own traditional land. Thus the Luo (1.5 m. in 1969) are concentrated in the west, on the Lake shore in Nyanza Province, as are the Kisii (0.7 m.) and the Luhya (1.5 m) to the north of them in Western Province. The Kamba (1.2 m.) live in Eastern Province to the east of Nairobi stretching towards the coast. The various Kalenjin groups (1.2 m.) are found in the vast Rift Valley Province. The Kikuyu, the most numerous tribe (2.2 m.), live predominantly in Central Province, to the north of Nairobi, though they have spread westwards into the Rift Valley and into the Highlands, partly as a result of settlement schemes and the transfer to African ownership of formerly European-owned farms.

The following list,[9] based on the 1969 Census data, gives a good picture of the location of population by tribe and of the tribal composition of the Provinces:

Central Province	96% of all people in Province are Kikuyu; 73% of all Kikuyu in Kenya live in Central Province.
Coast Province	62% of all inhabitants are from those groups classed as coastal; 98.4% of all those people live in Coast Province. 11.5% of inhabitants are Taita/Taveta; 95% of Taita/Taveta live in Province.
Eastern Province	54.5% of inhabitants are Kamba; 87% of Kamba live in Province. 39% of inhabitants are Embu/Meru; 97% of Embu/Meru live in Province.
North-Eastern Province	96.4% of inhabitants are Somali-speakers: 95% of Kenyan Somali live in Province.
Nyanza Province	63% of inhabitants are Luo: 87% of Luo live in Province. 31% of inhabitants are Kisii; 95% of Kisii live in Province.

Rift Valley Province	51% of inhabitants are Kalenjin-speakers; 95% of Kalenjin live in Province. 15% of inhabitants are Kikuyu; 15% of Kikuyu live in Province. 7% of inhabitants are Masai; 97% of Masai live in Province. 7% of inhabitants are Luhya: 10% of Luhya live in Province.
Western Province	88% of inhabitants are Luhya; 80% of Luhya live in Province.
Nairobi	47% of African people in Nairobi are Kikuyu; 9% of Kikuyu live in Nairobi. 16% of African people in Nairobi are Luhya; 4% of Luhya live in Nairobi. 15% of African people in Nairobi are Luo; 4% of Luo live in Nairobi. 15% of African people in Nairobi are Kamba; 5% of Kamba live in Nairobi.

CHAPTER 2

THE COLONIAL INHERITANCE[1]

Kenya is no longer *White Man's Country*[2] but before Kenya achieved national Independence in December 1963, a fundamental determinant of the nature of its economy and of the policies of its government was the existence of wealthy and – by tropical African standands – relatively large non-African communities. The future had not been foreseen, and further European immigration had been encouraged after the second world war. A European Settlement Board was set up in 1948 and about 500 European ex-service men were settled on farms during the 1950s.

By the time of Independence, changes had been in progress for several years, stimulated by the 'Mau Mau' Emergency of the 1950s. In 1960, the year in which agreement on self-government was reached, the total population was estimated to be 8.1 m., of which 7.8 m. were Africans. The European population numbered 61,000 and the Asian 169,000. There are no data of the racial distribution of money income, but it is clear that, despite the overwhelming numerical preponderance of Africans, non-Africans received a high proportion of the total. Eighty per cent of the value of the marketed produce of agriculture came from the European-owned farms and estates; 55 per cent of the total wage-bill accrued to non-Africans, though they amounted to only 10 per cent of the labour force. Profits from manufacturing and trade were received almost entirely by non-African individuals or companies. The predominance of the non-African population in the receipt of money income was more than matched by the predominance of non-African ownership in the monetary economy. Africans received money income from wages and from the sale of agricultural produce, and it is this sale of produce which constituted virtually the whole of the monetary output of the African-owned economy. It amounted to no more than 3 to 4 per cent of the gross domestic product in 1960. The remainder derived from the non-African economy, though of course much of the work was performed by African wage-earners.

Pre-Independence agriculture was characterized above all by the division of the land between Europeans and Africans. Asians were virtually excluded from the ownership of agricultural land, and Africans were prohibited from acquiring land in the 'White Highlands', which by the Agricultural Ordinance of 1955 became officially invested with the more neutral title of the Scheduled Areas. The Scheduled Areas occupied some 7½ m. acres, or about 3.1 m. hectares, which was not far short of the acreage of the non-scheduled areas, the former 'reserves' or Native Trust Lands.

European farming had at one time largely concentrated on cereals. By 1960 the efforts made after the second world war to develop mixed farming had achieved considerable success, but in addition to the mixed farms there was estate production of permanent crops produced for export – coffee, tea, sisal – and livestock ranches in areas where the rainfall was unsuitable for crop production. Livestock and dairy produce accounted, roughly equally, for about one-quarter of total sales from the Scheduled Areas; coffee, tea, and sisal contributed 45 per cent; cereals, mainly wheat, provided another 15 per cent of the total, and the remainder of total sales was made up of a number of crops, including cotton, tobacco, pyrethrum, sugar, and oilseeds.

Livestock, together with a very small value of dairy produce, also accounted for about one-quarter of sales from the non-scheduled areas, and coffee, a crop which Africans had only recently been permitted to cultivate on any scale,[3] accounted for another one-quarter; 14 per cent was provided by cereals, mainly maize, and a number of minor crops accounted for the remainder of sales, of which the most important was cotton. Farming in the non-scheduled areas was primarily for the household consumption of the farmers, and although cash-cropping was becoming increasingly important, by 1960 perhaps only about 15 per cent of total output was marketed.

The smallness of the shift in African agriculture towards cash cropping by 1960, partly caused by administrative and legal restraints on such development (as notably in restrictions on coffee cultivation by Africans), and partly by the limited development of transport in the African areas, was also in part the consequence of the fact that the activities of Kenya's highly developed and controlled structure of marketing and credit focused on the Scheduled Areas. Although the government agricultural service dealt with both African and European farming, the statutory boards, committees, and organizations concerned with marketing, mainly administered by the farmers themselves, were primarily concerned with the Scheduled Areas. In marketing fresh meat, the Kenya Meat Commission dealt only marginally with the African areas. Kenya Co-operative Creameries and the Kenya Farmers Union were the instruments of the European farmers. The determination of producer's prices was dominated by the European farming interest. The setting of the price of maize, the staple diet of African wage-earners, is the outstanding example of a policy in the interest of supposedly European farmers (although, in fact, Africans supplied more than half the maize marketed through official channels) against the interest of African consumers. The main sources of credit were oriented to European farming and denied to Africans particularly because of their lack of a security to offer in the absence of registered title to land.

Great changes in land tenure and in the occupation of land began towards the end of the colonial period. They were a response to a belief in the inability of the African reserves under existing tenure systems and agricultural practices to accommodate the expanding African population, as well as to the Emergency. There were two kinds of change. One was the transfer of land from European ownership and the settlement of African farmers upon it. The other was the 'commercialization' of African-occupied land by means of consolidation and adjudication and registration of title. Both kinds of change were advocated in 1955 by the East Africa Royal Commission, the analysis and recommendations of which had been described by *The Economist* newspaper as 'Adam Smith in Africa'. The Royal Commission proposed the abandonment of the 'tribal approach' to land, including the 'racial approach to the Highlands question', and prescribed 'individualization of land ownership and mobility in the transfer of land'.

The commercialization of land was a feature of the Swynnerton Plan (A Plan to Intensify the Development of African Agriculture in Kenya) of 1954, which argued that the reform of African land tenure was a prerequisite of agricultural improvement. Consolidation, enclosure, and registration of title, it was argued, would make credit obtainable for improvements and enable progressive farmers to acquire more land. The African lands would be enabled to move away from being overwhelmingly devoted to production for subsistence towards a commercial agriculture.

There had already been some individualization of land-holding in different parts of the country, even in the absence of machinery to adjudicate and register titles. A landless agricultural class had already developed in the form of squatters on European farms, who provided wage-labour and were allowed to cultivate some land for their own subsistence. The political circumstances were favourable for government action. Under the Emergency Regulations, introduced in 1952 to combat the Mau Mau rebellion, many potential opponents of change in African tenure were in detention, in parts of the country people who had formally lived scattered on their holdings had been gathered together in villages, making consolidation and redistribution of the land easier, and money was available to support policies which might help to defeat and to remove the causes of the rebellion.

Consolidation of land and registration of title began in 1955 and by the year before Independence about half the land of high potential had been consolidated and enclosed, and about half of that had been registered. Registration had, in fact, been completed in Central Province, but had not proceeded significantly elsewhere, where the pressures from the rebellion were less severe. The land-tenure changes were supported by credit and extension services and by the final removal of restrictions on the growth of cash crops, notably coffee. The value of produce sold from small-holdings increased from £5.1 m. in 1955 to £9.5 m. in 1960 and to £11.6 m. in 1963. The contribution of coffee to total sales increased from 6 per cent to 27 per cent. However, the large farms retained their dominant position in production for the market. In 1963 78 per cent of total sales were by the large farms, compared with 86 per cent in 1955, and there was no evidence of any marked rise in the marketed proportion of total output of small farmers. The large farms also remained the source of the bulk of agricultural exports. Nevertheless, by the end of the colonial period Kenya had made decisive progress towards the establishment of a commercial agriculture of small farmers in the traditional African areas.

It must not be presumed that this development showed the Swynnerton medicine at work. It is arguable that it was the final removal of the constraints imposed on African commercial agriculture that was responsible rather than the changes in land tenure, which were neither a necessary nor a sufficient condition for progress.[4]

The commercialization of land was accompanied by the growth of inequalities in land holding. The development was expected by the author of the Swynnerton Plan: '. . . able, energetic or rich Africans will be able to acquire more land . . .' But it is arguable that the land-tenure changes were also not a necessary condition for this development. It has been suggested that 'a general pattern of consolidation among the "large progressive farmers" long preceded the Swynnerton Plan (which to some degree was simply a ratification and enforced generalisation by the colonial government of the behaviour of the few).'[5] The adjudication and registration of land has been continued since Independence, though the operation of the market in land has not been untrammelled as District Land Boards have the power to veto a land sale if it would leave the seller landless.

The process of differentiation within the African population associated with the tenure changes and the removal of restrictions on cash cropping had not only a personal but also a tribal and – to a large degree the same thing – a regional dimension. Opportunities were more eagerly grasped in some areas than in others, aided by more favourable circumstances in some areas than in others. Nyanza and Central Provinces had roughly the same value of marketed output until 1957, after which date Central Province drew rapidly ahead, so that by the time of Independence its marketed output from small farms was roughly twice that of Nyanza Province.

In 1959 it was decided by the Kenya Government that the racial allocation of land should be abandoned, and this decision paved the way for African ownership of land in the White Highlands. Schemes for transferring European farms to Africans began to be devised in 1960. Farms were to be purchased from Europeans and sold to Africans. Funds were raised from the World Bank (IBRD) and the Commonwealth Development Corporation (Colonial Development Corporation, as it then was) for the purchase of farms and their settlement at a 'low density' to provide annual monetary incomes, in addition to subsistence and loan charges, of £100 and more. The following year the UK Government agreed to provide funds for land purchase, and this programme was expanded at the end of 1962 into what became known as the Million Acre Scheme. 'High density' settlement was planned under this scheme with the intention that settlers should be able to obtain a net annual income of between £25 and £70. By the time of Independence, 236,000 hectares or nearly 600,000 acres had been purchased and 10,000 families settled under the Million Acre Scheme, and a further 1,000 or so families had been settled on low-density schemes. Small-scale African farming had been firmly established in the Highlands. The influx of Africans into large farming had begun, but remained unimportant until after Independence.

The existence of the non-African population, both as producers and consumers, provided the initial stimulus for the development of manufacturing and processing in Kenya. The earliest developments were in the processing of the products of European agriculture, but as the size of the market expanded, particularly during and after the second world war, and with the increased use of tariff protection, the manufacturing sector of the economy became more diversified. It was not only the European and Asian communities of Kenya which provided a market for Kenya manufactures. Kenya had for long been associated in a common market with Tanganyika and Uganda, and the early impetus to the development of industry in Kenya resulting from her relatively large non-African population put her in a strong position to capture the markets of her common-market partners. By the late 1950s Kenya had become the manufacturing centre for the whole of East Africa, and something like 20 per cent of the output of her manufacturing industry was sold to Tanganyika and Uganda. It should not be thought, however, whatever the origin of the market for Kenya manufactures, that by the time of Independence it was solely a matter of the non-African demand. A number of products had a widespread market among Africans – shoes, cigarettes, beer, and grain-milling products, for instance.

In the middle 1950s manufacturing and construction accounted for about 20 per cent of GDP in the monetary economy (as large, in fact, as that of agriculture and livestock production), and manufacturing alone for 13 per cent. Industry was still heavily oriented towards agricultural processing. Food, beverages, and tobacco industries together produced one-half of the gross production of manufacturing industry.[6] Repairs to transport equipment was an important activity (11 per cent of gross production) fostered by the growth in the number of motor vehicles and by the location in Kenya of the railways and harbours and airways headquarters for the whole of East Africa. The ownership of industry was divided between Kenya Europeans (grain milling; dairy produce; pig products; sisal products; canning), East African Asians (sugar milling; bakery products), and what are now known as 'multinationals' (tobacco; footwear; pharmaceuticals; cement; paints; soap), but with expansion and a scarcity of capital in the locally owned firms the participation of the multinationals was increasing.

The construction industry had received a great stimulus during the war. The stimulus continued into the post-war years with the demands of development plans, which were heavily oriented towards public works, continued military expenditure, construction arising from the Emergency, and the expansion of facilities for the East African common services. Much of the industry was in the hands of Kenyan Asian firms, but international construction companies were becoming of increasing importance by the time of Independence.

Wholesale and retail trade accounted for 17 per cent of gross domestic product recorded in the monetary economy in 1960. Large-scale commerce in exporting, importing and in the distribution of domestic production was divided between European firms, some of them branches of international companies, and Asians. Asians were widely engaged also in small-scale retailing, and they were to be found in the smallest and remotest centres. Africans had hardly begun to enter large-scale commerce and their trading activities were carried on in a very small way and largely in the rural areas.

The existence of the non-African communities, particularly the Europeans, was responsible for the development of technical, financial, and government services to a much greater extent than might have been expected from the low average level of income in the population as a whole. European residents demanded public and private services appropriate to their own level of income. European agriculture was associated with a highly developed structure of marketing and advisory services. The position of Kenya at the centre of the common arrangements in East African substantially increased the activities of government. These factors account for the remarkable development of the city of Nairobi. Its growth was cumulative. The original railway construction encampment became the seat of government for Kenya and for those activities (notably in transport and communications) administered in common for the whole of East Africa; it developed as the centre for the provision of services to agriculture and manufacturing, and as the location of most manufacturing activity, and became the natural location for the headquarters of international firms entering the East African market. By the time of Independence Nairobi had long been established as a centre relevant to a level of income and way of life totally different from that of the vast majority of the population of Kenya.

The part played by Africans – except as wage-earners – in manufacturing, construction, and trade was of little importance. Of course, the smallest enterprises escape the statistical net (surveys of manufacturing, for instance, were confined to firms with five or more employees) and so understate the role of African business activity. But African participation and initiative in any but the smallest manufacturing, construction, and trading activities remained negligible until the end of the colonial period.

The inheritance of independent Kenya was, therefore, a modern economy the structure of which had been fashioned largely in response to the existence of a non-African population. Change had already gone some way in agriculture, although not far enough to destroy the central position of the former White Highlands. In other sectors of the economy change had hardly begun. In the few years preceding Independence the economic growth of the post-war period was halted by the uncertainties of the future. There was a sharp downturn in construction; employment declined; capital flowed out; the Government's finances deterioriated and Britain had to provide grants-in-aid. In the event, many of the fears proved groundless.[7] Jomo Kenyatta declared that 'The Government of an independent Kenya will not be a gangster Government. Those who have been panicky . . . can now rest assured that the future African Government . . . will not deprive them of their property or rights of ownership. We will encourage investors . . . to come to Kenya . . . to bring prosperity to this country.' When economic growth began again it was firmly within the structure established in the colonial period. The years since Independence have seen enormous changes, but there has also been a noteworthy continuity with the past.

CHAPTER 3

ECONOMIC STRUCTURE AND GROWTH

A well-developed system of national accounts exists for Kenya which can be used to describe the structure of the economy and its pattern of growth. It can also be used to throw light on changes in the standard of living, but only within limits.

Economic Structure

The first feature of the Kenya economy revealed by an examination of the national accounts is the existence of a large non-monetary, 'subsistence' sector, or semi-monetary economy as it is now officially titled. Most of the production in the semi-monetary economy is agricultural, and a large part of the food consumed by the rural population is produced and consumed without the intervention of a monetary transaction. The accounts also show other, smaller, elements of subsistence production, including building and construction. However, there are reasons, which are discussed later, for thinking that the relative contribution of the non-monetary sector to the welfare of the population is greater than its relative importance in the national product. Even so, the accounts indicate that nearly one-fifth of total production of goods and services (total GDP) in 1977 took place in the semi-monetary sector, and in 1964 as much as 27 per cent of total GDP had been non-monetary. It is clear that the semi-monetary sector is a very substantial component of the economy, of fundamental importance to the life and welfare of the majority of the population.

Within the monetary economy, agriculture is of course a major sector, accounting for between a quarter and a third of total monetary GDP. Its importance in the total appears from the figures (see Table 3.2) to have increased over time, accounting for a little under a quarter in the first full year of Independence, and much nearer a third in 1977. In one sense this is doubtless a perfectly true statement, but its meaning cannot be correctly interpreted in isolation from the reasons for the increase. It does not mean, in fact, that Kenya was becoming 'more agricultural', in the sense that more of its resources were being devoted to agriculture, the output from which was growing faster than the output from other sectors of the economy. In reality, the reverse is the case. The growth in the importance of agriculture in GDP has in fact nothing to do with any action by Kenyans, it is the result of the world price rise for Kenya's agricultural exports, notably coffee. The export price of coffee rose from KShs. 10/71 per kg in 1974 to KShs. 43/33 in 1977. The price of tea rose from KShs. 7/82 per kg to KShs. 20/44. In 1975 the contribution of agriculture to monetary GDP was 18 per cent, yet two years later it was only marginally under 30 per cent. No shift of resources into agriculture could have accounted for such an enormous change over so short a time. Its contribution has increased because world prices have increased, a fact that is confirmed by the contribution of agriculture to monetary GDP when output is measured in constant, 1972 prices, just under 18 per cent. In fact, when measured in constant, 1972 prices the contribution of agriculture is exceeded by that of manufacturing and several other sectors, including commerce and transport.

TABLE 3.1

Gross Domestic Product at Factor Cost

(percentages)

	1964	1977
Semi-Monetary	27	19
Monetary	73	81

TABLE 3.2

Monetary GDP by Industrial Origin

(percentages)

	1964	1975	1977
Agriculture	23.3	17.3	29.5
Manufacturing	14.8	18.1	16.0
Building	4.9	7.1	4.0
Trade, transport, etc.	23.8	19.3	21.4
Finance and other private services	15.7	16.1	13.2
Government	17.5	22.1	15.9

Note: Agriculture includes forestry and fishing.
Manufacturing includes mining and quarrying.
Trade and transport includes restaurants, hotels, storage, communications, electricity, water.

Nevertheless, in common parlance Kenya would undoubtedly be described as an 'agricultural country', and the basis for this description would have nothing to do with any particular level of commodity prices. It has much more to do with the fact that the population of Kenya is overwhelmingly rural, and largely dependent on the soil for its livelihood. The description reflects the importance of non-monetary as well as monetary agriculture. It also reflects a difference between the approach of the layman and the national accountant to the structure of an economy. The national accounts identify activities which may not ordinarily be distinguished. Of course, everyone knows that agricultural produce needs to be stored, transported, and processed, that an agricultural economy of any degree of sophistication requires banks and other financial services, and needs government to provide law and order, education and health, as well as direct services for agriculture. Yet the existence of all these activities, which are put into various different categories in the national accounts, would not prevent an economy from being described as 'agricultural'. And this description indeed has its advantages, in that it draws attention to the fact that a substantial amount of non-agricultural activity has its foundations in agriculture, as for example in the importance of agricultural commodity processing in manufacturing.

Another feature of the structure of the economy is revealed by figures of the share of wages and salaries in total money income. In Kenya the non-wages part of money income is not all a return to the owners of capital. In agriculture, in particular, a large part of the output that enters the money economy is produced by family labour, not by paid employees. Small-holder agriculture using unpaid family labour is important in the production not only of marketed foodstuffs, but also of cash crops such as coffee, tea, and sugar cane. Non-wage income – 'operating surplus' in the terminology of the national accounts – therefore includes a substantial income not from ownership but from labour.

Unfortunately, the national accounts do not distinguish the income of these small-scale enterprises, which includes a large element of non-wage labour income, from the profits of large-scale enterprises using paid employees. However, the relatively small proportion of wages and salaries in total income in the monetary economy, and the variation between productive sectors, is an indication of the importance of non-wage labour incomes in some sectors, notably in agriculture. In 1977 in the monetary economy as a whole, 45 per cent of GDP was accounted for by payments to employees of enterprises, that is, wages and salaries, and 55 per cent by 'operating surplus'. In monetary agriculture the proportion of employees' remuneration was less than 12 per cent; in contrast, it was 45 per cent in manufacturing and 83 per cent in the building industry. In government, of course, the proportion was virtually 100 per cent.

These figures of the relative importance of employee remuneration and surplus, were themselves substantially affected by the rise in agricultural prices. In 1975, before the great rise in prices, in the monetary economy as a whole the proportions were the reverse of those in 1977, employee remuneration accounting for 55 per cent and surplus for 45 per cent. In agriculture, employee remuneration was 27 per cent, and surplus 73 per cent. The sharp increase in the importance of operating surplus in agriculture between 1975 and 1977, from 73 to over 88 per cent, reflects the rise in agricultural prices, and the increased revenues of family farmers.

TABLE 3.3

Labour Cost Component of Monetary GDP, 1977

(percentages)

Total Monetary GDP	45
All enterprises	34
Agriculture	12
Manufacturing	45
Building	83

Source: *Economic Survey*, 1978, Table 2.3.

TABLE 3.4

Use of Resources in Monetary Economy

(percentages)

	1964	1970	1977
Gross Investment	16	25	25
Public Consumption	20	20	21
Private Consumption	64	55	54

Source: *Statistical Abstract*.

The flow of resources in the monetary economy into capital formation has been high. In 1977 about 25 per cent of total resources was devoted to fixed capital formation, the proportion having risen from 16 per cent in 1964.[1] In 1977 roughly 40 per cent of investment was in buildings and construction, 20 per cent in transport equipment (a higher proportion than in the immediately preceding years, but lower than in 1964), and the other 40 per cent in other forms of machinery and equipment. Public investment was in buildings and equipment to the extent of 66 per cent, compared with 16 per cent for private investment.

The sector which was the largest single claimant on investment in 1977 was transport, to which 20 per cent of investment was devoted. Government services, claiming 18 per cent were next in importance, followed by manufacturing with 17 and agriculture with 12 per cent. In 1964 the share of agriculture was higher (17.4 per cent) and of manufacturing lower (14.9 per cent); transport was then also the largest claimant on investment resources (26.3 per cent), which it has commonly been. In 1964 the share of government services was 11 per cent, compared with 18 per cent in 1977, though until the middle 1970s it was commonly more than 20 per cent.

TABLE 3.5

Monetary Fixed Capital Formation by Industry, 1977

(percentages)

Agriculture	12.1
Manufacturing	16.8
Electricity and water	9.1
Trade and hotels	7.8
Transport	20.1
Dwellings	6.5
General government	18.1
Other	9.4

TABLE 3.6

Public Sector Capital Formation
as
Proportion of Total Monetary Capital Formation

(percentage)

1974	1975	1976	1977
49	46	46	43

Source: *Economic Survey*, 1978, Table 2.9.
Note: Public as percentage of total net of traditional dwellings.
Current prices.

TABLE 3.7

Finance of Capital Formation

(percentages)

	1973	1974	1975	1976	1977
From abroad	20	39	35	14	−3
Domestic saving	80	61	65	86	103

Source: *Economic Survey*, 1975–8 issues.

The proportion of resources in the monetary economy devoted to public consumption was only marginally higher (21.4 per cent) in 1977 than in 1964 (19.5 per cent), though it was at times more substantially higher in the intervening years. But there are no indications of a trend of rising public authorities' consumption. Public consumption has risen more as a proportion of total consumption in the monetary economy than as a proportion of total resources. In 1964, 23 per cent of consumption in the monetary economy was public and 77 per cent private; by 1977 the proportion of public consumption had risen to 28 per cent and that of private had fallen to 72 per cent. Together, the increasing importance of investment and public consumption between 1964 and 1977 reduced the proportion of total resources in the monetary economy remaining for private consumption from 64 to 54 per cent.

Table 3.7 shows that commonly a high proportion of capital formation has been financed by domestic saving.

Consumer Prices

Kenya experienced remarkably stable retail prices during the 1960s. Indeed, over the five years from the end of 1959 to the end of 1964 the Nairobi lower-income index of consumer prices showed an increase of only 7 per cent, and the value of the index was actually unchanged from 1962 to 1964. Even by the end of 1969 the index had increased by no more than 20 per cent over the decade. The 1970s have been very different. The lower income index rose by 78 per cent over the five years 1970–5; in the following three and a half years, to the end of March 1978, the increase was 39 per cent. These figures are from different indexes, using different weights, so no precise comparison of the figures would be fruitful, but the general picture is strikingly clear. It is an unfortunate fact that the price changes of individual commodities have been such that the index weighted with the expenditure pattern of the lower-income consumers has increased more than those weighted by the expenditures of middle-income and of upper-income consumers. With 1975 = 100, the three indices had the following values at the end of March 1978: Lower Income 150; Middle Income 135; Upper Income 137. The explanation for this different experience of the three income groups is not the obvious one, that food which bulks large in the lower-income index has increased in price by more than other things. The index for food, in fact, is lower than the all-items index for the lower-income consumers, though it is marginally higher for the other two income groups. It appears to be a rise in house rents which is mainly responsible for the high increase in the lower-income index. Rent has a high weight in that index (22.9 compared with 41.0 per cent for food, and with 16.0 for rent in the middle-income index) and the rent component had a value of 173.9 in March 1978, compared with a value of 152.2 in the middle-income and of 137.8 in the upper-income index.

Although the price index is an important indicator of changes in the cost of living of urban dwellers, it is not easy to say what relevance it has to the rural population. In the first place, the rural population is less dependent on the market than the urban population because of the importance of own-produced food. Secondly, the prices recorded in Nairobi cannot be taken as an indicator of prices elsewhere. A study of prices in rural markets showed that the price of maize in different parts of the country varied from about 66 to 88 per cent of the Nairobi price.[2]

TABLE 3.8

Price Changes for Nairobi Lower-Income Group

(end-December)

1959	1960	1961	1962	1963	1964
100	102	104	107	107	107
1964	1965	1966	1967	1968	1969
100	106	109	111	112	112
1969	1970	1971	1972	1973	1974
100	101	107	112	128	149
1974	1975	1976	1977	1978	
100	118	129	156	164	

Sources: *Statistical Abstract*, Wage Earners' Index of Consumer Prices in Nairobi, base July 1964, for years 1959–1969; Lower Income Index of Consumer Prices – Nairobi, base August 1971 for years 1969–74; Lower Income Index of Consumer Prices – Nairobi, base January–June 1975, for years 1974–8.

Note: 1978 figure is for end-March.

An analysis of the inflationary process in the middle 1970s came to the conclusion that the rise in prices at that time was the combined outcome of the increase in import prices, a liberal credit policy and stock accumulation, food shortages because of drought, and increases in official producer prices for wheat and maize.[3] The subsequent acceleration in the rate of price increase in the second half of the decade can hardly be unconnected with Kenya's export boom, though the relationship is undoubtedly complex.

Labour Force and Employment

The size of the labour force cannot be measured by adding those seeking work to the number in paid employment, because of the importance of self-employment and family labour, particularly in agriculture. One estimate suggests that the modern sector provides paid employment for about a fifth of the total labour force,[4] and another[5] that wage employees constitute about 13 per cent of the economically active population. Nevertheless, great attention must be given to the number in paid employment because it is large, there is a serious problem of unemployment, and it has been said that 'the creation of jobs is the most important issue confronting the Kenya economy'.[6] In 1977, recorded wage employment totalled a little over 900,000, and the Development Plan had a target of 1,161,000 paid jobs in the modern or 'formal' sector by 1978.

The concept of the 'informal sector' has come into use in Kenya since the report of a mission from the International Labour Organisation in 1971.[7] There is some discussion of the informal sector in later chapters, and at this point it is worth simply setting out the definition adopted in the government's *Economic Survey*: 'The "informal" sector covers a great variety of occupations – street markets, "open-air" garages, hawkers, sellers of newspapers, shoe-shine boys, etc.'[8] The sharp rise in employment in the informal sector between 1975 and 1976 – 28 per cent, compared with a rise of 4.7 per cent in formal-sector wage employment – was said to 'reflect the relative difficulty of finding employment in the modern sector of the economy'.[9]

TABLE 3.9

Distribution of Economically Active Population, 1977

(thousands)

Wage employment in modern sector	903
Self-employment in modern sector	57
Informal urban sector	104
Other activity	5,736
Economically active population, approx.	6,800

Source: *Economic Survey*, 1978.

TABLE 3.10

Distribution of Employment Between Private and Public Sectors

(percentages)

	1964	1970	1977
Private	68	62	58
Public	32	38	42

Source: *Statistical Abstract* and *Economic Survey*, 1978.

So far as formal-sector employment is concerned, Tables 3.11 and 3.12 show its distribution between industries, for both private-sector employment alone, and for all employment, private and public. The public sector provides 42 per cent of all employment, mainly in agricultural services and forestry, in transport and communications, because of the publicly owned railways, harbours, and postal services, in manufacturing, because of the railway workshops, and in the category 'other services' which includes teachers and civil servants in the central and local administrations. 'Other services' in fact, account for 64 per cent of public employment, and education alone for more than 110,000, or 31 per cent.

TABLE 3.11

Private Sector Wage Employment by Industry

(percentages)

	1964	1977
Agriculture	51	39
Manufacturing	13	18
Construction	2	6
Trade and transport	16	15
Other services	17	22
Total private employment (thousands)	393.4	526.5
Total public employment (thousands)	182.0	376.4

Source: *Statistical Abstracts.*
Note: The classification of industries has been changed slightly between 1964 and 1977, but the broad percentage distributions of private employment are not significantly affected.

TABLE 3.12

Total (Private and Public) Wage Employment by Industry

(percentages)

	1968	1972 Old Series	1972 New Series	1976
Agriculture	31	31	34	28
Manufacturing	12	13	12	13
Construction	5	5	5	6
Trade and Transport	18	12	13	13
Other services	33	38	35	40
Total employment (thousands)	606.4	719.8	719.8	857.5

Source: *Statistical Abstracts.*

Employment in agriculture has been affected by the conversion of large farms employing wage labour into small holdings and co-operatives,[10] and fewer were employed in private agriculture in 1976 than in 1964 (198 compared with 202 thousand). The share of services has been increased in particular by the increased share of employment provided by education, which was 9 per cent in 1968 and 14 per cent in 1976. Employment in most branches of transport and communications changed very little between 1968 and 1976, and total employment declined from 51,000 to under 48,000, largely because of a fall in railway employment from 14,000 to 5,000. Private manufacturing increased its share of employment by a significant amount, but the volume of manufacturing output trebled between 1964 and 1977, whereas employment in the private manufacturing sector not quite doubled.

TABLE 3.13

Wage Employment by Province

(percentages)

	1964	1977
Nairobi	26	26
Central	15	16
Nyanza	7	7
Western	3	5
Coast	13	13
Rift Valley	29	25
Eastern	6	8
North Eastern	<1	<1

Source: *Statistical Abstracts* and *Economic Survey*, 1978.

It is remarkable how little the distribution of employment between Provinces has changed. Nairobi remained with a quarter of total employment in 1977, as it had at the time of Independence, and continued with the neighbouring Central Province to provide 40 per cent of all employment. The only change of significant size is the quite small decline in the proportion of total employment provided in the Rift Valley. The number of jobs in that Province has increased, of course, from 168,000 to 226,000 between 1964 and 1977, but in the early years of Independence the Rift Valley was affected by the departure of White farmers, and employment decreased and did not begin to rise above its 1964 level for four years. In Uasin Gishu District, indeed, employment did not reach its 1964 level until after 1970.

Africans were always the vast majority of employees, but before Independence non-Africans made up about 10 per cent of the total; by 1973 the proportion of non-Africans had fallen to under 4 per cent. The number of Europeans in employment had begun to decline well before Independence, from its maximum of 23,000 in 1960 to 16,000 in 1964. In 1973 there were only 9,500 Europeans employed. Asian employment continued to rise to a peak of nearly 43,000 in 1966, and had fallen to 20,000 by 1973. The employment of non-citizens of

Kenya has declined even more than that of non-Africans: in 1968 non-citizens accounted for 8.4 per cent of total employment and by 1977 for only 1.7 per cent.

It follows from the nature of the economy, in which wage employment occupies a small part of the economically active population, that there is no simple measure of the number of unemployed, such as is available in an economy in which only a few of the economically active are not either in employment or registered as unemployed. The World Bank mission noted: 'On the basis of urban surveys conducted recently, the average urban unemployment rate alone is around 11 per cent. The rate of unemployment among school leavers and new entrants to the job market is much higher – probably about 21 per cent.'[11] But in Kenya a lack of jobs may be reflected in a rise in economic activity in the informal sector, or in a smaller migration from the countryside to the towns, rather than in open urban unemployment. So the unemployment problem is in fact best seen as an employment problem, namely a slower rate of growth in the number of wage-jobs and other productive employment opportunities than is required if standards of living are to be maintained and increased in the face of rapid population growth and limited availability of good quality land. Indeed the ILO mission which visited Kenya under the World Employment Programme, argued that open unemployment was only an incomplete reflection of the underlying unemployment problem, and that attention should be focused on the broader problem of 'the working poor'.[12] However, the situation remains paradoxical because even though there is open unemployment there is a shortage of labour in agriculture, and the production of tea, coffee, sugar, and sisal has suffered as a result. 'We must, therefore,' the Minister of Finance and Planning remarked in his 1978 budget speech, 'rethink the precise nature of our unemployment problem and the policies we need to adopt to provide jobs to those without, when the country is under-producing and under-exporting because of labour shortages.'

Economic Growth

The increased use of resources for investment (see Table 3.4) indicates the extent to which the Kenya economy has been oriented towards growth, and the growth rate since Independence has indeed been impressive. Between 1964 and 1972 GDP at constant prices grew at a cumulative rate of 6.8 per cent a year.[13] Allowing for the increase in population, this growth in GDP amounted to an annual rate of increase in GDP per head of between 3.5 per cent and 3.8 per cent.

In 1973 monetary GDP at constant prices was 7 per cent greater than in 1972. But then international events took their toll. The increase in 1974 was only 4 per cent, and in 1975 it was less than 1 per cent.

Growth during most of the period since Independence took place, as has been noted already, at remarkably stable prices. The collapse in the rate of growth after 1973 was accompanied by a sharp rise in the rate at which prices were increasing. The price index for lower-income consumers increased by 11 per cent between 1973 and 1974, by 18 per cent in the following year, and by 9 per cent in the year after that. The dramatic change from a long period of relative price stability and rapid growth to a period of rapid price rises and slow growth, which followed the increase in the price of oil towards the end of 1973, completely overthrew the forecasts of the Development Plan for 1974-8, which had just been drawn up. The Plan set out a growth target of 7.4 per cent a year, which was higher than that of earlier Plans, and which was almost reached in 1973. But that was the last year over which satisfaction could be expressed. The official Economic Survey analysed the situation in the following words:[14]

> The direct and indirect effects of the rise in oil prices, together with the impact of the most severe recession experienced in the industrial countries since the end of the Second World War, further compounded in 1975 the poor growth rate of the economy experienced in Kenya in 1974. The further decline in economic activity in 1975 reduced the number of people in paid employment by 2 per cent, the first fall in a decade. In the past two years Kenya's terms of trade have deteriorated dramatically, a hugh balance of payments deficit has been incurred, the growth rate of the economy has declined to about 1 per cent, and real per capita income has fallen.

However, although the consequences of the higher oil price remains a burden on the economy, there was succour round the corner in the form of booming export prices. In 1976 the export price of coffee was 130 per cent, and in 1977 it was 317 per cent above its 1975 level. The export price of tea was 23 per cent above its 1975 level in 1976 and 134 per cent above in 1977. In 1976 GDP increased by over 5 per cent at constant prices and incomes by 1.7 per cent a head; the number in paid employment increased by 4.7 per cent. The recovery in the growth rate continued in 1977 when GDP at constant prices increased by 7.3 per cent, which was the highest figure achieved for nearly a decade. This growth combined with a marked improvement in the terms of trade increased the real resources available in 1977 by nearly 14 per cent. GDP per head increased substantially on average, but there was a marked shift in favour of agriculture, and farmers benefited but real wages declined, prices rising more than money wages. The era of high growth may have returned, but not the era of stable prices. The index rose by 21 per cent during 1977.

It is not intended to provide a blow-by-blow account of economic developments from year to year. But this outline of events in the years 1973 to 1977 does serve to show the openness of the economy and its susceptibility to changes in the world economy outside the control of Kenyans.

The economy is also highly susceptible, it might suitably be remarked at this point, to domestic events which are largely beyond control. The fortunes of agriculture, and hence the economy as a whole, are frequently affected by either too little or too much rain. Sometimes there is too much rain for some crops but not for others. The outlook for 1978 during the early months of the year was for a continuing, though not too drastic, decline in export prices from the levels of 1977, and the effect of the fall in the price of coffee would be compounded by a fall in production because of excessive rain. However, the good rainfall of 1978 would help the rest of agricultural production.

Incomes and Earnings

The relationship between the growth of GDP and the growth of the incomes and welfare of the people of Kenya is an exceedingly complex matter. The concept and measurement of income in the circumstances of Kenya, with a large part of the population having access to an income in kind, and with the importance of informal sector activity, is as complicated as that of unemployment, and the difficulty is compounded by the need to give attention to the distribution of income which makes averages of limited meaning.

In the first place, of course, it is necessary to allow for population growth, which is rapid. The economy needs to grow quite fast in order

TABLE 3.14

GDP and Private Consumption per Person

(K£)

	1964	1972	1974	1976	1977
GDP: current prices	36.3	54.6	69.3	91.2	113.0
GDP: constant prices	43.6	54.6	55.6	55.6	57.7
Private consumption:					
current prices	n.a.	37.3	48.6	63.3	74.4
constant prices	n.a.	37.3	37.3	38.2	n.a.

Source: *Economic Survey* and *Statistical Abstract*.

Note: GDP in 1964 scaled up by ratio of GDP in 1972 at 1972 and 1964 prices (*Economic Survey*, 1975 and 1977, Table 2.1).

Private consumption (*Economic Survey*, Table 2.6) divided by implied population size (Table 2.1) to give per capita figures. Constant price series from *Statistical Abstract*.

Constant 1972 prices.

to stand still in terms of average GDP per head of population. GDP in total, monetary and semi-monetary, was higher by 81 per cent in 1977 than in 1974, but per head it was only 63 per cent higher because of population increase. Then there are the effects of price changes. GDP per head measured at constant prices was not 63 per cent higher in 1977 than in 1974, but a mere 3.8 per cent.

So far only relative changes have been considered. Some absolute figures are given in Table 3.14. GDP per head even in current prices of K£113 shows Kenya still to be firmly in the poorest group of countries in the World Bank's conventional classification.[15] In terms of 1972 prices it remained in 1977 well down towards the bottom end of the group. Private consumption per head in 1976 at 1972 prices was K£38.2, equal to less than Shs. 15/– a week, or Shs. 73/– a week for a family of five.

TABLE 3.15

Average Earnings per Employee

(K£ p.a.)

	1974	1977
(a) Current Prices		
Private sector		
Agriculture	96	135
Manufacturing	427	597
Transport	636	709
Total	285	399
Public sector	402	588
Total	332	478
(b) Constant Prices		
Private sector		
Agriculture	109	105
Manufacturing	486	464
Transport	724	552
Total	324	310
Public sector	458	458
Total	378	372

Source: *Economic Survey*, 1978, Tables 5.11 and 5.13.
Note: Constant prices of January–June 1975.

Table 3.15 shows some figures of earnings in paid employment. The low position of agriculture is noteworthy. It is partly because the other industrial groups contain a higher proportion of managerial and supervisory employees. To compare earnings per employee with GDP per head is certainly not comparing like with like. Though it is still not comparing like with like, and though only the broadest and most tentative conclusions could be drawn, it would be more relevant to compare earnings in paid employment with the average per head of the sum of semi-monetary product, employee remuneration, and operating surplus in agriculture, where the main return to family labour is to be found. The average per head for this total, 'grossed up' for a family of five, is K£255 in 1974 and K£429 in 1977. It is of some interest that the figure for the earlier year is K£30 less than, and in the later year K£30 more than, the figure for average earnings in paid employment in the private sector. The question of whether wage-earners are an élite to be counted among the rich is taken up in Chapter 9.

A reader living outside Kenya, and thinking implicitly in terms of the level of incomes and prices and patterns of consumption with which he is familiar, must beware of interpreting these figures of GDP and consumption per head (even leaving aside the dispersion concealed within the average) in those familiar terms when they are converted at the going rate of exchange. In terms of US dollars, the GNP per head in 1976 is quoted as $US7,890 in the United States, $US4,020 in Britain, and $US240 in Kenya.[16] These figures show GNP per head in Kenya to be 3 per cent of that in the United States and 6 per cent of that in the United Kingdom. The figures would, however, be quite misleading if they were taken to show that 'on average' the standard of living or economic 'welfare' (if that elusive concept may be introduced) in Kenya was only 3 per cent of that in the US and 6 per cent of that in the UK. It is now generally acknowledged that comparisons of this kind between countries as different in the way of life of the majority of their people as Kenya and the US and the UK are invalid, and exaggerate the poverty of the less-developed country. An adjustment to allow for the inappropriateness for comparisons of the official foreign exchange rates results in an increase in the percentages to 6 per cent of the US and 9 per cent of the UK per capita levels. But these figures still give an exaggerated impression of the poverty of Kenya, as does the corresponding calculation which shows Kenya's average GDP per head as only 80 per cent and consumption per head as no more than 77 per cent of India's.[17] Exchange rates are not the only difficulty in the way of international comparisons. But because of the dispersion around the average, the comparison of averages is in any case a fairly meaningless exercise. The question of income levels, welfare, and standard of living is taken up again in Chapter 9, in the context of a discussion of income distribution and economic inequality within Kenya, and in that context the difficulties of comparisons are highlighted.

CHAPTER 4

AGRICULTURE[1]

For all the developments in other sectors of the economy, Kenya remains essentially an agricultural country. And it is in agriculture that change since Independence has been most dramatic and yet continuity with the past has been most marked. The changes in the ownership of land and in the system of land tenure are the result of the application and intensification of policies adopted before Independence. The characteristic distinction of colonial times between the large farms and the small remains a fundamental feature of the agricultural economy, though more than a little eroded. Agricultural marketing arrangements and price-fixing policies betray the strong influence of the past.

The Land

Only a small part of Kenya's land area is suitable for agriculture or intensive animal husbandry. On one estimate,[2] 46 m. of Kenya's 56.9 m. hectares are unsuitable for such use, although much of that area could be commercially utilised as range lands. The official definition, about which there is controversy however, defines the quality of agricultural land in terms of rainfall. Only 19 per cent of the land classified as of high, medium, or low potential falls into the first two categories, and can be considered as really suited to agriculture. This area amounts to only 17 per cent of all land. The proportion of high and medium potential land various enormously between different parts of the country, from 100 per cent in Nyanza and Western Provinces to zero in North Eastern Province. See Table 4.1.

The variations between Provinces in the proportion of good land are matched by opposite variations in the area of such land per head of population. See Table 4.2. The Provinces with a high proportion of good land are densely populated and have a small area of good land per head. The good land per head of population[3] in the Rift Valley – the centre of the former White Highlands – suggests why that Province can be called 'the granary of Kenya'[4] despite the fact that only 20 per cent of its land is of high or medium potential.

In earlier times the fundamental distinction between Large Farms and Small Farms was expressed at the distinction between the Scheduled Areas and the non-scheduled areas, and earlier still between European and Native lands. Table 4.3 shows the allocation of land between large farms, small farms, and various other uses. The area under large farms

TABLE 4.1

Categories of Land by Province

(percentages)

Province	As proportion of agricultural land High and Medium potential	Low potential	As proportion of all land High and Medium potential
Central	96	4	70
Coast	17	83	14
Eastern	19	81	17
Nairobi	30	70	24
North Eastern	–	100	–
Nyanza	100	–	100
Rift Valley	20	80	19
Western	100	–	90
Kenya	19	81	17

Source: *Statistical Abstract*, 1977, Table 81.

TABLE 4.2

High and Medium Potential Land in Relation to Population

(hectares per person, 1969)

Province	ha
Central	0.55
Coast	1.24
Eastern	1.41
Nairobi	0.03
North Eastern	–
Nyanza	0.59
Rift Valley	1.42
Western	0.56
Kenya	0.91

Source: Data in *Statistical Abstract*.

has been reduced under the programmes to transfer land from European to African ownership, in the course of which large farms have been divided into small-holdings, but the large-farm area remains large.[5] Table 4.4 shows the areas nominally under the different types of large farm. However, the figures in Tables 4.3 and 4.4 are misleading for several reasons. Estates and ranches remain as large enterprises, but many mixed farms are being worked as smallholdings. The recorded large-farm area contains farms which are cultivated by 'squatters' as small-holdings and co-operatively owned farms which are in effect a collection

TABLE 4.3

Estimated Land Use

(m. hectares)

Recorded small farms	3.5
Recorded large farms	2.7
'Gap' farms	1.0
Forest land	1.8
Other use	1.9
Range land and other unsuited to cultivation	46.0
Total land area	56.9

Source: Statistical Abstract and references in text.

TABLE 4.4

Large Farm Area by Type of Farm, 1976

(m. hectares)

Mixed farms	1.1
Estates	0.4
Ranches	1.2
Total	2.7

Source: Percentage distribution of land between types of farm in Agriculture Census of Large Farms, 1975 and 1976, *A Brief Review of Farming Activities*, CBS, Ministry of Finance and Planning, Nairobi, March 1978.

of small farms. That subdivision is taking place on a significant scale is indicated by the statement that 'illegal subdivision of once economically viable holdings in the mixed farm areas is on the increase despite Government's declared policy to discourage the practice'.[6] Something approaching 0.3 m. ha of the large mixed farms are thought to be small farms *de facto*. Other large farms, though still operated as such, also include substantial areas cultivated by farm workers for their own subsistence. The effective size of the area operated by large mixed farms (see Table 4.4) therefore tends to be greatly exaggerated by the statistics. On the other hand, large 'group' ranches have been formed on land outside the old Scheduled Areas, particularly on government land in Coast Province, and these are excluded from the large farm statistics.

The implications of what has been happening to the group-owned large farms have in fact now been acknowledged by the government, and subdivision in suitable locations is no longer to be discouraged but assisted. The development plan for the period after 1978 includes a Group Farm Subdivision Project. It has been officially recognised that in general a farmer's aspiration is to own and farm an individual small-holding, and that subdivision of the mixed farms will both meet the wishes of the owners and result in better farming than an attempt to maintain the farms as large-scale units. The project will implement orderly subdivision where the owners wish to subdivide, and where climate and soils make satisfactory small-holder commercial production feasible, and smallholders will be assisted under a Mixed Farm Improvement Project. The existing rehabilitation project for group-owned large farms is to be confined to the rehabilitation of coffee plantations.

Because of the unofficial subdivision of large farms, the recorded small-farm area understates the extent of small-holder farming. There are also other small farms, particularly in the Rift Valley, which were not caught in the survey on which the figures in Table 4.3 are based, the existence of which is being revealed by subsequent inquiries.[7]

Some farms fall outside the definition of small farms, being larger than 20 hectares, but are not recorded as large farms because they are located outside the old Scheduled Areas. It is thought that there may be some 40,000 of these 'gap farms' and the area attributed to them in Table 4.3 is a guess.

'Land reform' in Kenya, which began before Independence, as was explained in Chapter 2, has been of two distinct types. The transfer of land from European to African ownership, the first type of land reform, had proceeded to the extent of around 1¼ m. hectares by the middle of 1976. At their full extent the Scheduled Areas under European ownership had occupied about 3.1 m. hectares. Something approaching a half of the transferred area has been settled as small farms by individual families, mostly as high-density settlement, but some as under the *Harambee* scheme as relatively low-density settlement. On average, holdings under these settlement schemes amount to about 12 hectares. Although nominally high-density,[8] the holdings on settlement schemes are many times larger than the great majority of holdings in the traditional small farm areas. Recent surveys have indicated that the majority of small farmers have holdings of less than one hectare, and nearly a third of them have holdings smaller than half a hectare.[9]

Table 4.5 shows the transfers of land in the former Scheduled Areas from European to African ownership under various settlement schemes[10] and by private sale. The figure for the area transferred by private sale is for 1973 or 1974, so that it understates the area transferred by 1978. In September 1978, although there was still substantial non-African ownership of estates and ranches,[11] there remained in European hands only thirty-five mixed farms, covering perhaps 60,000 hectares, which qualified for inclusion in the British-financed land transfer programme. And this large-scale land reform had been

TABLE 4.5

Land Transfers

(a) To Small-holder Settlement

Scheme	Area (ha)	Number of holdings	Average size of holding (ha)
Million Acre	470,000	35,000	13.4
Harambee	6,500	400	16.25
Haraka	105,000	14,000	7.5
Total	581,500	49,400	11.8

(b) To Large Farms

Scheme	Area (ha)	Number of holdings	Number of families
Ol Kalou	56,000	86	2,000
Shirika	109,000	105	12,000
Private sale	600,000	n.a.	n.a.

Note: Million Acre – the final version of the pre-Independence Land Transfer Programme. The subdivision of large farms was discontinued in 1971. Some of the land purchased under the scheme was unsuitable for sub-division and was set up as large units, mostly co-operative ranches. The rest mainly high density settlement.

Harambee – a low-density scheme not carried to the extent originally envisaged, namely 20,000 acres a year for four years.

Haraka – formerly known as Squatter Settlement Schemes on land from which European owners had been excluded on grounds that farms were inadequately managed. *Haraka* settlements were hastily and cheaply established on smaller plots than in other schemes.

Ol Kalou – abandoned farms taken over and operated as large units by Department of Settlement, with settlers having small plots for production of food.

Shirika – scheme started in 1971 for co-operative farming of large units by landless and unemployed. A plot of about 1 hectare provided for each family for own cultivation. Farms managed by manager appointed by Department of Settlement, but with intention eventually to transfer responsibility to the tenants' co-operative.

Private sale – credit for purchase available from Agricultural Finance Corporation. Agricultural Development Corporation buys European farms for sale or lease to Africans.

Sources: *Development Plan, 1974–1978*, pp.225–30, for data on Million Acre, *Harambee, Haraka*, and Ol Kalou schemes, and for information on *Shirika*.

Statistical Abstract, 1977, Table 82(b) for June 1976 data on *Shirika* programme.

Development Plan, 1974–1978, p. 57 for information on private transfers.

Gerald Holtham and Arthur Hazlewood, *Aid and Inequality in Kenya*, 1976, Ch. 5, Part One, 'The Land Transfer Programme'.

accompanied remarkably enough, by a significant growth of production rather than by the stagnation that might reasonably have been expected.

The second leg of the land reform, adjudication, and registration to replace communal by individual tenure, had proceeded to completion in some areas by the time of Independence, and continued in others at a rapid pace. Even though the process has not been implemented in the sparsely populated North Eastern Province, there is a view that it is being applied too indiscriminately in areas, such as those devoted to migratory pastoralism, where it is inappropriate. As a proportion of the 30 m. hectares of registrable land[12] outside North Eastern Province, by the end of 1977 nearly 17 per cent had been registered, a further 14 per cent had been adjudicated but not yet registered, and in more than 6 per cent the adjudication process was underway. The area in each Province registered, adjudicated or under adjudication as a percentage of registrable land is shown in Table 4.6.

TABLE 4.6

Land Registered, Adjudicated, or under Adjudication as a Percentage of Registrable Land, end 1977

Province	Percentage
Coast	19.6
Central	99.3
Eastern	6.6
Rift Valley	64.1
North Eastern	0
Nyanza	82.7
Western	92.5

Source: *Economic Survey*, 1978, Table 8.19.

It was not to be expected that the process of adjudication and the allocation of title would leave the distribution of land unchanged. In Chapter 2 it was pointed out it was not intended to do so by the original proponents of the land reform. The Swynnerton Plan foresaw[13] that with the commercialization of land 'able, energetic or rich Africans will be able to acquire more land and bad or poor farmers less, creating a landed and a landless class.' The settlement programme has given land to many thousands of landless households, but together with adjudication it has given the opportunity to some for the accumulation of land. A study of one division showed that the beneficiaries were the rich, including 'outsiders', and that as a result of adjudication, socially *Things Fall Apart.*[14] However, it would be a mistake to attribute all changes of this kind to the land reform because consolidation of land among the larger and more progressive farmers long preceded the Swynnerton Plan.[15]

However the responsibility is allocated, there is a large and growing class of landless probably numbering more than 400,000,[16] and on the other hand there is no doubt that men (and women) of wealth have been able to acquire land on a large scale. Some acquisition has been perfectly proper under the rules; some has been a good deal less so. Some of the allegations – on such an issue it is rarely that evidence stronger than rumours and allegations can be assembled – seem to be no more than that the land market is in fact working and that the poor, however ill-advisedly, are selling land they have been allocated.[17] But it is also widely alleged that 'big men' by pressure and trickery, or by taking advantage of official positions, have been able to acquire large holdings, often with the help of bank loans.[18]

In September 1978 President Moi announced that the allocation of plots was suspended because there were too many people with too much land trying to get more when most Kenyans had none. There were calls for 'a national land reform' and for ceilings to be put on land ownership by an individual.

Products

The apparently simple question: What is the relative importance of the different products of agriculture in Kenya? admits of no simple answer. Even if the question is interpreted as being purely quantitative – for who is to judge the relative importance of a food crop and the goods which can be acquired from the sale of a cash crop? – there is no simple answer, for two reasons. One reason is that the importance of the different products in value terms fluctuates violently with the fluctuations in world market prices. The rise in the price of coffee after 1975 meant that the contribution of coffee to the total value of agricultural production was quite different in 1977 from 1975. The second reason is that there are no regular and comprehensive figures of the total production of many agricultural products.

It may seem strange in a country where the statistics are as well developed as in Kenya, that there is this lack of production figures. The lack is certainly no reflection on the statistical services, but follows from the nature of the economy and the sources of statistical information. Most statistics, in all countries, are a by-product of other activities, administrative or commercial.[19] Data on agricultural production are generated when crops flow past a recording point, which is usually the point at which the crop is sold. Regular crop production statistics are, therefore, a by-product of marketing. In Kenya, a large part of the production of many crops which are important in agricultural activity and in the welfare of the farmers, of which maize is the outstanding example, is not marketed and does not flow past a recording point at any stage. The greater part of the output of such crops is consumed by the growers, or sold unrecorded in local markets. For such crops it is only from specially mounted sample inquiries, which are costly and necessarily subject to error, that estimates of the total amount produced can be obtained. There is also, it may be said in passing, a further problem once an estimate has been made of the quantity produced, of converting it into value terms so that comparisons can be made. The quantity produced can all be valued at prices found to rule in local markets, and that is what has to be done, but it is conceptually a doubtful exercise to value own-consumed production in this way and only limited meaning can be attached to the arithmetic outcome.

Although large differences between recorded and total production are found mainly in food crops, where a large part of total output is not sold, there are also differences with crops that are produced only for sale. It is legal sales that are recorded, and at times when a higher price can be obtained from illegal sales than through the official marketing channels, or when there are other reasons for unofficial marketing, the official records can fail to measure the amount actually produced. In 1977 and 1978, for instance, it was suspected that a great deal of coffee was being smuggled out of Kenya as a way of exporting foreign exchange, as well as being smuggled in from neighbouring countries, so that recorded sales could either overstate or understate the size of Kenya's production.

Table 4.7 showing the value of sales of a selection of products must be read with these considerations in mind. There is no doubt about the importance of coffee and tea, or of the change in their importance with the price rise of 1976–7, but the importance of some other products, of which maize is a notable example, is grossly understated by the figures of recorded sales.

TABLE 4.7

Gross Marketed Production of Crops and Livestock

(percentages of total and total K£ m.)

	1970	1973	1975	1977
Coffee	26	27	22	46
Tea	16	14	14	22
Sugar cane	4	4	5	3
Wheat	6	3	5	3
Maize	3	7	11	5
Cattle	16	13	12	5
Dairy produce	8	9	7	5
Other	21	23	24	11
Total K£ m.	85	123	162	415

Source: *Economic Survey*, 1978, Table 8.3 and *Statistical Abstract*, 1975, Table 83.

The amount of food sold varies widely from year to year, changes in the size of the harvest having their main effect on the surplus available for sale.[20] Of course, there is not complete ignorance of the amount of food crops consumed on the farm or marketed through informal channels. There are sample inquiries and crop forecasts conducted by both the Central Bureau of Statistics and the Maize and Produce Board. The diet of Kenya's population is predominantly of cereals, and in particular of maize, and in a matter of such importance, where harvest failures can cause hunger and good weather gluts, the Government cannot afford to be in ignorance. The proportion of the maize crop sold varies from year to year, but statements about the proportion marketed differ independently, one suspects, of these real variations. 'The Maize and Produce Board only handles a very small proportion of the total maize crop. This was estimated at about 10 per cent in 1966.'[21] 'Maize, being the staple food, is the most important crop in Kenya. Marketed sales of maize, however, amount to less than 20 per cent of total production.'[22] The Integrated Rural Survey indicates that a little under one-third of smallholder production was sold, but this figure includes sales on local markets which are excluded from the figures in Table 4.7.[23] The crop forecast put out in 1978 says that in the 1977–8 crop year small farmers sold about 27 per cent of their production, or about 360,000 tons out of a total of 1⅓ m. tons, but almost all of the sales were made through local traders. The tonnage sold through the Board in 1977 from all sources was 424,000 tons.

A heroic calculation which values the total maize crop in 1977 at the price of purchases by the Maize and Produce Board shows the value of maize produced to be not 'less than 10 per cent of that of coffee', and not '20 per cent of that of tea', which are the proportions of recorded marketed output, but 40 per cent of the value of coffee and over 80 per cent of the value of tea.[24] These figures, however inaccurate, certainly give a more realistic impression of the importance of maize in the agricultural economy than the figures of marketed output.

Cattle and milk are other products where total production is very much bigger than recorded sales. The Integrated Rural Survey shows small-holders as producing 840 m. litres of milk in 1974–5, and selling, both in recorded and unrecorded sales, some 38 per cent of it. Recorded milk production amounted to 250 m. litres in 1974 and 231 m. litres in 1975.[25]

A further indication of the inadequacy of the figures of gross marketed production as a measure of the production of food crops, though an indication to be used with caution, may be obtained by comparing the value of food produced by small-holders for their own consumption with gross marketed production after the value of crops which small-holders do not produce for their own use is deducted.[26] The deduction of the value of these crops leaves a figure for the value of the remaining items of K£50.3 m. in 1974 and K£65.9 m. in 1975. The value of smallholders' consumption of their own produce in the year of the Integrated Rural Survey, 1974–5, was K£96.2 m.[27]

TABLE 4.8

Gross Recorded Marketed Production

(total K£ m.; share of large and small farms, percentages)

	Total	Large Farms	Small Farms
1964	60.4	59	41
1967	66.9	49	51
1972	105.9	47	53
1973	123.3	49	51
1974	148.4	49	51
1975	162.0	44	56
1976	250.0	49	51
1977	415.1	49	51

Source: *Economic Surveys.*

The relative importance of large and small farms in total recorded marketed output is shown in Table 4.8. The contribution of the small farms has increased since Independence, but there has been no sign of a trend increase since the late 1960s.

The Small Farms

Knowledge about the small-farm economy is increasing. In the past, when cash cropping was little developed, and indeed discouraged, there were naturally no statistical data about the small farms, because the statistics were of marketed output. With the development of cash cropping by small farmers more of their activity came to be recorded, and various special inquiries were mounted. A programme of Integrated Rural Surveys was started, the first conducted in 1974–5, and these are providing a great deal of information. It must be emphasized, however, that despite the relative profusion of data now available, the small-farm economy is still only dimly and patchily illuminated, and it would be rash to base too confident or dogmatic conclusions on the data which exist. Not everything is yet known by any means about that sector of the economy upon which nearly three-quarters of the population is dependent for its livelihood.

That this is so is indicated by the state of knowledge on what might seem to be the most straightforward and basic fact about the small-farm economy: the number of small farms. The number, of course, is changing, but so is statistical coverage. The 1974–5 survey concluded that there were 1.48 m. holdings in the main small-farm areas; in the second survey carried out in 1976 the number had risen to 1.7 m. The new data also revealed a higher proportion of very small farms among the total.[28] Table 4.9 shows the percentage distribution of holdings by size from the two surveys. New information in the future may improve on both of them, but it seems safe to conclude that about a third of the farms, and perhaps as much as a half, are smaller than one hectare. It is as well that most farmers have incomes from other sources than farming[29] because a hectare is little enough land to support a family, even though smaller holdings go with smaller families.[30] It is not a very small holding, however, for a woman to cultivate with a hoe.

TABLE 4.9

Distribution of Small Holdings by Size

(IRS-1, 1974–5, and IRS-2, 1976–7)

Size of Holding (hectares)	Number of Holdings (thousands)		Percentage of Holdings	
	IRS-1	IRS-2	IRS-1	IRS-2
less than 0.5	208	508	14	30
0.5–0.9	267	405	18	24
1.0–1.9	400	362	27	21
2.0–2.9	222	156	15	9
3.0–3.9	133	88	9	5
4.0–4.9	104	59	7	4
5.0–7.9	104	67	7	4
8.0 and over	44	59	3	3
Total	1483	1704	100	100

Source: *Integrated Rural Survey, 1974–75*, Table 7.1 and L.D. Smith, 'Low Income Smallholder Marketing and Consumption Patterns,' FAO Marketing Development Project (KEN 75/005), Nairobi, Sept. 1978.

There is considerable variation in holding sizes between different parts of the country. Table 4.10 gives a summarized distribution by Province. The differences cannot be related in a simple way to any single determinant: they will reflect population density, the nature of the agricultural economy, the historical development of land tenure, and doubtless other influences.

Table 4.11 is one way of showing the production and consumption pattern of the small farms, averaged over Kenya as a whole. A relatively high proportion of output is sold, but still less than half the total. Food crops, both for sale and home consumption, are the predominant product, though livestock and milk production are perhaps surprisingly large. 'Export crops', despite the great expansion in their production by small farmers in the period since Independence, still contributed under a tenth of the value of small-holder output. That was in 1974-5, of course, and the rise in the price of tea and coffee, as well as increases in production, means that the corresponding figures for 1977 would be substantially bigger.

TABLE 4.10

Size Distribution of Small Holdings by Province

(percentage)

Province	Less than 1 hectare	1.0–3.9 hectares	4 hectares and over
Central	17	65	18
Coast	39	42	19
Eastern	27	57	16
Nyanza	42	44	14
Rift Valley	35	43	22
Western	39	41	20
Kenya	32	51	17

Source: *Integrated Rural Surveys, 1974–75*, Table 7.1.

TABLE 4.11

Small Farms: Type and Use of Output, 1974–5

(percentages of total output)

(*a*)	
Food crop output	58
Export crop output	9
Livestock and milk output	33
(*b*)	
Food crop sales	20
Export crop sales	9
Livestock and milk sales	16
Food crop own use	38
Livestock and milk own use	17

Note: Export crops = coffee, tea, cotton, pyrethrum.
Source: *Integrated Rural Survey, 1974–75*, Table 8.24, and L.D. Smith, 'Low Income Smallholder Marketing and Consumption Patterns', FAO Consultant, September 1978.

Table 4.12 shows that the distribution of small-farm output between different products, and the extent to which output is sold, vary widely between Provinces. There is clearly a very important 'agro-ecological' influence here – there is virtually no coffee at the Coast, for instance – though it is not the only influence. Table 4.13 makes it clear that the small proportion of export crops in small-holder output for Kenya as a whole is very much the consequence of the complete or relative unimportance of export crops in all but Central and Eastern Provinces. In those two Provinces, in contrast with the others, sales of export crops rival sales of food crops in size.

TABLE 4.12

Small Farms: Type and Use of Output by Province, 1974–5

(percentages of total output)

	Province					
	Central	Coast	Eastern	Nyanza	Rift Valley	Western
(*a*)						
Output of:						
Food crops	47	50	44	83	39	64
Export crops	13	–	14	6	3	1
Livestock and milk	40	50	42	11	58	35
(*b*)						
Sales	48	45	54	38	47	36
Own use of:						
Food crops	35	36	27	51	28	45
Livestock and milk	17	19	19	11	25	19

Source: *Integrated Rural Surveys, 1974–75*, Table 8.24 and unpublished survey data.

TABLE 4.13

Small Farms: Sales of Produce as Proportion of Total Output by Province, 1974–5

(percentages)

Province	Food crop sales	Export crop sales	Livestock and milk sales	Total sales
Central	12	13	23	48
Coast	14	–	31	45
Eastern	17	14	23	54
Nyanza	32	6	–	38
Rift Valley	12	3	32	47
Western	19	1	16	36
Kenya	20	9	16	45

Source: *Economic Survey*, 1978, Table 8.8 derived from *Integrated Rural Survey, 1974–75.*

The extent to which farmers produce particular products varies within as well as between Provinces. Although some products are widely, almost universally produced, others are produced by only a minority of farmers. Table 4.14 shows the proportion of small farmers in each Province producing each of the products listed at the time of the 1974-5 survey. The Table does not say anything about the extent of production, so that a farmer producing a large quantity of a particular product has the same weight in the Table as a farmer producing a very small quantity. This fact reduces the information provided by the Table, and at present there are no data to provide a fuller picture.

TABLE 4.14

Percentage of Small-holders Growing Selected Crops by Province, 1974–5

	Province						
Crop	Central	Coast	Eastern	Nyanza	Rift Valley	Western	Kenya
Maize (l)	95	94	99	80	59	74	86
Maize (h)	67	19	30	36	92	73	50
Beans	98	28	86	39	22	79	69
Potatoes	86	2	52	1	8	–	32
Sorghum	1	2	16	75	1	37	30
Millet	–	–	19	34	51	45	24
Coffee	45	1	44	21	5	5	27
Tea	18	–	18	7	15	4	12
Pyrethrum	8	–	7	18	16	–	9
Cotton	–	5	2	17	5	20	9

Note: Maize (1) local maize; Maize (h) hybrid maize. Potatoes, English potatoes.
Source: *Integrated Rural Survey, 1974–75*, Tables 9.2–9.8.

Despite this deficiency, there are several matters of importance to which Table 4.14 draws attention. First of all, reference needs to be made to what is not in the Table. It would be wrong to imagine that Table 4.14 lists all the crops grown by small farmers, or even all that are of importance for their welfare. One omission is cassava which is widely grown in some areas, and is of importance as a 'famine crop': when other crops fail it provides at least a minimum subsistence. Coconuts and cashew nuts are important at the Coast. Fruit and vegetables are grown, particularly bananas. Large areas are cultivated with cow peas and pigeon peas. Finally, mention must be made of sugar cane, a crop which receives further notice later.[31]

Table 4.14 does show that cultivation of maize is almost universal, and that a large proportion of farmers in three Provinces grow the high-yielding hybrid maize.[32] For Kenya as a whole, maize contributed 45 per cent of the value of small-holder food crops in 1974–5. There are marked differences between Provinces in the attention given to the other food crops listed in Table 4.14. It is to be noted that even in Central and Eastern Provinces, where sales of 'export crops' are large, they are grown only by a minority of farmers. Less than half the farmers grow coffee in each of these Provinces, and less than a fifth grow tea. Although the proportions will almost certainly have increased since 1975, it seems likely that the direct benefits of the coffee and the tea price boom in 1976 and 1977 will have been felt by a minority of farmers, even in the Provinces where coffee and tea are particularly important crops.

The rural survey data make it possible to examine the distribution of crops by size of holding.[33] This is an important matter, because questions such as this can be asked of the data: Did the coffee and tea boom benefit not only a minority, but a minority composed of the larger farmers? There is no consistent pattern which applies to all crops. Certainly coffee is not confined to the larger farmers. Although a smaller proportion of farmers with the smallest holdings (less than half a hectare) grow coffee than the average, this is also true of farmers with the largest holdings (5 hectares and over). A higher proportion of middle farmers, with holdings of between 0.5 and 4.9 hectares, grow coffee than the average proportion for all holdings. With tea it is different: less than the average proportion grow tea on holdings of less than 2 hectares, and more than the average proportion on all larger holdings, but 2 hectares is hardly the holding of a wealthy man. For beans and sorghum, there is no particular relationship between the size of holding and the proportion of farmers growing the crop. For local maize, more than the average proportion grow the crop on holdings of less than 5 hectares, and less on the larger holdings. Hybrid maize is grown by a smaller than average proportion of farmers on holdings of less than 2 hectares, but not much smaller.[34]

A relationship that is evident from the rural survey data is between the scale of farming operations and the volume and proportion of total output which is sold.[35] With maize, for instance, growers producing an output valued at more than Shs. 300/- sold 22 per cent of their crop, whereas growers with outputs of lower value sold only 6 per cent. The same phenomenon is revealed in the fact that a high proportion of total sales comes from a small proportion of farmers. Maize farmers with sales of over Shs. 1,000/- a year made up 5.8 per cent of all smallholder maize farmers, but they were responsible for 71.4 per cent of the total sales of small-holder-produced maize. The pattern was similar with other food crops. The 9.5 per cent of small-holder milk producers with sales of over Shs. 1,000/- a year supplied 60 per cent of total sales of small-holder-produced milk. The underlying phenomenon, of course, is that small farmers produce food in the first place for their own consumption, so that it is the surplus over their own needs that is sold, so that the larger producers have the largest sales. Most small farmers have little to sell.

TABLE 4.15

Small-holder Coffee Production

	Quantity (thousand tons)	Percentage of total production
1964	16.6	40
1966	28.5	50
1967	28.8	60
1969	25.6	49
1970	30.4	52
1972	27.8	45
1974	39.3	56
1976	37.7	47

The progress of small-holder coffee must always be seen against the historical background in which coffee growing by Africans was completely prohibited until 1933, when there was a limited relaxation of the ban, and became really free from restriction only in 1949,[36] though later there were controls on planting under the International Coffee Agreement. By the time of Independence, small farms were already contributing 40 per cent of total output, and the proportion since then has commonly been around 50 per cent. There is no increasing trend in the share of small-holders – the largest share was 60 per cent in 1967 – and the distribution of the total crop between estates and large farms on the one hand, and small-holders on the other varies from year to year with the particular circumstances. For instance, the small-holder share declined from 53 per cent in 1975 to 47 per cent in 1976, which was a dry year in which estates, but not smallholders, were able to increase their yields by irrigating. The circumstances of 1977 were peculiar and large amounts of coffee were smuggled into Kenya.[37] Although over 97,000 tons were delivered to the Coffee Board, it is thought that Kenya's own production amounted to less than 90,000 tons.

Tea was later on the scene than coffee as an important small-holder crop.[38] It was thought to be an impracticable crop for small farmers[39] because of the need for factory processing and speedy delivery of picked leaf to the factory. Nevertheless, tea growing was begun in Nyeri District in 1952[40] and a processing factory was established in 1957. The belief in the technical impracticability of small-holder tea production proved unfounded, and Table 4.16 shows the remarkable expansion of cultivated area, number of growers, and output during the first decade of Independence. The cultivated area per grower increased after 1964–5 but has remained almost constant since 1971–2. Output per hectare increased sharply in 1976–7. Small-holders produced about a third of total output in 1977 as compared with about a fifth five years earlier. See Table 4.17. Small-holder tea growing is under supervision of a statutory body, the Kenya Tea Development Authority, and the extension of cultivation has been supported by the construction of 'tea roads' to speed the transport of picked leaf to the factory.

TABLE 4.16

Small-holder Tea Production

	Area (thousand ha)	Number of growers (thousands)	Production (thousand tons)
1964	5.1	22.3	n.a.
1971–2	26.2	66.9	11.3
1974–5	37.2	97.3	16.1
1976–7	43.6	115.6	27.7

	Area, ha, per grower	Production tons/ha
1964–5	0.23	n.a.
1971–2	0.39	0.43
1974–5	0.38	0.43
1976–7	0.38	0.64

TABLE 4.17

Share of Small Farms in Production of Tea and Sugar Cane

(percentage and tons)

	Tea		Sugar Cane		
	Small farm share percentage	Total Production (thousand tons)	Small farm share percentage (a)	(b)	Total Production (thousand tons)
1972	21	53.3	8	n.a.	1,062
1973	26	56.6	16	11	1,545
1974	27	53.4	38	25	1,719
1975	28	56.7	47	27	1,655
1976	31	62.0	50	30	1,653
1977	32	86.3	48	33	1,888

Source: Tea: *Economic Survey* (small-holder production 1971–2 as percentage of marketed production 1972 etc.).
Sugar cane: *Economic Survey* ((a) small-holders plus co-operatives; (b) small-holders).

Production of cane for processing into sugar (sugar cane had always been grown in small amounts for direct consumption – chewing) also increased enormously during the 1970s. Small-holder production in 1977 was nearly four times what it had been in 1973. The tonnage of cane produced by small-holders and co-operatives in 1977 was ten times what it had been in 1972. Although not a significant item in traditional diets, the use of sugar has become widespread, not only in the towns. The upsurge in sugar consumption resulted in the early 1970s in the need for large imports to meet the demand; and consumption was no doubt encouraged by a consumer price set at a level well below the world price.

The desire to conserve foreign exchange stimulated the implementation of policies to achieve self-sufficiency in sugar. Small-holder production was encouraged and sugar factories established. Some small-holder production has taken place under a highly organized and controlled cultivation system with an associated nucleus estate to provide two sources of supply for the factory, as in the extremely successful Mumias scheme in Western Province.[41] In other cases, small-holder production has been less highly organized. The producer price of cane was greatly increased from the middle 1970s and in 1977 was nearly three times what it had been in 1970 and 1971.[42] The encouragement of small-holder production has been almost embarrassingly successful. The 1974–8 Development Plan saw the problem as one of ensuring a sufficient supply of cane to utilize factory capacity.[43] Towards the end of 1978, however, there were complaints that the factories were unable to take all the cane on offer and much cane was being left uncut.[44] The Provincial administration was issuing warnings that farmers should not neglect food crops in their concentration on sugar. Two new factories were due to be brought into operation, which would bring the total number of large factories to seven.[45]

It should not be thought that the income of small farm households comes only from farming. An analysis of the rural survey data of income per 'adult equivalent', to get round the incomparabilities created by differences in household size, concluded that non-farm income accounted for 41 per cent of total income on average.[46] Regular employment provided 35 per cent of non-farm income (14 per cent of total income), casual employment 15 per cent, and trading, handicraft production and other such activities 26 per cent. Transfers and gifts accounted for 24 per cent of non-farm income, much of which must have come from relatives in employment and business outside the rural areas, indicating the close connection that remains between town and country dwellers. In fact, non-farm income, being more equally distributed than farm income, is an important equalizing influence, and the rural survey data suggest that the poor are those who have little land, land of low potentiality, and little non-farm income.[47]

The Large Farms

In the past in Kenya agriculture meant European farming: Africans were seen as merely cultivating for subsistence. This attitude is long gone and fogotten, though an echo lingered in the consideration given to the large-farm sector by government and the attention lavished on it.

TABLE 4.18

Large-Farm Area by Province, 1972 and 1976

(thousand hectares and percentages)

	1972	%	1976	%
Central	328	12.9	319	12.5
Coast	68	2.7	89	3.5
Eastern	275	10.8	292	11.5
Nairobi	27	1.1	26	1.0
North Eastern	–	–	–	–
Nyanza	25	1.0	26	1.0
Rift Valley	1,813	71.4	1,788	70.3
Western	2	0.1	6	0.2
Total	2,538	100	2,545	100
Forest land	150		144	
Total Kenya	2,688		2,689	

Source: *Statistical Abstract*, 1977, Tables 95 and 97.

TABLE 4.19

Large Farms: Size Distribution

(percentage of number of farms)

	1960	1976
Less than 300 ha	45	57
More than 300 ha	55	43
500–999 ha	19	15
500–1,999 ha	28	22
Number of farms	3,609	3,273

Source: *Statistical Abstract.*

Table 4.18 shows the location of the large farms by Province, with more than 70 per cent of their total area in the Rift Valley. Although the total area of the large farms as recorded has declined only little since Independence, despite the land transfer and settlement programmes, the size distribution has changed considerably. The modal farm size has remained, as it happens, at between 500 and 1,000 hectares: there were more farms in that size group in 1960 than in any other group, and that was still the case in 1976. But Table 4.19 shows that they now constitute a smaller proportion of the total, and that the proportional distribution of farms between those of less and those of more than 300 hectares has been reversed.

TABLE 4.20

Large Farms: Land Use 1976

(percentage of total area)

Crops	19
Temporary meadow and fallow	5
Uncultivated meadow and pasture	66
Forest and other land	10
Total area, thousand ha	2,689

Source: *Statistical Abstract*, 1977, Table 95.

The large farms are much less densely cultivated than the small, and that has always been so. Table 4.20 shows that only 19 per cent of the large-farms area was under crops in 1976, and in earlier years the proportion was even smaller. It must be remembered, however, that almost half the large-farms area is under ranching, and at least part of the reason is that rainfall is inadequate for successful mixed farming. About half the old Scheduled Areas was considered too dry for arable farming, and with the transfer of land to small-scale settlement that proportion of the remaining large-farms area must have increased. Although the intensity of cultivation would undoubtedly be higher if the large farms were converted into small – and after all there are small farms in marginal locations with inadequate rainfall though further such settlement is not necessarily desirable – the high proportion of 'uncultivated meadow and pasture' is not simply an example of the phenomenon observable in other parts of the world,[48] that the intensity of cultivation is a decreasing function of farm size. In the mixed-farming districts the proportion of uncultivated land ranges between 46 and 60 per cent of all land in large farms. In the major ranching district, Laikipia, it accounts for 94 per cent of the large farm area. The three districts which account for three-quarters of the total area under ranching contain 57 per cent of all uncultivated land, though only 43 per cent of all large-farms land.[49]

It was shown earlier that the large farms continue to provide around half of the marketed output of agriculture, most of it provided by the plantations, and that there is no trend towards a decline in that proportion. But this does not mean that the position of the large farms is assured. The existence of economies of scale as a justification for large farms has been questioned, and their efficiency is suspect. The large farms had always received a lion's share of government help to agriculture, in the way of credit, research, and other assistance, and help became even more necessary with the transfer of large farms into inexperienced African hands. Despite the assistance provided the large farms got into serious difficulties. The 1966–70 Development Plan noted that[50]

many of the new African large-scale farmers have run into serious trouble, first of all because most of them had to devote nearly all their savings to purchasing their farms, which left them with very little working capital . . . a number of farmers have gone heavily in debt . . . another significant factor is that very few of them had the skill and experience required . . . The unfortunate result . . . is that most African-owned large-scale farms have deteriorated since their change of ownership . . . On many farms production per acre is estimated at only around 20 per cent of pre-transfer levels . . .

Extension services for large farms were improved, training schemes were introduced, and funds made available. In 1975 a World Bank loan of K£6.5 m. was announced for the rehabilitation of ninety mixed farms and thirty-six coffee farms over a period of four years.[51]

The decision at that time to rehabilitate the ailing large farms appears to have been taken without consideration of the alternative of dividing them into small farms.[52] Yet it is argued that the advantages of small farms are great. They provide more (self-) employment than large farms. The machinery used on large farms has become more costly relative to labour and has become increasingly difficult to maintain. And there are perhaps far more unexploited technical possibilities in small- than in large-scale farming.[53] It can be argued on the other side that large farms are needed to produce wheat, of which there is insufficient, whereas more small farms would add to the surplus of maize, though if research had been directed at the difficulties of small-farm wheat production in the past some of them might have been overcome.

Whatever the balance of technical and economic advantage, increasing population and increasing landlessness will continue to exert pressure for subdivision. There are vested interests in the other direction linked with the extent of individual African large farm ownership, often by owners – the so-called 'weekend' or 'telephone farmers' – with a major interest elsewhere. But individual large farm ownership is not incompatible with small-scale farming of the land. It has already been pointed out that government policy has changed with respect to group-owned mixed farms and subdivision is to be assisted.

It is officially acknowledged[54] that 'most farm products can be produced very successfully on small-scale farms. In the long-run, therefore, a considerable amount of land currently used for large-scale farms will be sub-divided.' The argument against large farms is applicable particularly to mixed farms and coffee estates. It has perhaps less force when applied to tea and sugar estates. With these crops the need for a large-scale processing plant[55] requiring regular supplies to be economic, and on the other hand the need for speedy processing if quality is not to suffer, has always been taken to speak in favour of large scale cultivation. The development of smallholder production has taken the form of a nucleus estate with 'outgrowers'. Recently, however, the necessity for the estate had been questioned and it begins to appear perfectly feasible to produce both sugar and finished tea efficiently from small-holder supplies.

Marketing[56]

The marketing of agricultural produce in Kenya is complex and controversial. A large part is played by statutory boards, particularly for the most important products. In milk marketing a producers' monopoly, Kenya Cooperative Creameries, has a major role. The origins of the highly organized marketing system are to be found in colonial days when it was created to support the White farming interest. Prices, which are fixed by government at various points in the marketing chain, have often been set for political reasons, to favour particular groups, generally producers, on an arbitrary basis. As a result prices have often not served to balance supply and demand.

Although the maketing system 'works', collecting and distributing local foodstuffs, export crops, and farming inputs, one examination of the system[57] concluded that

> The flows of commodities and inputs through Kenya's agricultural marketing system do not take place as smoothly or as cheaply as they should . . . both food and export marketing are often performed at relatively high cost . . . production is lower and less efficiently distributed than it might be . . . Among the most critical problems . . . are those stemming from the high degree of regimentation and control.

The marketing of maize, which has a particularly stormy history, illustrates, though in an extreme form, the difficulties that arise in agricultural marketing. The arrangements for the marketing of maize have failed to guarantee a supply to deficit areas or a market for surplus areas; they have failed to prevent the necessity at times to import and at others to export maize, both at a loss. There have been times of severe national shortage accompanied by widespread hunger, as well as local shortages when maize was in surplus elsewhere. The pricing system has discouraged efficient locational specialization in maize growing, and has spawned a forest of controls which have turned farmers and traders into criminals. These deficiencies are extremely serious in the marketing of the country's major foodstuff.

The producer price of maize has been kept high to encourage production and to please the farmers, so that in surplus years exports can take place only at a loss. To pay for these losses and the other costs of marketing, including storage, the consumer price is set with a wide margin over the producer price. The high price that must be paid to buy maize encourages local production in deficit areas which are marginal for maize growing and where other activities would be more economic. The wide margin creates an incentive for producers to market outside the official system, selling direct to the consumer at below the official consumer price but above the official producer price. To limit this diversion of trade from the official channels it has been made illegal to transport maize across district boundaries without a permit, or even within a district except in very small amounts.[58] But the incentive is strong enough for there to be widespread evasion of the controls, which has been assisted by the greater availability of motor transport in rural areas now than in the past.

Illegal trade is costlier than legal trade – round about routes, bribes, fines – so that there are higher costs than need be both in the official and unofficial marketing channels. Only the Maize and Produce Board may legally store maize, and unless it exports at a loss a run of good harvests makes it unable to meet its obligation to buy all maize on offer. This situation arose in 1972. It arose again with the 1977–8 harvest. As a result of the Board's inability to buy, the controls over the movement of maize were lifted from October 1977 to June 1978, when they were reimposed. During the period of freedom, the Board was undercut by private traders and was unable to sell on the internal market. The story is likely to be repeated with the harvest of 1978–9.

Critics of the system who support a freeing of the maize market have nevertheless seen the Maize and Produce Board as having necessary functions in holding a strategic reserve, exporting surpluses which cannot be stored, and exerting some stabilizing influence by acting as a buyer and seller of last resort.[59] The problem is to determine how these services are to be paid for, because to meet the costs out of a margin between the buying and selling price invites unofficial marketing and the reimposition of controls. With free marketing, it is argued, the Board would be unable to trade on a large enough scale to raise the finance required to meet its costs. Government finance has been proposed on the grounds that the maintenance of a strategic reserve against harvest failure, given the high cost of importing,[60] is a proper function of government, and as it is a political decision to set the producer price above export parity, to meet the losses on exports would also be a proper use of government funds. It might also be thought that if subsidies for manufactured exports are desirable, there is also a case for subsidizing the export of maize, which would after all bring in foreign exchange.

A change in the marketing arrangements appeared possible with the announcement by President Moi in September 1978 that there was to be an economic review in which particular attention would be paid to the role of statutory boards, and to whether they were all necessary.

CHAPTER 5
MANUFACTURING

In the shops of Kenya one can buy Johnson's Baby Powder, Bournvita, Harpic, and Vaseline Hair Tonic made in the factories of Kenya. These are some of the many products with internationally known names which were at one time imported and are now locally manufactured. This process of 'import reproduction', that is, not simply the substitution or replacement of imports by local products, but the local manufacture of the previously imported brand, is a noticeable feature of Kenyan manufacturing industry. Nor has it escaped notice, frequently critical. It is said to involve a 'resource use . . . almost totally out of tune with local needs and conditions', which requires a 'reliance on advanced country imports for men, technology and finance', while 'income distribution and tastes are perverted to provide a market for the goods produced'.[1] These are strong words, and there is doubtless some truth behind them. But the whole truth is less simple, and to approach it one needs to start at the beginning.

Products

The statistical categories employed in this chapter do not convey much information about the particular products of Kenya's manufacturing industry, and it is worth starting out with some more impressionistic information. Some manufactures are processed local raw materials, particularly those provided by agriculture and animal husbandry. These manufactures include bacon and canned meat, butter, flour and meal, tinned fruit and vegetables, and timber products. Cement may also be included in this category, as well as beer and soft drinks – if water is counted as a locally produced raw material. Between a quarter and a third of the total output of manufacturing industry is of products where the existence of locally produced raw materials provides a major basis for the industry.[2]

In a relatively small, poor country the demand can be expected to be small, particularly for products which are not basic necessities. But it is not too small for the manufacturing of a wide range of products to have been established, though generally on a small scale and often with the encouragement of high protection from imports. Despite the low general level of incomes there are enough people with the means to demand most of the products familiar in richer countries. Textiles, clothing, footwear, soaps, detergents, toothpaste, bed frames and mattresses, electric lamps, batteries, pharmaceuticals, cosmetics, and shoe polish, as well as a wide variety of foodstuffs ranging from mass consumption maize meal to ice cream and lollies, are among the consumer goods manufactured for the local market. Building materials include, in addition to cement, metal window frames, plastic pipes, and paints. Intermediate products for other industries include agricultural chemicals, hollow cans, crown corks, electric cables, industrial gases, carbon papers, and typewriter ribbons.

The food and drink industries are the most important group within manufacturing, contributing more than one-third of the total output of manufacturing industry, and providing more than a quarter of total employment in manufacturing. Brewing is the single largest of them. These food and drink industries were even more dominant at the time of Independence, having since declined in relative importance with the growth of other sectors of manufacturing.

Chemical manufactures of various kinds comprise the second largest industrial group, as measured by its contribution to the total output of manufacturing. The term chemicals is interpreted broadly in the statistics, and includes the manufacture of soap and paint as well as the refining of petroleum. As a group these industries contribute just over a quarter of manufacturing output, but this figure is very much the consequence of the importance of petroleum, the value of the output of which is large because it includes a large value of crude oil imports. Petroleum refining itself is not a particularly important contributor to national product, and the employment it provides is tiny (fewer than 300 jobs). Mainly because of the great rise in the value of crude oil imports, the relative importance of the chemical industries as a whole has increased significantly, from about 11 per cent of total manufacturing output in 1963.

With these two broad branches of manufacturing accounting for some 60 per cent of the value of total output of manufactures, no other group of industries is of course anything like as large. Wood and paper products, including printing and publishing, account for about 10 per cent of output, textiles, clothing, and footwear also for 10 per cent, and other groups for smaller proportions. The only substantial change in the contribution of the different activities is in the manufacture and repair of transport equipment (excluding motor vehicles) the share of which has roughly halved since 1963. Despite this reduction in the relative importance of this group of activities, the railway workshops, the largest of these industries and the earliest established, remain the biggest manufacturing employer (more than 12,000 in 1977) providing more than a tenth of all employment in manufacturing.

Growth

At the time of Independence manufacturing accounted for about 12 or 13 per cent of Kenya's national product in the monetary economy, a contribution which had increased to 16 per cent by 1977. Although this increase in the relative importance of manufacturing was quite modest, because of the growth of other sectors of the economy, the output of the manufacturing sector itself had increased greatly, by nearly three and a half times.[3] (See Table 5.1). In 1977, 118,000 persons were employed in manufacturing industry, equal to 13 per cent of total wage employment. In private sector employment, the 94,700 in manufacturing amounted to 18 per cent of the total.

TABLE 5.1

Quantity Index of Manufacturing Production

1963	100
1964	115
1965	123
1966	129
1967	138
1968	149
1969	163
1970	180
1971	199
1972	209
1973	233
1974	253
1975	253
1976	299
1977	345

Source: *Statistical Abstract* and *Economic Survey*, 1978.
Note: Index with base 1969 = 100 for years 1964 to 1972 linked to previous Index with base 1964 = 100 to give value for 1963, and to later Index with base 1972 = 100 to give values for 1973–7, all converted to base 1963 = 100.

Size of Firms

There were 1,685 establishments engaged in manufacturing and repairs recorded in the 1972 Census of Industrial Production, giving employment to 106,414 persons.[4] Although only 22 per cent of all establishments had 50 or more employees, they accounted for well over 80 per cent of employment, value added, and output in manufacturing. Only 12 per cent of establishments had 100 or more employees, but they provided more than 70 per cent of employment and produced nearly three-quarters of total value added.

Some further light may be thrown on the size of firms by looking at the average employment per firm. In manufacturing as a whole, the Census shows the average number employed per firm in 1972 was only 63, but for the larger firms (100+) it was 371, for the middle sized firms 69, and for firms with less than 50 employees, no more than 14. The largest firms, as indicated by average employment per firm, were in the Transport equipment, Sugar, and Electrical machinery groups of activities, the average for the firms with 100 or more engaged being respectively 1,706, 704, and 633. There were also small firms with less than 50 engaged in these industrial groups, and their employment on average was 17, 20, and 22 respectively. There were obviously large establishments with very much more than the 100 employees which defines the group's lower limit; and among the firms having less than 50 employees, there were many very much smaller firms. There were 3,190 persons engaged in the smallest establishments in 1972 with an average employment per establishment of less than 9.

In all branches of manufacturing small firms are shown by the Census to be more numerous than large, but only in a few – clothing, furniture, non-electrical machinery, miscellaneous manufacturing – does the number employed in small firms exceed the number employed in large. In those branches of manufacturing, the value added in the small firms as a whole also exceeds that of the large firms. In all other groups except one, Printing and publishing, the proportion contributed by the larger firms is not less than three-quarters, and in most it exceeds 90 per cent. In all industrial groups, of course, value added *per firm* is much smaller for small firms than for large. The labour in small firms is not, however, of low productivity, and there are several industrial groups in which the average value added per person engaged in greater for small firms than for large. This is the case in Textiles, Clothing, Wood products, Machinery, and Transport equipment. The range of value added per person engaged, as is to be expected with the wide differences in productive processes and the use of capital equipment between the different industrial groups, is very wide. The lowest figure is K£276 in Wood products, and the highest K£2,527 in Petroleum and chemicals.

In summary, it is the fact that with few exceptions all branches of manufacturing in Kenya are dominated by the larger firms, though in most branches there is a substantial number of small firms which produce between them only a small part of the total value added.[5]

Public and Private

One basis for the differences in the size of firms is the difference between public and private sector establishments. No Census information is available for later than 1967, but in that year the average public sector establishment in the manufacturing and repair of Electrical

TABLE 5.2

Manufacturing and Repairs by Industrial Group, 1972: Establishments, Employment, Value Added

Branch	Establishments (number)				Employment (thousands)				Value Added (K£ m.)			
	Large	Medium	Small	Total	Large	Medium	Small	Total	Large	Medium	Small	Total
Food, drink and tobacco	61	47	215	323	19.4	3.1	3.7	26.2	20.0	3.1	2.1	25.2
Textiles, clothing, and footwear	31	29	295	355	12.5	2.0	3.5	18.0	6.5	0.8	1.7	9.0
Wood, paper, printing, and publishing	40	49	348	437	7.9	3.5	5.6	17.0	4.8	1.5	3.2	9.5
Petroleum, chemicals, rubber and plastic	22	19	89	130	4.5	1.3	1.3	7.1	9.6	2.2	1.1	12.9
Pottery, glass, and non-metallic minerals	8	10	32	50	2.6	0.8	0.5	3.9	4.1	0.4	0.4	4.9
Metals	21	3	109	133	5.3	0.2	1.4	6.9	4.6	0.4	0.7	5.7
Machinery	7	7	85	99	4.1	0.5	1.4	6.0	3.3	0.6	1.1	5.0
Transport equipment	11	7	29	47	18.8	0.5	0.5	19.8	6.0	0.2	0.3	6.5
Miscellaneous	2	5	104	111	0.3	0.3	1.2	1.8	0.2	0.2	1.1	1.5
Total	203	176	1306	1685	75.3	12.2	18.9	106.4	59.0	9.3	11.9	80.2

Source: *Statistical Abstract*, 1977, Table 130, 'Census of Industrial Production 1972, Summary of Results – All Establishments', and Table 133(d), (e), and (f), 'Large Scale Firms and Establishments, Manufacturing'.

Note: Full description of activities included in summary groupings above:

Food: Meat and dairy products; Canned vegetables, fish and oils and fats; Grain mill products; Bakery products; Sugar and confectioneries; Miscellaneous foods; Beverages and tobacco.
Textiles: Textiles; Clothing industry; Leather products and footwear.
Wood: Wood and cork products; Furniture and fixtures; Paper and paper products; Printing and publishing.
Petroleum: Industrial chemicals; Petroleum and other chemicals; Rubber products; Plastic products.
Pottery: Pottery and glass products; Non-metallic mineral products.
Metals: Metal products.
Machinery: Non-electrical machinery; Electrical machinery.
Miscellaneous: Miscellaneous manufactures.
Value Added = Contribution to Gross Domestic Product.

machinery, to take one example, employed 1,070 persons, whereas the private sector establishments in this activity had on average twenty-six employees.

The largest industrial enterprises, in fact, are in the public sector – the railway workshops, the Kenya Meat Commission and the Government Printer among them. The 1967 Census showed that in all but two branches of manufacturing in which there were both public and private enterprises (brewing and timber) the average size of public-sector establishments was substantially larger than those in the private sector. Some statistics of public- and private-sector manufacturing and repairs in 1967 are given in Tables 5.2 to 5.4.

TABLE 5.3

Manufacturing Industry, Public and Private, 1967

(percentage of total)

	Public	Private
Number of establishments	2	98
Number of employees	20	80
Gross product	15	85

Note: Gross Product = Output–Input.

TABLE 5.4

Average Gross Product per Establishment in Some Branches of Manufacturing, 1967

(£ thousands)

	Public Sector	Private Sector
Meat products	124	75
Dairy products	52	44
Printing	148	31
Electrical machinery	737	22
Shipbuilding and repairs	221	50
Motor vehicle repairs	494	19
Aircraft repairs	929	91

Source: *Census of Industrial Production, 1967.*

Within the private sector firms there is a wide dispersion of firm size. In several kinds of manufacturing there are firms with 500 or more employees. These are found in the manufacture of textiles, cement, footwear, beer and soft drinks, bread, hollow cans, metal windows, and in grain milling, canning and elsewhere. Of 160 or so firms with

100 or more employees listed in the Directory of Industries, 1974, nearly one-half had more than 200 employees, and 20 per cent had 500 or more.

Foreign ownership

Examples of brand names familiar elsewhere which are found attached to Kenyan products have been given at the beginning of this chapter. A large part of manufacturing is in the hands of multinational firms. Cow & Gate milk products, Bata Footwear, Metal Box cans, Union Carbide batteries, Firestone tyres, and the inevitable Coca Cola are just a few further examples. But the multinationals do not all operate under their familiar names. One of the largest manufacturing enterprises in Kenya, East African Industries, producing soaps and detergents, margarine and many other products, is a subsidiary of Unilever,[6] while Twiga Chemicals and Magadi Soda are local names for ICI.

Nevertheless, despite the extent to which manufacturing in Kenya has been taken up by the multinationals, foreign ownership of industry is by no means overwhelming. There are estimates for 1967 and 1972 (see Table 5.5). Roughly 60 per cent of the value added in manufacturing was by foreign firms in these years.[7] In food, drink, and tobacco, and in wood products foreign ownership was in a minority in 1972,

TABLE 5.5

Foreign Ownership in Manufacturing

(percentage of Gross Domestic Product from foreign firms)

(*a*) 1967	
Total manufacturing	57
Meat and dairy products	0
Grain mill and bakery products	21
Textiles	91
Footwear and clothing	84
Cement, Clay, and glass	100
Metal products	76
Railway rolling stock	0
(*b*) *1972*	
Total manufacturing	59
Food, drink, and tobacco	49
Textiles, clothing, and footwear	66
Wood and furniture	42
Paper and printing	76
Metal products	79

Source: (a) ILO Report, Table 73.
(b) *Census of Industrial Production 1972*, Table 4.14.

while in other sectors of manufacturing, notably paper and metal products, it was overwhelmingly predominant. It is possible that the foreign share has decreased since 1972 because of increasing participation in ownership by the Kenya Government. The 1972 figures may, in fact, overstate the extent of foreign ownership at that time because of the lower response rate from small establishments than from large, where foreign ownership is more important.[8] Locally owned firms are therefore not of negligible importance in Kenya manufacturing.[9]

In many branches of manufacturing the establishment of production by one foreign firm was rapidly followed by the entry of other firms. This bunching of investments is largely the result of the protection system, which means that if one firm decides to jump the barrier to imports and to produce locally, its competitors must needs follow suit. Such bunching is to be found in the manufacturing of paints, proprietary medicines, confectionery, baby foods, and razor blades, to refer to just a few instances. It is not to be assumed, however, that because of this competitive response the Kenyan market is particularly competitive. Once they are established, firms engage in the same mixture of competition and collusion that is common in other countries. Metal windows, paints, cement are industries where this pattern of behaviour is found. Foreign firms are also particularly active in the use of non-price competition, and are the major spenders on advertising.[10]

Established international products have come into production in Kenya through several different channels. In addition to the direct establishment of production by the foreign company, locally established firms have been licensed to produce, and there have been take-overs of existing companies by foreign firms. Products introduced into Kenya manufacturing through the licensing of existing firms include plastics, clothing, paper products, soft drinks, confectionery, and other foods. Take-overs of existing firms by foreign enterprises have occurred in paints, ice cream, canning, radio assembly, packaging, and many other industries.

The capital invested by foreign enterprises in manufacturing has by no means been provided entirely by the foreign investor. There has been equity participation by government through the Industrial and Commercial Development Corporation (ICDC), by the local stock exchange and other financial institutions, and for a time cheap bank credit has been available, though access to this was later restricted. It has been calculated that in the period 1964–70 some 30 per cent of all local capital, public and private, invested in manufacturing went into foreign-controlled companies, and that more than half of the funds, other than retained earnings, put into new investment by foreign-owned enterprises were locally supplied.[11]

Location

The geographical location of manufacturing is heavily concentrated. In 1972, one-half of all manufacturing establishments were located in Nairobi, and they accounted for one-half of the value of output and 55 per cent of the value added of manufacturing. Most of the remainder were located in five other towns, with Mombasa more important than the rest put together. Although a quarter of all establishments (and total employment in manufacturing) were located outside the six towns, they accounted for only 18 per cent of the value of output and 16 per cent of value added.

However, there have been great efforts to distribute industries more widely. Eldoret in the Rift Valley, for instance, is a fast-growing industrial area with plywood, textiles, chemicals,[12] and soft drinks among its recently established products. Thika, to the north of Nairobi, has a Leyland assembly plant and a plant manufacturing sulphuric acid. In Western Kenya various kinds of motor vehicle production have been established. There is a project for cotton spinning at Machakos in Eastern Province and for tractor assembly at Nakuru in Rift Valley Province. When the statistics became available for the later 1970s the location of manufacturing may appear less heavily concentrated than in earlier years.

Technology

It is possible to discuss the technology used in manufacturing, when a wide range of different industries and enterprises is involved, only in a very general way, in terms of some general proposition. The proposition about technology in developing countries that has been most discussed, is that it is often inappropriate to their factor endowment. Specifically, the proposition is that technology is too capital intensive for countries in which capital is scarce and there is much unemployed and underemployed labour.

Possible explanations for the establishment of inappropriate techniques include the existence of factor prices which do not reflect factor scarcities, the reproduction by multinational firms of the methods they use elsewhere, and the manufacture of 'inappropriate' products which require inappropriate methods to produce them. An extreme and absurd version of the inappropriate factor price argument would be that the existence of surplus labour with no opportunity cost, and of a zero value of leisure at the margin, make the 'appropriate' wage zero. More realistically, it may be argued that wages are kept high by trade-union pressure, minimum-wage legislation, and standards set for the rest of the economy by some firms for whom labour cost is unimportant. Whatever the reason for high wages, it is argued that they discourage the adoption of labour-using technologies. On the other side, measures to assist manufacturing investment, such as high depreciation allowances and other forms of subsidy to capital, make capital cheaper than it would otherwise be in relation to labour and encourage the use of capital-intensive techniques.

Multinational firms, it could be imagined, carry their technology with them, and operate on an international scale which makes it not worth while to adapt their technology to the particular economic environment of one of their smaller operations. The production of 'inappropriate' products is one element in a model of the industrialisation process which is discussed later; as a cause of capital intensity it carries the implication that there are products for the rich, which are necessarily capital-intensive in their manufacture, and products for the poor, the manufacture of which is labour intensive.

It is certainly true that in examining the capital-intensity of technology it is necessary to distinguish the choice of technique in any particular branch of manufacturing from the choice of particular branches, in other words, to distinguish between how things are produced and what things are produced. For if it is true that 'manufacturing is inherently capital-intensive',[13] it is even truer that some branches of manufacturing are inherently more capital-intensive than others – it is difficult to envisage a labour-intensive technology in petroleum refining.

In examining the technology in use in Kenyan manufacturing some standard of comparison is necessary, though difficult to devise. One possibility is to compare the capital-intensity of Kenyan manufacturing with that of some developed country. Although such a comparison must be very imprecise, as they recognized, the ILO mission found that the amount of capital per worker in manufacturing in Kenya was about one-third less than in the United Kingdom.[14]

More enlightening, perhaps, is a comparison between the behaviour of international firms which operate in Kenya and elsewhere. The information collected by the ILO mission on this question was impressionistic rather than systematic, but it did indicate that at least some firms used more labour-intensive methods in Kenya than they would have used in their home country. Even in operations where economies of scale would have allowed a high degree of mechanization, labour-intensive techniques were sometimes used. The mission quote an interesting instance in fabric printing. And although the Kenyan branches of international firms rarely carry out their own research and product design, 'this does not mean . . . that expatriate enterprises do not adapt products and processes for the Kenya market.'[15]

A comparison can also be made between the technology of international and of local firms in their Kenya operations. This comparison was also made by the ILO mission. At first sight it appeared that the international firms were more capital-intensive than local firms. They had a higher depreciation per worker and a lower share of labour in value added. But closer examination revealed the misleading nature of this conclusion based on manufacturing as a whole; a more careful comparison for branches of manufacturing in which both foreign and locally owned firms operated showed that the foreign firm was often a good deal less capital-intensive than the local firm. The overall greater capital-intensity of international firms resulted from the fact that industries in which there were no local firms had a capital-intensity above the average: it was the products international firms made, rather than the way they made them, that accounted for their high capital-intensity on average. Petroleum refining, sugar refining, cement and paint manufacture were among those branches of industry in which capital-intensity was greater than average and which were the preserve of foreign firms.

International firms were not less capital-using than local firms in every branch of industry in which both operated. In some cases the two types of firm, although in the same statistical category, Miscellaneous foods and Metal products, for example, may produce very different products, so that a proper comparison is impossible. In others, such as soft drinks and soap, international firms by the use of established brand names and high selling costs were presumably able to create a market large enough to make capital-intensive methods commercially attractive.

In the majority of branches of industry where the international firms were shown to use less capital-intensive technology than the local firms, the suggested explanation is that they employ more skilled supervisory staff and, because of better management, use them more effectively than local firms. Better supervision permits the use of production techniques which employ unskilled labour relatively efficiently. Firms deficient in technical supervision must rely more upon machines, so that their technology is more capital-intensive.

Whatever the explanation, the somewhat unexpected result of the comparison does suggest that production methods are not entirely rigid. This does not mean that all that is required to achieve an optimum technology is to establish factor prices which reflect factor scarcities. Techniques are not available generally to permit a free choice in response to price incentives. And technical change and development is faster in capital-using than in labour-using technologies. As a result, there is likely to be a trend towards the use of more capital, and it must be recognized that some labour-using techniques which are available would be uneconomic even at much lower wages than prevail. The ILO mission examined labour-using methods of manufacturing tin cans and concluded:[16] 'Their labour and capital productivities are too low compared to those of the automated techniques to make them viable at any realistic shadow wage rates. They are a vintage of techniques which have been overtaken by capital-intensive technological change.'

Although there has apparently been some adaptation of techniques to local conditions, subsidies to capital through the investment deduction system,[17] wages higher than the opportunity cost of labour, and the activities of multinational firms may have created an industrial structure which is more capital using and less labour using than would have been possible. It is not useful to stray too far into the world of might-have-been, but few conclusions on any other basis are possible. The World Bank summarizes its examination of the matter by saying:[18]

. . . the data do not indicate much deepening of physical capital . . . However, continued rising real wages would almost certainly lead to rising physical capital-intensity in the future. There is no evidence that trade policy has affected capital-intensity, although this is possible. There is also no evidence that physical capital-intensity is very high in Kenya, although it is always possible that some labor-intensive industries and processes have been precluded.

It does seem likely, as the ILO mission suggests, that the pattern of investment in the 1970s, which includes enterprises such as the motor tyre factory, have raised the capital-labour ratio. The high degree to which the domestic market for consumer goods is already satisfied by domestic production (see below) suggests that the further extension of manufacturing into intermediate products and capital equipment, the manufacture of much of which is more capital-using than many consumer goods industries, would work in this direction. This fact also suggests that the ILO is right in thinking that the scope for reducing capital-intensity is more dependent on changing what is produced, rather than by changing how any particular product is produced. But they are equally right in saying:[19]

How far one should attempt to change the pattern of demand beyond this (the effect of greater income equality) in order to favour labour-intensive goods is a difficult question. One needs evidence of the feasibility of making fundamentally new products which are labour-intensive, as well as new ways of making existing products, before any firm recommendations can be made.

One might add that one should also consider whether the people of Kenya would wish to be deprived of 'Western style goods' even though 'the economy becomes dependent on (capital-intensive) Western technologies to produce them'.[20]

Structure

The structure of manufacturing can be presented either in terms of the contribution of the different industries to total output, or in terms of their contribution to 'gross product', that is, to the value added in manufacturing.[21] See Table 5.6. Even in terms of output there does not appear to have been any radical change in the contribution of most of the different industries in the years after Independence, the only large changes being the decline in the contribution of food, drink, and tobacco, and the increase in that of 'chemicals and petroleum'. The changes are even less in terms of value added, the only two of any size being the increased share of 'chemicals and petroleum' and the decreased share of 'transport equipment'. It seems that the manufacturing sector grew rather than changed.

TABLE 5.6

Output and Gross Product of Manufacturing by Industry 1963 and 1975

(percentages)

	Output		Gross Product	
	1963	1975	1963	1975
Food, drink, and tobacco	55	34	38	34
Textiles, clothing, and footwear	8	10	10	13
Wood and paper	6	10	11	12
Petroleum and chemicals	11	26	9	15
Cement, clay, and glass	4	4	6	6
Metal products	6	7	5	7
Machinery	2	3	6	5
Transport equipment	8	4	15	8

Source: *Statistical Abstract.*

Note: Transport equipment excludes motor-vehicle repairs.
Rubber and leather products included with Textiles etc.
The distribution of total manufacturing output and gross product by industry is available for 1963 only for large firms, i.e. those with fifty or more workers. The figures for 1975 are for all firms. The difference in coverage makes no significant difference to the distribution. The proportion of both output and gross product of Food, drink, and tobacco deriving from large firms is somewhat higher than for all firms in 1975. In fact for gross product the proportion is less than 1 per cent different from that for 1963, suggesting no significant difference between the two years, though the output proportion remains substantially below that of 1963. The proportional contribution, both for output and gross product, is smaller for large firms than for all firms for Wood and paper, and larger for Petroleum and chemicals, as might be expected, the former activities being more open to small firms than the latter, but the difference is never as much as three percentage points. In the other industrial groups the proportional contribution for large firms is not significantly different from that for all firms.

This conclusion that the structure of Kenyan manufacturing has not greatly changed in the years since Independence is supported by figures of output divided into consumer goods, intermediate goods, and capital goods. One possibility is that industrial growth has been accompanied by an increase in the extent to which manufacturing industry as a whole produces its own requirements of machinery and intermediate goods. In practice many individual industries – especially in the way they are grouped for the statistics – do not produce exclusively one or other of the categories, consumer goods, intermediate goods, or capital goods. Any analysis which uses the available data to allocate industries as if they do necessarily departs from reality.[22] Nevertheless, an allocation of industries between the three categories can give a rough idea of their relative size, and a consistent allocation in two different years can give a rough impression of any change in their importance. The figures in Table 5.7 can lead only to the conclusion that there has been no significant increase in the extent to which manufacturing produces its own requirements of intermediate goods and capital goods. Indeed, there may in effect have been a decrease. In 1963 the oil refinery had barely got on stream and the gross product of the industry group, Basic industrial chemicals and petroleum, which is included in the category of industries producing intermediate goods, was very small. If this industrial group is excluded from the calculation, as in Table 5.8, the proportion of manufacturing gross product consisting of intermediate goods falls between 1963 and 1975 from 11 per cent to 8 per cent.

TABLE 5.7

End-use of Gross Product of Manufacturing

(percentages)

	1963	1975
Consumer goods	56	56
Intermediate goods	12	15
Capital goods	32	29

Source: *Statistical Abstract*, 1970, Table 93, and 1977, Table 133(b). Industries allocated according to allocation in World Bank, *Kenya*: *Into the Second Decade*, Table 20, p.344.

Quite apart from any actual decline in the percentage of intermediate goods, Tables 5.7 and 5.8 do suggest that they account for a rather small proportion of the gross product of manufacturing. Table 5.9, which is derived from the Input-Output Table for 1971,[23] further illustrates the position. It is not that an exceptionally small proportion of the output of manufacturing goes as an input into productive activity: the Table shows that very nearly one-third of total manufacturing output is used

TABLE 5.8

End-use of Manufacturing Gross Product, Excluding 'Basic industrial chemicals and petroleum'

(percentages)

	1963	1975
Consumer goods	57	60
Intermediate goods	10	8
Capital goods	33	32

TABLE 5.9

End-use of Manufacturing Output

(percentages 1971)

Input into manufacturing	8.8
Input into other sectors	22.9
Total intermediate products	31.7
Other uses:	
Private consumption and stocks	39.2
Gross fixed investment	3.1
Exports	26.0
Total other uses	68.3

Source: *Input/Output Tables for Kenya, 1971*, Table 3.
Note: Manufacturing consists of sectors 5–19 inclusive.
Value of output includes indirect taxes and import duties on imported inputs.

in this way, rather than as final output for consumption, investment, and export. What is noteworthy is that a very small part of manufacturing output – 8.8 per cent – is used as an input into *manufacturing*. Manufacturing serves other sectors of the economy. The beverages and tobacco industry produces inputs into the hotel and restaurant trade to the extent of 16 per cent of its output; 27 per cent of the output of sawmill products is an input into building and construction; metal products, such as nails, wire, and nuts and bolts, are supplied to agriculture and building. But manufacturing itself is to a large degree dependent on inputs from outside manufacturing, roughly equally from other domestic sectors and from imports. In 1971 the value of inputs amounted to 66.4 per cent of the value of output, of which domestic inputs accounted for 36.8 per cent, 8.8 per cent being from manufacturing and 28.0 per cent from other domestic productive activities; imported inputs amounted to 29.6 per cent of the value of output. The figures are set out for clarity in Table 5.10.

TABLE 5.10

Inputs into and Value Added in Manufacturing

(percentages of output, 1971)

Inputs from manufacturing	8.8
Inputs from other domestic activity	28.0
Total domestic inputs	36.8
Imported inputs	29.6
Gross value added	33.6
Gross Output	100.0

Source: *Input/Output Tables for Kenya, 1971*, Table 3.

'Finishing-touch' Industry

Because of the relatively small importance of intermediate products it has been argued that Kenyan manufacturing consists of industries in which imported materials and semi-finished products are simply given a 'finishing touch' to make them products of Kenya, and that this characteristic has become of increasing importance. There are two relationships involved in this argument: the extent to which a particular manufacturing process adds value to its inputs of materials and semi-finished products; the extent to which those inputs are imported.

TABLE 5.11

Gross Product as Percentage of Output in Manufacturing

	1963	1973	1975
All manufacturing	28.6	28.4	22.4
Basic industrial chemicals and petroleum	25.4	22.3	7.3
Grain mill products	20.6	14.4	9.3
All manufacturing other than Basic industrial chemicals and petroleum	28.7	28.9	26.4
All manufacturing other than Basic industrial chemicals and petroleum and Grain mill products	29.5	29.8	27.6

Note: All manufacturing excludes motor-vehicle repair.
Data for large-scale firms.
Source: *Statistical Abstract*, 1970, Table 93, 1977, Table 133(b) and (c).

The first of these relationships involves the difference between the Output and the Gross product of manufacturing. Table 5.11 shows the percentage of gross product in output for manufacturing as a whole and for certain industrial groups. It appears that less than a quarter of the value of the output of manufacturing is added or created in the manufacturing process, and that the new industries and firms established during the period since Independence are even more concerned with the last stage of processing than those existing in 1963, the proportion of value added having declined from 28.6 per cent to 22.4 per cent. The percentage is perhaps rather more than a 'finishing touch', but it certainly is not large: the corresponding figure for the United Kingdom is 38.6 per cent.[24] The reasons for the low figure and in particular for the decline in the percentage of value added, however, require further examination.

First of all, it is to be noted that for the first ten years of the period there was no decline in the proportion of value added, the whole of which took place between 1973 and 1975. Secondly, the percentage for manufacturing in total is as low as it is because of the extremely low values for just two industrial groups: Basic industrial chemicals and petroleum, and Grain mill products, particularly the former. If these two industries are excluded from the calculations the percentage for the rest of manufacturing is 27.6, and if the chemicals and petroleum group alone is excluded the figure is still no lower than 26.4. The two industries would be expected to have a low proportion of value added, because they are, indeed, concerned with a final processing of a raw material, crude oil in the one case, and maize and wheat in the other. No other industrial group has less than ten per cent of value added. But there is a further conclusion to be drawn from Table 5.11. It was the fall in the percentage of value added in these two industries, and particularly the sharp fall between 1973 and 1975 in Basic industrial chemicals and petroleum, which is the main cause of the decline in the percentage for All manufacturing. The decline in the percentage of value added in that industrial group was responsible for two-thirds of the six percentage points fall in the All manufacturing figure.[25] The great rise in the price of crude oil imposed by OPEC had its effect, of course, in 1974 and more fully in 1975. It is not surprising that the rate of value added in the industrial group which included oil refining should fall sharply after 1973: between 1973 and 1975 the value of inputs into the industry was multiplied five times, even though the volume of imported crude oil increased only marginally.[26]

Two-thirds of the fall in the percentage of value added in manufacturing can be accounted for directly by the world rise in oil prices, therefore. But the rise in oil prices would have been likely to increase the value of inputs and reduce the percentage of value added in all industries using oil as a fuel. This indirect effect, though it cannot be accurately measured, must have accounted for most of the remaining observed decline in the percentage of value added. There must be little left to explain in other ways. Although in some industries, in the period since Independence, growth has been accompanied by a fall in the percentage of value added in output, this fall has been offset by a rise in the percentage in other industries. There has been no general tendency for growth to be associated with a decline in the value added in manufacturing industry.

The relatively low proportion of value added in manufacturing is undoubtedly due in part to the fact that Kenyan manufacturing is only to a small extent devoted to intermediate products for further processing. But it is also due to the fact that Kenyan industry retains characteristics of its origins in the processing of raw materials produced by agriculture. In 1971, 15.6 per cent of the value of manufacturing output was accounted for by inputs from domestic agriculture. It is not the case that, because manufacturing produces only a small part of its own requirements for inputs, the remainder are imported.[27] Together with inputs from agriculture, inputs from other sectors of the domestic economy, including manufacturing, amount to 36.8 per cent of the value of manufacturing output. The sum of value added and domestically produced inputs totals over 70 per cent of the value of output, whereas imported inputs account for less than 30 per cent. See Table 5.10. Although that 70 per cent of output is not a measure of payments to domestic factors of production,[28] because it includes profits on foreign capital, it is a large enough figure to indicate that it is over-simplified to describe Kenyan manufacturing as a whole as engaged merely in adding the finishing touches to goods imported from abroad.

Markets

The main market for Kenya's manufactures is in Kenya. Some characteristics of this market are discussed later. In the past a major export market has been in the Partner States of the former East African Community, Tanzania and Uganda, and almost all the exports from Kenya to the other two Partners were manufactures. The break-up of the Community (see below, Chapter 7) and the subsequent closure of the Kenya-Tanzania border has potentially a serious effect, though in 1977 the sharp fall in exports to Tanzania was to a considerable extent offset by a rise in exports to Uganda.[29]

Statistics of the share of manufacturing output exported are not regularly available. In 1970 the proportion is said to have been about 18 per cent.[30] If 1970 is taken as 100, the value of output of manufacturing in 1975 was 312; the value of exports of manufactures was 265. These figures suggest that the proportion of manufactures going to export markets had declined, and it has been estimated that in 1976 the proportion was 13 per cent. Excluding oil products, the value of which was greatly increased, only about 8 per cent of manufactures were exported.[31] In 1977, exports of petroleum products accounted for more than half of all exports of manufactures,[32] whereas in 1970 they accounted for 29 per cent and in 1973 for only 25 per cent. As the value added to imported inputs in the petroleum industry is lower than in most other branches of manufacturing, the increasing contribution of that industry makes the export performance of Kenya's manufacturers look even more unsatisfactory.

Import substitution

Although the origins of manufacturing in Kenya are to be found in the processing of locally produced raw materials, the focus of industrialization, and policy towards industrialization, since Independence has been on import substitution. As the Development Plan published in 1974 stated, 'In the last five years, there has been a considerable amount of import substitution and this trend will continue in the next five years.'[33] There can be no doubt that import-substituting industrialization has been carried far, particularly in some industries, though the measurement of the degree of import substitution, the degree of self-sufficiency, achieved is not without its difficulties.

An obvious measure of the extent of import substitution and the degree of self-sufficiency is the proportion of total supplies of manufactures, home produced and imported combined, which is supplied by domestic production. In practice, however, the statistical and conceptual difficulties of this measure are considerable. It would be a fairly unambiguous measure for a particular single product, though it is unlikely that it would be statistically feasible to identify such a product. In principle, an increasing proportion of domestically produced transistor radio receivers in the total of imported and domestically produced sets would seem clearly to indicate a growing self-sufficiency in the product. It is by no means so clear what meaning could be attached to such a change in proportions for the statistical categories that are commonly available. Total supplies of electrical goods would include domestic products which contained imported parts which are included in the imports which have been added to domestic output to give total supply. A measurement of total supply as the sum of imports and domestic value added, instead of output, would create other difficulties. It would omit from domestic production inputs which are derived from other sectors of manufacturing – insulating materials, which are a product of the textile industry, perhaps – in which as a result of increasing production of electrical goods self-sufficiency is increasing. And when an attempt is made to deal with even broader aggregates, such as total manufactures, the difficulties are compounded.

One possibility is that the domestic production of manufactured consumer goods increases and imports are reduced, either absolutely or relatively, while the importance of imports in supplies of manufactures as a whole does not fall. The reason could be that the pursuit of import substitution in final consumer goods has increased the demand for imported materials and equipment. This is an effect of import-substituting industrialization on which there has been much comment, and the dangers of which have been stressed. However, a failure of the imported component of total supplies to decline with import substitution would not necessarily be the result of rising imports of intermediate products and capital goods for domestic manufacturing. It might, for instance, be the result of an increasing demand from agriculture for imported fertilizers, and though that might indicate an opening for further import substitution, the failure of the import ratio to fall would not be evidence of the dangers of import-substituting industrialization. On the other hand, an expansion of domestic manufacturing which does lead to a fall in the imported component of total supplies of manufactures may simply reflect the conventions of statistical classification. An increase in domestic production of a manufacture may cause a large increase in a non-manufactured import, as with petroleum refining and crude oil.

It is not an easy way out of the difficulty to deal with imports as a whole, manufactured and non-manufactured, in relation to some aggregate such as manufacturing output or value added or GDP. There are so many other influences on total imports that nothing could be deduced about import substitution. To cite only one relationship: imports are determined by exports and capital inflow, as the joint determinants of foreign-exchange availability. A constant ratio of imports to GDP is therefore likely to say more about exports and foreign investment than about import substitution.

The conclusion is not agnosticism about the meaning and measurement of import substitution but an emphasis on the dangers of hasty interpretation of aggregate ratios and on the need to look behind the figures if the reality they reflect is to be seen. With these warnings and considerations in mind it is possible to look at some indications of import substitution in Kenya.

It can be seen from Table 5.12 that imports in total have increased as a proportion of monetary GDP when valuation is at current prices. Although the proportion in 1976 was lower than the peak figure of 1975, it was still above the 1964 proportion. However, the statistical picture is again greatly affected by the increase in oil prices after 1973, which accounts for the exceptionally high ratio of imports to GDP in 1974, and when the effects of this and other price changes are removed it looks very different. In constant price terms, the ratio of imports to monetary GDP, far from being higher than at the beginning of the period, is substantially lower. In 1976 it was 28 per cent compared with 43 per cent in 1964; the figure did not fall below 40 per cent until 1972, and in 1971 it was 48 per cent. The figures at constant prices seem more relevant to the particular question of the nature and effects of import substitution (though not, of course, to other matters, such as the balance of payments) than figures which are determined by a change in the prices of imports. It is, therefore, difficult to sustain the view that when measured appropriately 'imports have grown at about the same rate as GDP',[34] and equally difficult to justify an implication that this is the result of the fact that import substitution does not reduce dependence on imports. It follows that although 'the policy of protecting import substitution industries *may* [italics added], in fact, increase Kenya's reliance on imports',[35] it does not, in fact, appear to have done so.[36]

TABLE 5.12

Ratio of Imports to GDP

(percentages)

	1964	1973	1974	1975	1976
At current prices	43.2	43.0	60.2	52.9	47.4
At constant prices	43.2	36.3	38.8	29.3	28.1

Source: *Statistical Abstract*, 1976, Table 44, 1977, Table 44.
Note: Imports of goods and services.
GDP in monetary economy at factor cost.
Constant prices of 1964. 1976 value from series at 1972 prices linked by average of overlap years of the two series, 1972 and 1973.

TABLE 5.13

Total Supply of Manufactures by Origin

(percentages)

	1964	1973	1975
Domestic Output	57.4	60.5	69.2
Imports	42.6	39.5	30.8

Source: *Statistical Abstract*, 1977, Tables 78 and 133, 1970, Tables 68 and 93.
Note: Domestic output of large firms, excluding motor-vehicle repairs.

Turning to the total supply of manufactures, Table 5.13 shows a marked decline between 1964 and 1975 in the proportion supplied by imports, and a corresponding rise in the proportion supplied by domestic industry, of manufactures as a whole.

Table 5.14 shows changes in the distribution of imports for different uses, namely consumption, intermediate use, and investment. In all three component tables the proportion of imports for final consumption declined significantly between 1964 and 1975, and the proportion for investment increased. When the distorting effect of the rise in oil prices is eliminated, it can be seen that the proportion of imports destined for intermediate use remained remarkably constant, the fall in the proportion going to final consumption being balanced by a rise in the proportion of imports for investment. To the extent that these changes reflect the process of import substitution, the growth of domestic consumer-goods industries resulted in the growth of imports of capital goods rather than of materials and components.

TABLE 5.14

End-use of Imports

(percentages)

	1964	1973	1975
(*a*) *Total Imports*			
Final Consumption	27.0	17.6	15.2
Intermediate use	57.9	61.8	66.7
Investment	15.2	20.6	18.1
(*b*) *Total Imports* less *Crude Oil*			
Final Consumption	29.9	19.1	20.5
Intermediate use	53.4	58.6	55.2
Investment	16.8	22.4	24.3
(*c*) *Manufactured Imports*			
Final Consumption	29.7	19.3	21.2
Intermediate use	52.5	57.1	53.1
Investment	17.7	23.6	25.7

Source: *Statistical Abstract*, 1976, Tables 77 and 66, 1970, Tables 68 and 60.

TABLE 5.15

Imports of Manufactures by Economic Class

(percentages)

	1964	1975
Consumer goods	33.0	22.4
Intermediate goods	18.0	23.5
Capital goods	49.0	54.1

Source: *Statistical Abstract*, 1970, Table 60, 1977, Table 67, World Bank, *Kenya: Into the Second Decade*, in p.344, Table 20.
Note: Imports as recorded in *Statistical Abstract* allocated to economic class as in World Bank, Table 20.

In a statistically convenient world, Table 5.15 would contain the same figures as Table 5.14(c), because they show the result of different ways of measuring the same underlying relationship – the use to which imported manufactures are put. The difference between the two tables is a useful warning against attempting too sophisticated an approach to the measurement of import substitution, and against putting weight on relatively small differences in the results of statistical computations. The nature of the available data makes it necessary in comparisons of imports and domestic production by economic use, to allocate groups of imports into one class of use or another, whereas in fact for many groups of imports a part is used for consumption, a part for intermediate use, and a part for investment. It is some consolation that the proportion going to final consumption is not wildly different in the two methods of measurement, nor therefore the proportion going as input into production, for both intermediate use and investment combined.

TABLE 5.16

Imports as Proportion of Total Supply of Manufactures by Economic Class

(percentages)

	1964	1975
Consumer goods	26.8	15.9
Intermediate goods	40.5	27.8
Capital goods	63.6	55.6
All manufactures	40.8	31.0

Source: *Statistical Abstract* and World Bank, loc.cit.
Note: Total Supply = Output of Large Firms + imports, both allocated to economic class as in World Bank, op.cit.

TABLE 5.17

Imports as Proportion of Total Supply of Particular Manufactures

(percentages)

	1964	1975
Food, drink, and tobacco	65.4	6.2
Textiles and clothing	73.6	40.6
Paper and printing	49.0	34.4
Chemicals, rubber, and petroleum products	39.6	24.3
Metals	59.4	43.8
Machinery	83.8	78.6
Transport equipment	58.9	60.4

Source: *Statistical Abstract*, 1970, Tables 68 and 93, 1977, Tables 78 and 133.
Note: Total Supply *equals* Output *plus* imports.

Table 5.16 shows that for manufactures as a whole, and for each of the three kinds of end-use, the proportion of imports in total supply declined substantially between 1964 and 1975. In each group Kenya became more self-sufficient. Certainly, the degree of self-sufficiency was greater in consumer goods than in intermediate goods, and greater in intermediate goods than in capital goods, both at the beginning and at the end of the period, but the 'rate of import substitution' of the three classes of goods has been in the reverse order.[37]

The contribution of imports to total supply of various groups of manufactures may be seen in Table 5.17 also to have fallen significantly, and in the case of Food, drink, and tobacco, dramatically. Only in Transport equipment does it appear that imports made a marginally larger contribution to total supply in 1975 than in 1964.

Incentives

Investment in manufacturing has been encouraged by the establishment of a reputation for stability and order, rather than by the offer of excessively generous tax concessions. The Government advertises that the effect of tax allowances is that 'an industrialist can write off 120 per cent of his investment against taxable income over a period of a few years'. However, the tax rates are relatively high and allowances not conspicuously generous, and there is no provision for tax holidays. Even so, it has been suggested that the investment-deduction system, which allows a deduction of 20 per cent of the value of new fixed assets against pre-taxed profits in the first year, with provisions for a carry-over, unnecessarily deprives the government of revenue, because it 'probably has little effect on the incentive to invest'.[38]

The availability of loans and equity participation by government in manufacturing investment is another form of financial incentive. Reference has already been made to the activities of the ICDC in providing finance, and there exists in addition the Development Finance Company of Kenya (DFCK), the Industrial Development Bank[39] and the East African Development Bank, which was established under the 1967 Treaty for East African Cooperation, and survived the demise of the East African Community. The supply of domestic finance, reducing the capital that has to be contributed by the foreign investor and spreading his risk, is an important incentive.

The political climate for investment was set before Independence when it was made clear by the pronouncements of Jomo Kenyatta that the British were not to be succeeded by 'a gangster government', and that the new Government would 'encourage investors . . . to come to Kenya'. In 1964 the Foreign Investment Protection Act entitled holders of Approved Enterprise Certificates to transfer profits and capital out of Kenya, and this right is probably a more important incentive to investment than the reliefs from taxation.

The Foreign Investment Protection Act was amended in 1976 in certain respects. As a result of these amendments the Act makes it clear that, although loans may be designated and repayment guaranteed in foreign currency, equity investment must be denominated in Kenyan currency, so that there is no guarantee of the original foreign-exchange value of the investment and the investor carries the exchange risk. Moreover, it is made clear that although the provision of foreign exchange for the repatriation of capital gains is not ruled out, the foreign-investment guarantee does not apply automatically to such transfers. These provisions were made retroactive to 1964 when the Act originally came into force. The Government claimed that there had been no change either of policy or in the way the Act was administered, but merely a removal of 'ambiguities that have up till now existed in the original wording of the law . . .'[40] But the Minister of Finance and Planning felt it necessary to acknowledge that 'a certain amount of fear and dismay has been built up amongst foreign investors following the publication of these amendments' and to issue the assurance that 'foreign investment continues to be welcome here. All that we have done is to define more precisely the foreign exchange that will be guaranteed to an investor . . . But we have defined the *status quo*.'[41]

The provisions for the transfer of profits are an important incentive for investment, particularly because of the operation of the other major form of incentive, protection. Protection is given by import duties, by licensing and quantitative restrictions, and by remissions and drawbacks of duty paid by manufacturers on imports used in production. Individual investors are able to negotiate special protection for their investments, and the possibility of restrictions being imposed on imports of their goods to protect domestic production by a competitor is a great incentive for a manufacturer to undertake production in Kenya.

The protection accorded to manufacturing is in effect a subsidy to manufacturers, and to their profits. The provisions for the conversion of the profits of foreign companies into foreign exchange means that the protective system provides a subsidy for the expatriation of foreign exchange. Protection and permission to export profits together confer great benefits on the foreign investor. The question of the benefits or losses imposed on the economy of Kenya is discussed later.[42]

Assessment

With a background of the facts of Kenyan manufacturing it is possible to examine a variety of critical opinions on the nature of the industrialization process.

One model of industrialization in a developing country, important elements of which some claim to have detected in Kenya, has an initially rapid growth in 'the simpler forms of import substitution',[43] mainly of consumer goods, and a sharp deline in growth once the 'easy' stage has been passed with the easy options taken up. The protective policies pursued to foster the initial growth of manufacturing not only encourage undesirable forms of import substitution, but also serve to inhibit further growth, particularly in the production of intermediate goods and capital equipment. Although protection for the finished product against competing imports encourages investment in domestic production, the products of this manufacturing process are domestic products in only a very limited sense. Much of the protected investment is foreign, often by multinational firms, and is in 'finishing touch' manufacturing which relies upon imported inputs, and in which domestic value added and in particular benefits to the domestic economy, given the expatriation of large profits, are small. By engaging in only the final stages of processing, the investor is able to leap the protective barrier which would impede the entry of his product as an import, at least for a time to obtain a market protection from his competitors who have not invested in local production, and yet to minimize his commitment and risk in the local market.

In addition to providing protection for the finished product against competing imports, so as further to assist the domestic producer of final products, the protective system in the model allows free entry of intermediate products. This second characteristic of the system of protection provides a specific encouragement for manufacturers to use imported inputs and directly discourages the domestic production of intermediate goods, thus reinforcing the tendency of manufacturing investment to concentrate on the final-stage processing of consumer goods. It also encourages the use of production methods which use imported capital rather than local labour. Profits are increased in the protected industries, which has two adverse effects: the outflow of foreign exchange in the repatriation of profits is increased; firms are able to pay wages out of line with incomes that can be earned in other activities.

The outcome, in this model of industrialization, is that a time is reached when the substitution of domestic products for imports of finished consumer goods has been carried very far and provides little further scope for industrial development. The possibilities for industrial growth must then be sought in the production of intermediate goods and capital equipment and manufactures for export. But the protective system which fostered the easy stage of import-substituting industrialization itself impedes the 'deepening' of the industrial structure, the extension backwards into 'earlier' stages of processing, which is now required if growth is to continue. The widespread restriction of imports makes it possible to sustain too high a rate of exchange between domestic and foreign currencies, which limits export markets for manufactures by making them expensive. And, of course, the vested interests which have been created in the existing arrangement exert powerful pressure against a radical change in the protective system.

It cannot be denied that some features of this model are to be found in the Kenyan experience of industrialization. The system of protection has in general, on the one hand, protected final products and, on the other, exempted imported inputs, hence encouraging their use and discouraging their domestic production, though this was less true after the middle 1970s when tariffs were imposed on imported raw materials. Until 1976 there were no tariffs on capital equipment, thereby discouraging its domestic production and encouraging capital-using methods of production. Since the early 1970s the tariff has to some extent become redundant, the effective restriction of competition being achieved by a system of import licensing. The controls can put enormous power in the hands of existing local producers, as when a prospective importer must obtain a 'letter of no objection' from producers possessing an Approved Enterprise Certificate before he is allowed to import the product. The licensing system was not new, and its scope had been gradually extended to protect domestic producers, but its impact was greatly increased in 1972 when it was used as a means of conserving foreign exchange, as it was also in 1975. But in 1977, when foreign exchange was plentiful because of the export boom, 12,100 licences were issued as compared with 5,300 in 1975.[44] Although imports of intermediate products which are produced in Kenya are restricted, and there have been times when restrictions, by accident or design, have affected the import of other inputs into manufacturing,[45] in general the effect of the licensing system has been similar to that of the tariff.[46]

The protective system did not develop according to a 'coherent strategy, but piece by piece in response to pressures and temptations of various kinds'.[47] The result was a structure of effective protection (see Chapter 7(e) for a discussion of this concept) with a wide dispersion of rates and little connection between the protection rate and the need for protection,[48] that does not best serve the objectives of development. But it is understandable how such a protective system has grown up. To encourage an investment in manufacturing, protection of the product was offered;[49] common sense would suggest that protection given to the product should not be offset by taxing inputs into the protected industry. But this is a case where common sense is not an adequate guide to the disadvantages flowing from such a policy. The disadvantages of the protective structure have been acknowledged by the Kenya

Government. One indication that this is so is the 1973 Budget Speech in which the Minister declared that 'our long term objectives would be reached more easily with a more even tariff structure . . . our tariffs should not encourage the excessive use of imported raw materials and capital goods', while the budget speech of the previous year had already given 'due warning . . . that the Government proposes to lower the protective barriers around domestic industry.' Among the objectives of policy on indirect taxation, it has been stated, is 'to induce industry to adopt more labour-using techniques by raising import duties on imported capital goods'.[50] In 1976 a 10 per cent duty was imposed on a number of items of capital equipment.

The argument of the critics of the protective policy seems therefore to have been accepted. The practice, however, appears mixed. In 1974 an Export Compensation Scheme, providing a subsidy of 10 per cent on the value of exports of manufactures, was introduced. In the 1977 budget the duty on a wide range of imported raw materials, which had earlier been zero, was raised from 10 or 15 per cent to 20 per cent. On the other hand, much larger duty increases were applied to provide greater protection for domestic textile and clothing manufactures. On clothing the duty was raised from 50 to 70 per cent, and an *ad valorem* duty was imposed on second-hand clothing, an import of importance to the poor, at a rate of 100 per cent. Early in 1978 the import of textiles was banned. The administration of the system can result in its being much more restrictive than the statements of policy would suggest. And more complex, powerful, and specific barriers to competition with particular domestic producers have been raised, as in the virtual monopoly given in the middle 1970s to the Firestone tyre factory established at Nairobi in 1971.

However, despite some of its features, the model of the industrialization process above is certainly not a perfect likeness of Kenyan industrialization. Manufacturing, as was shown earlier in this chapter, is by no means totally devoted to the production of substitutes for imported consumer goods; it is not properly described as 'finishing touch' manufacturing; and it is not overwhelmingly dependent on imported inputs. Nor had the predicted collapse in the growth of manufacturing following the exhaustion of the easy opportunities occurred by the end of 1977. It might have seemed to an observer of the statistics that the high mark of industrial growth was reached in 1971 when the index of manufacturing output showed a growth of 10.6 per cent, which fell to 5.0 per cent in the following year. But in 1973 the growth was up again to 11.5 per cent, though then the collapse, or at least decline, appeared really to set in, with a growth of 8.6 per cent in 1974 and of zero in 1975. But even this proved to be a false twilight, perhaps largely the result of the world economic upheaval, because in the following year the rate of growth of manufacturing output was at the record figure of 18.2 per cent, and in 1977 it was 15.4 per cent. (See Table 5.1 for the Index figures.) It would be pointlessly offering hostages to fortune to predict subsequent movements of the Index; all that need be said is that up to that time the constraints on further manufacturing development imposed by the protective system and the existing industrial structure with its vested interests, had not proved all-powerful. It would seem that the model draws attention to dangers and possibilities rather than describes an inevitable progression of events.

There is another model of industrialization in developing countries in which some observers find a representation of Kenyan reality, elements of which were mentioned in the introduction to this chapter. It has some features in common with the first model, but its emphasis is much less on the consequences of a wrong price structure created by ill-advised protection, and much more on the inequality of income distribution and the evils of foreign investment and the multinationals.[51] Its proponents would doubtless reject with scorn the idea that matters can be put right by juggling with the tariff and 'getting prices right'.

This model emphasizes that the process of import substitution in the form of the local manufacture of the previously imported multinational brand creates an industrial structure in which inappropriate goods are produced by inappropriate methods. The goods are produced to the (inappropriately high) international standards of the brand, which are costly to produce so that demand is confined to the rich, and to achieve which production is necessarily by the (inappropriately capital-intensive) internationally used method. The firms pay wages, particularly to managers, at rates vastly above the general level of incomes, thus increasing inequality. They bring in their inputs from abroad so that domestic production does not reduce the need for imports. Because their product is alien to, and inappropriate for, the life of the masses of the population, they serve a small market, so that costs are high and they can operate only with high protection, with its attendant disadvantages. Even to get the small market they supply among the rich, heavy advertising and the distortion of tastes is necessary. The pattern of consumption of the rich in poor countries is made to conform to that in rich countries, and to diverge from that of the mass of the population of their own country. And the scope for industrialization based on the demands of the rich is very limited because so many of the goods demanded by the rich cannot be produced, even with high protection, on the small scale provided by the national market.

It will be clear that this model has some features in common with the other model of the industrialization process and these have already been discussed. Perhaps the most distinctive feature of this model is its emphasis on the 'transfer of tastes' and the social divisiveness of the products of the multinationals. That the phenomenon of import reproduction is a real one is clear from the brand names that have been mentioned earlier. The issue is the extent to which import reproduction of goods for the rich is a dominating feature of Kenyan industrialization, and the extent to which it is to be deplored. A consequential question is whether anything can or should be done about it. The question can be explored from both sides by examining, first, the nature of the products, and then the nature of the market.

Among the most important sectors in Kenya manufacturing are food and textiles, including clothing and footwear. These industries, although they produce some luxuries, do not mainly produce 'inappropriate' products for the rich. The manufacture of blackcurrant juice from imported fruit makes a good debating point[52] but it is of total insignificance, and totally atypical. Kenya's factories produce maize meal, cheap cigarettes, plastic sandals, cooking fat, soap (not only 'import reproduction' toilet soap), and enamel and aluminium holloware – all products which, although maybe not all available to the poorest, are certainly items of mass consumption and by no sane stretch of the imagination luxuries for the rich.

It is untrue, to look now at the question from the other side, that manufacturing industry in Kenya finds its market among the rich, unless rich is to be given so relativistic a definition as to lose its commonsense meaning. It might reasonably be expected that the main market for manufactures would be found among a minority of the population, the majority having money incomes too small, even in the aggregate, to constitute a market for anything but an extremely limited range of manufactured goods. However limited the range of manufactures available to the poor, it must be a very small minority indeed that purchases no manufactures. And most of what the poor do buy will be domestic products. It is, indeed, imported manufactures, rather than the products of domestic industry, that find their market among the rich.

Certainly, even in the urban areas the purchases of the poor are very restricted. In the budget used for computing the urban low-income price index, 70 per cent of all expenditure on goods (something like one-third of expenditure is on services – rent, transport, education, etc.) goes on food, drink, and tobacco. About half the expenditure on food is on manufactures, mostly maize meal and wheat flour, but also bread, sugar, and cooking fat. Clothing and footwear take 15 per cent, and fuel a further 6 per cent. There is not much left for anything but a limited range of other manufactures. This budget relates to households with incomes of up to KSh.699/- a month, or K£419 a year.

The pattern is not greatly different in the budget for middle incomes of between K£420 and K£1,499. Food, drink, and tobacco, clothing, and fuel together account for 87 per cent of expenditure on goods, although the range of consumption of manufactured foods is considerably wider than in the low-income budget, and the amount spent is much greater. For incomes above K£1,500 a year the proportion of expenditure on services is much higher, approaching one-half of all expenditure, because of high expenditures on rent and transport.

But to find the market for Kenya's manufactures one must not look solely to the urban areas. Indeed, when the urban population is so small a proportion of the total, it would be surprising if it did provide the main market. Agricultural small-holders make significant purchases of some manufactures, though undoubtedly the expenditure of the poorest is negligible. The Rural Survey[53] shows that the average rural household spends K£108 a year. Of this total, K£65 or 60 per cent is spent on food, a perhaps surprisingly high proportion given that it is additional to consumption of own-produce, £16 on clothing, and K£3.25 on 'appliances, utensils and furnishings'. Even households wth the smallest holdings, less than 1 hectare, which presumably include a high proportion of the poorest households, spend K£83 a year, of which K£56 goes on food and K£10 on clothing.

Although to 'gross up' these average expenditure figures to provide an estimate of aggregate demand is a very dubious exercise, it is a way of obtaining some very rough indication of the size of the market provided by rural households. There are 1.483 m. holdings, so that an average expenditure of K£16 on clothing represents an aggregate expenditure of K£24 m. The output of manufacturers of clothing in 1974 was only K£15.1 m., but the expenditure figure will also include textiles (output of K£25.7 m. only part of which for sale to consumers) and footwear (output of K£7.6 m.). Allowing for high mark-ups between the manufacturer and the rural consumer, and for expenditure on imports, particularly second-hand clothing, rural households must constitute a sizeable part of the market for domestic clothing and consumer textiles. The same conclusion is suggested by the figures of expenditure on other identified manufactured products. The average expenditure on sugar and sweets of nearly K£9 a year constitutes an aggregate expenditure of K£12.8 m. at consumer-market prices; the value of the output of domestic manufacturers of this item, at factory-gate prices, is K£12.9 m. Aggregate expenditure on drinks and beverages amounts to K£10.4 m., on fats and oils to K£6.2 m., on furnishings to K£3.0 m., and on appliances and utensils to K£1.9 m. The average money income of these households is K£118 a year, and although there is certainly a wide dispersion around this average, and some households will have a very much smaller income, there cannot be enough households who could on any reasonable interpretation be called rich, to provide a significant part of the total expenditure. In fact, only 12 per cent of the households have an income of over K£400 a year. The evidence, incomplete and fragmentary as it may be, provides no support for the view, however correct it may be for some countries, that Kenyan manufacturing finds its market by satisfying the 'perverted tastes' of the wealthy.

The 'perversion of tastes' is the familiar 'demonstration effect', the disadvantages of which have long been recognized. It is not clear that the disadvantages of the 'rising expectations' created by the demonstration of higher standards of consumption inevitably outweigh the beneficial incentive effects, and it is even less clear that policies to deal with the disadvantages are available in which the cure is not worse than the disease. Kenya's development policy, after all, aims at least in some respects to emulate the rich countries, and the move to the consumption of superior goods is part of the process of development. Other patterns of change are conceivable; in Kenya they are 'non-agenda'. And just as it is easy to exaggerate the extent to which Kenyan manufacturing is concerned to serve the rich, so is it easy to exaggerate the disadvantages of the transfer of tastes. It might readily be agreed that a transfer of tastes from maize meal to cornflakes would not be an important ingredient of development. But could the same be said for a shift from thatch to iron for roofing, or the stimulation of a demand for plastic sandals? It has, in fact, been argued that local materials are potentially available that would provide improved roofing without the high import content and high capital intensity of the manufacture of corrugated iron, and that plastic sandals are an 'inappropriate' product because the alternative exists of sandals made from old motor tyres. If consumers believed themselves to be as well off or better off using some other roofing material, and if they preferred motor-tyre sandals, then it would be reasonable to declare corrugated iron and plastic sandals to be inappropriate products. There is a case here for research into improvements of the alternative products and for the advertising of their benefits. But unless such activity persuades consumers – and with the consumers of these two products, and of many others, we are not dealing with a small, wealthy minority – that the alternative products are to be preferred, it cannot reasonably be maintained that the transfer of tastes is detrimental – not to consumers' welfare, at any rate. And it would be a great error, compounded perhaps of ignorance and arrogance, to assume that because people are poor they have no preferences of any importance, and can be provided like cattle with what is good for them and cheap. In reality, the purchases of even the poorest consumers reflect marked preferences which are expressed in a choosiness for particular varieties or styles in such widely different products as clothing, where it might be expected, foodstuffs, and oil lamps.[54]

It is not as if the availability of corrugated iron and of plastic sandals precludes the availability of alternative products. By definition, 'appropriate' products are not capital-intensive, so that there are no significant economies of scale in their manufacture. The demand for plastic sandals does not, therefore, raise the cost of motor-tyre sandals by limiting the size of their market. They are available for those who wish to buy them, and their availability is not affected by the availability of plastic sandals. It is simply that, for many people, for many uses, plastic sandals are a superior product for which they are prepared to pay. The buyer's standard of living is higher with plastic sandals than without them. Of course, distortion of factor prices may make plastic sandals too cheap relative to motor-tyre sandals, but that is another question. It does not alter the fact that higher standards of living are often associated with the consumption of so-called 'inappropriate' products, the taste for which has been created by their being made available by modern-sector manufacturers and by imports.

Doubtless there can be a transfer of tastes to products the social utility of which (one's judgement may suggest) is small. This is hardly a problem confined to poor countries, and it provides an argument for intervention (if one's judgement is shared by those who make policy and those for whom it is made!). It is not an easy matter to know how to intervene. It is not a question of regulating the behaviour of domestic producers. The demonstration effect is exercised by imports, by the cinema, by tourists and returning travellers. To insulate the population from the disease would not be easy, and the draconian measures that would be required do not seem to be practical politics in present-day Kenya, even where it is judged that the welfare loss would be outweighed by other benefits. There is a role for fiscal policy and for research and promotion of alternative products. It can also be argued that there is a case for a tougher and more sceptical attitude on the part of the Kenya Government to overseas manufacturers than has, perhaps, been the case in the past, and that 'stricter scrutiny of investment proposals and a more critical appraisal of applications for protection are necessary to achieve appropriate import substitution',[55] which brings us back to the discussion of the first model of the industrialization process.

The Informal Sector

Nothing has been said so far of that underworld of industry, the so-called informal manufacturing sector. It is a safe bet that the statistical inquiries, even the Census of 1972 which included a sample of establishments in which less than five people were engaged, do not catch in their net a variety of manufacturing activities which, although the value of their output may in total not be large – but who can tell? – are nevertheless of significance for the livelihood not only of those engaged in them, but also of the consumers of their products.

It is difficult to find a concise definition of 'informal sector' Commonly the sector is defined negatively, as embracing activities which 'are largely ignored, rarely supported, often regulated and sometimes actively discouraged by the Government',[56] or by reference to the characteristics in which it is the reverse of the formal sector: ease of entry; reliance on indigenous resources; family ownership; small scale; labour-intensive and adapted technology; lack of formal training; unregulated markets. More concretely it has been said that the 'key characteristic of informal sector technology is its emphasis on repair and improvisation and in the use of scrap and of available tools.'[57] Informal-sector manufacturing is often undertaken without benefit of permanent buildings or legally occupied sites, on wasteland in the open air. Its labour, where not self-employed, is not subject to minimum-wages legislation or to the protection of legislation governing safety and hours of work.

Although the term 'informal' sector has only recently become popular, the existence of large numbers engaged in 'informal activities' in less-developed countries has been long recognized, with easy entry, and low requirements of skill and particularly of capital, as their major characteristics. For this reason they have sometimes been thought of primarily as unproductive, parasitical service activities – parking boys, for instance – equivalent to the 'disguised unemployment' identified in the under-employed economies of the 1930s, of which the match seller was the archetypal example. What is new is a recognition that the informal sector is not all – though it may be in part – a sump for those who have sunk down to the bottom layer of economic life. The productivity of many informal-sector activities has now been recognized, and sometimes even exaggerated, seen through rose-tinted spectacles as an economic and appropriate adaptation to the income level and factor endowment of a country in which consumers are poor and cannot afford quality, in which labour is plentiful and capital scarce, and sharply distinguishable from those highly inappropriate factories of the multinationals.

That there are important productive activities in the informal sector is clear. Not even all service activities are parasitic – the contribution of the informal sector to motor maintenance is an important case in point. But there are also goods manufactured in the informal sector which are widely consumed by the poor.

A wide range of products is manufactured in the informal sector.[58] Many of its products are substitutes for those obtainable from the formal sector. Furniture, including beds, chairs, and tables, and window frames and other products for the building trade, are examples. But the informal sector also satisfies needs which are not satisfied by formal manufacturing industry, and it is in meeting these needs, where not only the material and method of manufacture, but also the design of the product are specific to the informal sector, that the inventiveness and innovativeness of some informal-sector production is particularly to be found. Simple machines are among such products, some for use in informal manufacturing: metal-working machines to construct bicycle carriers is an instance.[59] A cutter for maize stalks, so that they can be cut into lengths for feeding to cattle, is another machine manufactured and devised in the informal machine-making industry, the demand for which results from improvements in animal husbandry. A consumer good of importance to the poor, and essentially a product of the informal sector, is the so-called 'candle' made out of scrap metal – a motor-oil tin and the lid of a dried-milk tin – which, selling for less than a shilling and burning paraffin, provides a low-cost form of lighting now widely used in Kenya. Charcoal-burning stoves and vessels for cooking and washing are other widely used consumer goods manufactured in the informal sector.

Although informal-sector activity may to some extent justifiably be seen as an 'appropriate' use of resources, producing goods appropriate to the purchasing power of the poor, it is necessary to realize that it is in no way a 'traditional' sector. On the contrary, it is in general producing products unknown in traditional society in Kenya with materials equally unknown. It is no less modern than the formal sector of multinational manufacturing, and is dependent on the formal sector for much of its material and some of its markets.

The informal metal-working industry is a good example, for it is 'directly dependent on the detritus of the modern car industry'.[60]

If too rosy a view has sometimes been taken of the informal sector, this is perhaps particularly with regard to its workers, many of them wage employees, for whom life is not by any means a bed of roses. The exclusion of informal-sector employment from the protection of labour legislation implies the probability, though certainly not the inevitability, of wage levels lower than in formal sector employment, with longer hours and worse conditions of work. A vivid picture of the dynamism and activity of the informal sector is given by the statement[61] that 'in parts of the Burmah market, near the Nairobi Stadium, the din of metal being beaten and reworked is maintained from dawn till nightfall. There is no hush at the lunch hour, as there is in Nairobi's formal Industrial

Area next door.' But the working conditions of the workers are the dark side of that feverish activity. This consideration has led to the comment[62] that 'what stands out about the so-called informal sector is that most of what it covers is primarily *a system of very intense exploitation of labour . . .*' Exploitation it may be, as one can give many meanings to that emotive word. It is difficult, however, to see much exploitation, or exploitation long endured, of employees by informal-sector employers. The ease of entry into informal manufacturing on one's own account must militate against that kind of exploitation. Some will see the workers of the informal sector exploited by the multinationals[63] – but who is not exploited by them in the eyes of some? It would perhaps be best to turn away from so theoretical an approach and to try to look more dispassionately at the effect of the activities of the informal sector. What then in fact stands out is that it provides opportunities for earning a livelihood to many who lack so good an alternative. And it provides a range of goods to the poor which assists them as producers, widens their range of consumption, and improves their standard of living beyond what they could achieve without it, and beyond what they have achieved in the past. There are no doubt ways in which it could be assisted to do this more effectively, and on a wider scale. Informal-sector activity is in fact already benefiting from the production of craftsmen by Village Polytechnics, and for its further development the informal sector requires positive assistance from the authorities rather than grudging toleration and at worst outright suppression.

CHAPTER 6

THE SERVICES SECTOR

A large part of the output of the Kenya economy consists of services. Even with the inflated value of agricultural output resulting from exceptionally high prices, services contributed 50 per cent of gross domestic product in the monetary economy in 1977. Revaluation of the outputs of the different sectors of the economy at 1972 prices raises the contribution of services to 57 per cent. Government services are the largest component of the services sector, accounting for 16 per cent of GDP at current prices in 1977. The group of activities covered by the title 'trade and transport' contributed 15 per cent. This chapter looks at three important components of this group of activities: trade or commerce; rail, road and air transport; and tourism. Though these are all service industries, the discussion in fact strays outside the services sector itself and looks at such matters as investment in roads and hotels which are included in other components of the national accounts.

(a) TRADE

The Asian trader, no less than the European settler, was a potent symbol of African subordination in colonial society. Even though the big business of commerce was in the hands of European firms with international links, the Asian trader was the 'non-African' at whom remarks such as 'traders take advantage of the ignorance of the rural consumers' and 'the poorest consumers frequently pay exorbitant prices for inferior goods',[1] were really directed.

The important issue was succinctly put in the 1966–7 Development Plan:[2]

> No other economic activity is in direct contact with so many people as commerce. As long as the people as consumers depend on retail shops that are overwhelmingly owned or operated by non-Africans, they will conclude that, although Africans have gained control over the political and administrative machinery of the country, the economic life of the nation is still in the hands of non-Africans.

The Plan document concluded that 'the present situation in commerce has a tremendous psychological impact, and a planned Africanization of the commercial sector is therefore one of the Government's important objectives.'[3]

Here was a totally understandable basis for a policy of Africanizing trade, without any need to pretend that it was 'Kenyanization' that was the aim. The Government committed itself to 'respect the constitutional safeguards against discrimination', but it was clear that the 'psychological impact' had very little to do with citizenship status, and made it essential that 'the present concentration of the trading activities in the hands of non-Africans must be reduced by actively promoting rapid entry of Africans into commerce.'[4]

The clear argument for Africanization from 'psychological impact' was supported by less pellucid economic reasoning. The existence of exploitation by the foreign trader is a staple belief the world over, and truth is less often allowed to emerge from objective economic analysis. Similarly, that high cost and inefficiency result from having too many shops is a common contention. It is frequently, if illogically, combined with allegations of monopolistic practices. All these familiar arguments are to be found in the Development Plan document. It cannot be doubted that there were inefficiencies in the trading system inherited by independent Kenya, nor that traders exploit the consumer, when they can, and engage in restrictive practices, when they can. There is, after all, the authority of Adam Smith for the view that traders never meet without conspiring against the public. It is perhaps more open to doubt that the existence of 'far too many small shops' made it possible for commerce to be 'characterized by restrictive practices which restrain competition'.[5] Anyway, from the analysis of the situation, three policy objectives emerged: growing African participation in trade; a better spread of trading facilities throughout the country; greater efficiency with lower mark-ups and fewer middlemen. There was also a desire expressed for modernization of trading practices and the disappearance of 'the bazaar system of haggling [which] went out of fashion in Europe a long time ago'.[6]

Whatever has been achieved towards the other objectives, and there is nothing said on the matter in the assessment of progress contained in the 1974–8 Development Plan,[7] nor in the annual *Economic Surveys*, Africanization has certainly gone ahead, though the figures are likely to include a good number of African 'front men' for businesses which remain essentially in non-African hands.[8] The latest available figures are from the 1971 Survey of Distribution. These show that the proportion of establishments in retail and wholesale trade owned wholly or mainly by Kenyans increased from 48 per cent in 1966 to 80 per cent in 1971, and in retail trade alone from 55 to 89 per cent. The proportion of the value of total sales in businesses owned by Kenyans is smaller than that for the number of establishments, because it is the larger businesses that remain in non-Kenyan hands, and that proportion increased between 1966 and 1971 from 30 to 54 per cent for all establishments, and from

44 to 81 per cent for retail establishments. Figures are not available for African citizens as distinct from Kenyans, including non-Africans, but it is a fair bet that the change in the proportions indicate the progress of Africanization, as there can have been few sponsored transfers of businesses from non-citizens to non-African citizens. The Development Plan document published in 1974, in a reference to the transfer of businesses to Kenyans, remarks that 'with the implementation of a new list, published recently, naming over a thousand establishments to be Kenyanized, a large part of the task will have been accomplished.'[9]

The major instrument of Kenyanization was the Trade Licensing Act of 1968, under which lists of non-Kenyan businesses which it was required should be sold to Kenyans were published from time to time. Loans were available to Kenyans for purchasing and operating the businesses taken over. The Commercial Loans Revolving Fund Scheme of the ICDC[10] was directed particularly to those who had acquired businesses from non-citizens. District Joint Loans Boards provided credit to small businesses in rural areas who neither qualified for ICDC assistance nor had access to funds from the commercial banks. The Kenya National Trading Corporation, in addition to its intended role as a state-trading organization, trading on its own account, also assisted the Africanization of commerce by appointing African agents to handle the products for which it had been given a monopoly.[11]

The plans for the Africanization of commerce fully recognized the need for both capital and credit if the programme was to be a success. That these components of the programme have been adequately supplied is less than certain. The inexperience of the new African shopkeepers has sometimes led them into difficulties from allowing too much credit to customers and failing clearly to distinguish income from revenue. The ILO mission believed that 'one of the greatest hindrances to the success and growth of small-scale trading is the lack of adequate training facilities',[12] and that the small amount spent by government on training needed to be expanded in order to avoid business failures. Credit has also been a difficulty, particularly after the KNTC began to demand cash payments from its distributors.[13]

Retail trade is a business where below the formal sector, with its agencies and licences and access to credit, the informal sector operates. Minor trading perhaps conforms most closely to the conventional image of the informal sector in which it provides barely productive, if not entirely parasitic, occupations for the unemployed. In principle, even the smallest-scale activity required a trading licence, and there was considerable harassment from time to time of unlicensed hawkers. The ILO mission complained that alongside Kenyanization the system of trade licences and KNTC agencies served to protect the monopoly profits of those who gained access to business through these means. The mission recommended the liberalization of the licensing system so that those operating without benefit of licence would cease to be in conflict with the law. The Government accepted this recommendation.[14] The 1974–8 Development Plan[15] acknowledged the fact that the licensing laws 'act as a deterrent to the promotion of business enterprises, especially in the "informal" sector' and stated that 'the Government will relax the conditions for issuing trade licences for citizens'. The effect on the informal sector however, must have been double-edged. Certainly, illegality disappeared and harassment with it, but if restrictive licensing raised prices and earnings in the protected sector, by the same token it gave improved opportunities to those who competed with the protected sector outside the law. It would not be only the former recipients of monopoly rents who would lose from a greater freedom to trade.

Although the 1971 Census of Distribution is rather long out of date, the data on the structure of distribution and the comparison with 1966 remain of interest. The increase in citizen ownership between the two censuses has already been remarked upon. Another striking change is the greater concentration of trading activity in Nairobi. In 1966, 30 per cent of all the establishments covered, were located in Nairobi, and this proportion had risen to over 40 per cent in 1971, despite the desire of Government to spread the network of distribution. In 1971, 55 per cent of all establishments were located in Nairobi and Mombasa together, and they accounted for 75 per cent of total sales. Retail establishments were less concentrated in the two main towns, but even for those, 52 per cent, with 59 per cent of sales, were in Nairobi or Mombasa. This concentration is particularly striking when it is recalled that less than 7 per cent of the population lived in these two cities at the time of the 1969 population census.

The great majority of establishments in distribution, particularly retail distribution, are shown by the censuses to be small. Ninety-one per cent of establishments had fewer than ten employees in 1971, and 72 per cent had fewer than five. For retail establishments the corresponding figures are 96 and 82 per cent. The size of establishments did not change significantly between 1966 and 1971. The predominance of small establishments is also reflected in the figures for the value of sales. The modal size of establishment measured this way had sales of between K£10,000 and K£50,000 a year in 1971, and a quarter of all establishments were in that class. A quarter of all retail establishments were also in the modal class, which had the same value of sales. Fifty-two per cent of establishments (66 per cent of retail establishments) had annual sales of less than K£10,000, and as much as 21 per cent (26 per cent for retail) had a value of sales of less than K£1,000 a year or K£20 a week.

(b) TRANSPORT

The story of Kenya's rail and air transport in recent years is largely the story of the decline and fall of economic integration in East Africa. Road transport in Kenya, although not an East African common service, was also affected by the frictions that developed between the East African countries during the decay of economic cooperation.

The integration arrangements in East Africa, which had their origins in early colonial days, at one time embraced a common market, a common currency, a common tax system, and joint research, communications, and transport services, including railways and airways.[16]

Railways

The origins of the Kenya railway system are described in Chapter 1. After the Uganda border was moved westward in 1902 the railway lay wholly within Kenya, traffic with Uganda being carried by Lake steamer from the railhead. The railway was extended into Uganda within its revised borders in the late 1920s, and was opened to traffic with Kampala at the beginning of 1931. The line to Uganda is not an extension from the Lake terminal at Kisumu, but runs to the north of the Kisumu line from Nakuru to Eldoret and on to the Uganda border at Tororo. There are spurs from the main line northwards from Nairobi to Nanyuki, from near Naivasha to Nyahururu (formerly Thomson's Falls), and from near Eldoret to beyond Moi's Bridge (formerly Hoey's Bridge). There is also a link with the Tanzanian system at Moshi, and a spur from Konza to the potash works at Lake Magadi (see Map). In 1976, 2,329 kilometres of line were open to traffic.

The railway was initially administered as a department of the Kenya Government, and its revenues and expenditures were combined with the other finances of government. In the 1920s the railway finances were separated from those of the Kenya Government, and a separate administration established. In 1948 the Kenya and Uganda Railways and Harbours Administration was amalgamated with the Tanganyika Railways and Port Services to form a single system under the East African Railways and Harbours Administration. As part of the major reoganization of the co-operation arrangements between Kenya, Tanzania, and Uganda, under the 1967 Treaty for East African Cooperation, which established the East African Community, the administration of the railways was divided from that of the harbours, and separate Corporations were established. The headquarters of the East African Railways Corporation was retained in Nairobi, which had been the EAR&H headquarters, and the headquarters of the Harbours Corporation was set up in Dar es Salaam. Under a programme of regionalization of the railways administration, regional railway headquarters were established in each of the three countries, the Kenya regional administration being distinct from the central administration, even though both were in Nairobi. Increasing difficulties in operating the co-operation arrangements, including the joint railway system, led to the dissolution of the Community and almost all its institutions. A Kenya Railways Corporation was set up in early 1977 to administer the railway system.

Although the history of the break-up of East African Railways has its own plot, it can be understood only as part of a play which was being enacted on many different stages – customs, income tax, airways, posts and telecommunications, and other joint services of the East African countries on which the curtain fell over a period of a year or so. The strains on the economic integration arrangements in East Africa had been operating from the beginning. In fact, they were responsible for the separation of the railways' finances from those of the Kenya Government, and the establishment of a separate railways administration in the 1920s, which was designed to enable the differing interests of Kenya and Uganda to be harmonized.[17] The series of reorganizations and expedients to which the integration arrangements were subjected were all designed, while maintaining the overall gains from co-operation, to achieve an equitable distribution of the benefits between the three countries. The emphasis on measures to achieve an equitable distribution of benefits became more important with the approach to Independence, when the power of the colonial authority to ensure the continuation of the integration arrangements would disappear, and their continuation would depend on consent arising from perceived advantages. The most ambitious of the reorganizations, and the one embodying the most complex provisions concerning the distribution of benefits, was that which flowed from the 1967 Treaty. One element in the whole scheme for achieving an equitable distribution of the benefits of continuing cooperation was a reallocation of the headquarters of the various common services, which had in the past been concentrated in Kenya. It was as part of this reallocation that the changes in the railways administration were made which have just been described.

It did not take long for troubles to engulf the newly founded East African Railways Corporation. It inherited the problems of the previous administration and acquired some of its own. One long-lived problem for the railways, road competition, is discussed below, and it was a fundamental cause of the financial difficulties which are indicated by the change in the out-turn of the Corporation's finances from a surplus of Shs. 3 m. in 1966 to a deficit of Shs. 8 m. in 1967, which had increased to Shs. 26 m. in 1970. The administrative structure imposed by the Treaty, and particularly the duplication of buildings and appointments, created by the attempt to decentralize in the name of regionalism, reduced efficiency and added to costs.

The financial problems developed in an atmosphere of growing suspicion and hostility between the Partner States which the railway served. The fundamental reason for the hostility between the Partner States' Governments was the feeling, particularly strong in Tanzania, that despite the reforms introduced under the Treaty, Kenya was benefiting unduly from the integration arrangements at the expense of the other members of the Community. It was this feeling that lay beneath and exacerbated whatever other difficulties were facing the railways, as well as the airways and all other spheres of co-operation between the Partner States.

In the past this belief in the benefits accruing to Kenya was almost certainly misplaced with regard to the railways, because the heavy traffic on the Kenya–Uganda line made the operations in Kenya the most profitable part of the system. It is possible that this was no longer true, or was at least less true by 1973. There had been a fall in Kenya traffic because of import restrictions in Kenya and economic disruption in Uganda, and there was increased traffic in Tanzania. There was also a view in Tanzania that the Kenya Government was more concerned with the interests of private road-hauliers than with those of the railways and was allowing excessive competition to damage the revenues of the railway in Kenya. Whatever the truth of the situation, the existence of a belief in Tanzania that she was subsidizing the other parts of the railway system gave plausibility to rumours that she was planning to withdraw from the EARC and administer her own railways.

The financial problem of the railway was compounded by a failure to transfer funds accumulated in the other regions to the Kenya headquarters, perhaps partly because of exchange-control delays.[18] On top of it all came the rise in oil prices which quadrupled the railways' fuel costs. From time to time the Corporation was unable to pay its workers and the Railways Training School was closed for a time. The report in June 1974 of a Select Committee of the East African Legislative Assembly alleging gross mismanagement and dishonesty – which some say the committee set out determined to discover – added to controversy about railway affairs. Agreements between the Governments were not implemented, and the inability to pay for spare parts resulted in the passenger services in Kenya, though not in Tanzania, being closed down in February 1975. Passenger services were resumed later in the year, but there was no radical improvement in the situation of the Corporation, though by then the central headquarters had so little control over the regions that the system was being in effect operated under three separate administrations which began to prepare for formal separation. The Kenya region started to order equipment for its own system, and began to require payments for services to the other Partner States to be in

Kenya currency. The transfer of rolling stock between the Partner States was discontinued. In 1977 the break up of the common railway system was formalized and the Kenya Railways Corporation was established.

Although the passenger services of the railway were well used, freight carriage has always been the predominant business, contributing over 90 per cent of total revenue. The major part of the freight traffic is between Mombasa and Nairobi. At one time, before the development of road transport, that section of the system carried not only all Kenya's exports and imports, but also virtually the whole of the external trade of Uganda. Petroleum products were the largest item of up-country traffic, and were of great importance for the finances of the railway. The balance of traffic was to be greatly changed by the weakening of restrictions on the development of road transport.

Roads and Road Transport

Kenya's road network was little developed before the 1960s. Although roads existed over most of the country which were passable in the dry season at least, there were few roads of high quality. In 1956 there were less than 400 miles of bitumenized road in the whole country, equal to under 2 per cent of the total road mileage. In 1966 there was still a substantial length of the main road to Uganda without a bitumen surface and in poor condition. The road between Nairobi and Mombasa was not bitumenized, except for a short distance outside the two cities, until 1968, while the main road from Nairobi to the Tanzanian border was reconstructed and bitumenized only in 1971.

To an economist the improvement of the main roads to a high technical standard was not a priority claim on resources. The 1963 IBRD report took the view that 'the improvement of the Nairobi–Mombasa road and the international road between Nairobi and Tanganyika . . . have much less claim than interior roads needed to support the development of agriculture.'[19] The IBRD mission believed that the roads should be complementary to, and not competitive with the railway, and 'the short-term economic function of the roads should primarily be to augment the railroad system in the haulage of freight.'[20] There was also the railways lobby, which feared increased competition on the railways' most profitable route when an improved road reduced road-haulage costs between Nairobi and the Coast.

There is scant evidence for much notice being paid to these considerations, and improvement of the main roads went ahead. The 1966–70 Development Plan allocated K£12 m. for main trunk roads and K£10 m. for all other roads, but it denied that this emphasis on trunk roads would 'be at the expense of programmes of road building aimed at fostering continued development of agriculture'.[21] The Plan for 1970–4, in allocating 46 per cent of its expenditure on roads to trunk roads, claimed that 'major emphasis is being directed toward feeder and other minor roads in rural areas.'[22] The Third Plan, for 1974-8, promised that 'greater emphasis will be given to the improvement and maintenance of secondary and rural access roads than has been the case over the last five years.'[23] Nevertheless, expenditure on trunk roads and primary roads in the four years of the Plan varied between 53 and 67 per cent of total expenditure on road construction.

Looking back it can be seen that to argue against the tarring of the main roads, particularly the Nairobi-Mombasa road, was crying in the wind. Some improvements in main roads were undoubtedly economically justified by the volume of traffic they were carrying, though improvements can appear self-justifying by their traffic-inducing effect. That not too much attention was paid to the desirability of road development that was 'complementary to, and not competitive with the railway', to repeat the proposition of the IBRD, may be deduced from the fact that the road to northern Tanzania, where there was no direct rail route, remained unimproved for several years after the Nairobi-Mombasa road, which ran alongside the railway throughout its length, was reconstructed and tarred. But the construction of a 'proper' road between the Capital and the Coast had acquired a symbolic value independent of its economic return. Its completion was cause for much celebration. A statement once made to the effect that 'our people have the right to drive in their cars to the coast in comfort',[24] may have been carrying things a bit far, and cries out for analysis of the meaning attached not only to 'right', but also to 'people'. But the new road certainly also improved the journey for the large number of people who travel by *matatu* taxi and bus.

By 1977 a very great development of the road network had been achieved, though the standard of construction was sometimes low, resulting in the need for frequent repairs. The standard of design has also sometimes proved inadequate, as on the Nairobi-Mombasa road, where vehicle weights have greatly exceeded what had been expected.[25] Axle-load limits were imposed on vehicles, but not for long, it being objected that restrictions on road transport hindered the Africanization of business. That maintenance has been a problem may be deduced from the emphasis in the Third Plan document that 'all types of new construction will be treated as second priority to maintenance.'[26]

Between 1963 and 1977 the total road mileage increased by 20 per cent, and the bitumenized proportion of the total rose from 4 per cent to nearly 9 per cent. This may not appear to be a startling improvement – the bitumenized mileage was increased by two and a half times – but it did mean that a large part of the main roads in the heavily populated areas of the country were tarred. Although only 62 per cent of the roads classified as International Trunk Roads, and 31 per cent of those classified as National Trunk Roads are tarred, the untarred mileage is largely through sparsely populated areas, such as along the route followed by the road towards Ethiopia. Between 1970 and 1977 the bitumenized length of the former category increased by 22, and of the latter by 84 per cent. For what are called Primary Roads, however, the bitumenized length was increased by 155 per cent, from 7 to 17 per cent of the total length of such roads. It is the improvement of these roads, which 'link provincially important centres to each other, or to higher class roads' which must have brought a substantial proportion of the population within reach of a tarred road.

The improvements to the road running 'parallel' to the railway heightened the railway's problem of road competition. Despite the poor condition of the roads, there had for many years been a road-rail problem such as most countries faced with the development of motor transport.[27] Competitive behaviour by the railway was constrained by a published tariff which required lengthy procedures to change. The tariff differentiated between commodities not according to the cost of carrying them, but according to what the traffic would bear. This system of charging provided cross-subsidization between different traffics, and the bulk carriage of petroleum products – highly charged but low cost – was a particularly profitable business on which the finances of the railway had become heavily dependent. This charging policy was viable so long as the high-rated traffics, which were profitable to road hauliers as well as to the railway, were not competed away. The scope for this to occur was limited by restrictive licensing of road transport.

At about the same time as the new road between Nairobi and Mombasa was opened to traffic there was a relaxation of the restrictions on road transport. Investments were made in road vehicles for the haulage of petroleum products (many of them, it was said, were owned by well-placed Kenyans), and there was a diversion of this highly profitable traffic from the railway. By 1974 about half the total oil transported to Nairobi from the Mombasa refinery had been diverted to the road.[28] The new road also generated a great deal of other traffic, some of which would otherwise have been carried by rail. The change in the relative positions of road and rail may be judged by the fact that in 1966 the railway earned 72 per cent of the total revenue from the carriage of freight, and the road-transport industry only 28 per cent; by 1977 the railway had become less important than road transport, receiving only 46 per cent of the revenue compared with road transport's 54 per cent.

Although changes were delayed by cumbersome procedures, adjustments were made in the railway tariff which limited the diversion of traffic to the roads. The volume of traffic carried by rail and the total revenue continued to increase, but the reduction in the tariff for high-rated traffics such as petroleum products reduced their profitability and contributed to the serious adverse turn in the railway finances.

Both road and rail transporters were faced with a changed future, with the decision in 1974, already forseen in the 1970–4 Development Plan,[29] to construct a pipeline for petroleum products from Mombasa to Nairobi. It was argued that the volume of oil to be transported in the future would require heavy investments in the existing means of transport, and that a pipeline would be more economic. The damage to the road was again brought into the argument.[30] It is not clear what consideration was given to the economics of transporting oil products by rail alone, with a prohibition on the use of motor transport. The pipeline was brought into use early in 1978.[31]

The 1970–4 Development Plan set out the transport policy that was to be pursued with some clarity.[32] It was to be essentially a 'pricing solution' to the problem of distributing the traffic between the different modes of transport. Modifications in the railway tariff to allow charges to reflect costs were favoured, as was progress toward greater freedom in licensing road hauliers. Both policies had been recommended in the large-scale East African Transport Study, the report of which had been submitted to the East African Governments in 1969. Kenya's policy, 'recognising that the country has moved from a monopolistic to a competitive transport scene', was 'to permit and encourage each mode of transport to offer the service . . . which it is peculiarly capable of providing.'[33] A realistic gloss was put on these unexceptionable statements in the 1974–8 Plan, which suggests alarm at the way road transport had been developing. The Plan declared that the objectives of road–rail coordination were to make maximum use of the railway and to avoid the high cost of repairing 'roads ruined by vehicles which transport goods that should have been moved by rail'.[34]

The government is itself a participant in the road transport industry. In 1966 Kenatco (Kenya National Transport Company) was formed as a wholly owned subsidiary of ICDC, taking over an existing co-operative transport company which had got into financial difficulties. Kenatco made heavy losses in its early years, but a successful period ensued. Kenatco developed its freight business in several directions, but particularly important was its haulage to and from Zambia. Kenya developed a sizeable export trade to Zambia from 1966, and the bulk of the goods were transported by Kenatco. Kenatco also carried Zambian copper and other goods as a return load when Zambia's normal outlets were cut by the fighting in Angola and the closure of the border with Rhodesia. Large vehicles with trailers were used for the traffic, and up to 300 were operating through Tanzania to Zambia in 1974. This business was badly hit by Tanzania's imposition at the end of the 1974 of a ban on heavy-duty vehicles operating into Tanzania from Kenya. Tanzania's complaint was at the damage being caused to the roads, which can be believed when the similar difficulties on the Nairobi–Mombasa road are remembered. But the decision must also be seen in the context of the deteriorating relations at the time between the Partner States of the East African Community.

After this setback, Kenatco continued its business with Zambia using other vehicles, though it lost the traffic in Zambia's exports to the newly opened Tazara railway from Zambia to Dar es Salaam. Then, with the increasing tension between the Partner States, the Kenya–Tanzania border was closed in February 1977. Apart from the loss of its route to Zambia, Kenatco suffered the loss of nearly one-third of its long-haul vehicles, which were in Tanzania when the border was closed, and were detained there. The company made up for some of its loss of Zambian business by operating to Uganda and Rwanda and to the Southern Sudan.

Passenger transport is mainly a business for the roads. The licensing of passenger vehicles was modelled on the British arrangements, and has protected, though not with complete success, the monopoly of large operators. Within Nairobi the monopoly Kenya Bus Services Ltd. operates, and long-distance journeys are dominated by East African Road Services, both large foreign-owned companies. The defence of restrictions has been along the lines familiar from the experience of transport licensing in other countries. Controls were necessary to avoid cut-throat competition, to allow regular, scheduled services, and for safety. In Kenya there was an additional feature, as licensing was an instrument of Africanization. Licences were being issued mainly to Africans, and by 1973 they already accounted for nearly 80 per cent of the holders of passenger licences. But Africanization, and competition, also developed through illegal, unlicensed operators. The *matatu* car or mini-bus, operating without benefit of licence, is the transport manifestation of the informal sector. Despite police harassment the unlicensed sector thrived and played an important role not only within the towns but also in long distance passenger transport. The ILO mission were very taken with the *matatu*. They believed they were beneficial for employment and for income generation and distribution. They noted that *matatus* competed with 'the public bus transport monopoly mainly in areas where there is heavy traffic at peak hours and where the transport companies make big profits' and remarked, somewhat naïvely it appears to anyone familiar with, for example, the discussion in the 1930s about London buses, that 'there are hardly any *matatus* in areas where these companies are not making profits.'[35] Despite that remark, which in fact concedes much of the monopoly bus companies' case, the Kenya Government was persuaded by the plea for liberty. In June 1973, by Presidential decree, all vehicles under 3-ton tare weight were exempted from licensing.[36]

Airways and Airports

East African Airways had its origins in a private company operating from Wilson Airport, Nairobi. It was established as a public corporation in 1946, with its capital subscribed jointly by Kenya, Tangangika, and Uganda. As the national airline of East Africa it had a monopoly of domestic routes. Its operations ceased to be purely domestic in 1949 when it began flights to Mozambique and South Africa. The Corporation commenced flying to London in 1954, began operating jet aircraft in 1960, and became a major carrier between Europe and East Africa when it introduced Super VC 10 flights in 1966. The airline's main international traffic, on which it depended for its profit, derived from Nairobi, and its domestic traffic was least unprofitable in Kenya. The internal services in Tanzania were particularly costly to operate, involving long distances and small loads.

The Treaty for East African Cooperation provided for the continuation of the headquarters of EAA and its main workshops at Nairobi. The Corporation got off to a good start after any uncertainty about its future as a joint airline seemed to be settled by the Treaty. It soon ran into trouble, some of its own making, and some as part of the general strains within the Community.

The administration of EAA left a great deal to be desired, and its commercial judgment was bad. Its finances were badly hit by a euphoric and ill-judged extension of services to North America and the Far East, the high losses on which soon forced their abandonment. There were financial losses from incompetence, if not from corruption. Uncollected debts amounted to 37 per cent of revenue in 1970. A net operating surplus of Shs. 14.3 m. in 1968 had become a deficit of Shs. 60.8 m. in 1971. The Partner States put new capital into the Corporation and arrangements were made with a foreign airline to provide technical and managerial assistance. By 1974 the financial position of the Corporation had taken a turn for the better, and the worst appeared to be over.

This optimism proved to be ill founded and EAA became increasingly a victim of the deteriorating relations between the Partner States. By the end of 1976 the manifestation of the disagreements between the Partner States of the Community which particularly affected EEA, it was claimed, was the failure to transfer funds accumulated in the other countries to the country in which the headquarters was located. The Nairobi headquarters of EAA had to pay the bills, but was being deprived of revenue. It is unclear how quantitatively important this issue was in reality, but it served as one ingredient in an increasingly acrimonious situation in which there were well-publicized squabbles between the EAA Board members from the different Partner States. In any case, EAA was overwhelmingly in debt, there were doubts about the Corporation's ability to pay wages and salaries, some of its aircraft were grounded at Nairobi for its failure to pay landing fees, and flights were stopped when the oil companies required cash payments for fuel.[37] There were growing rumours that each of the States was to establish its own airline in expectation of the collapse of EAA.[38]

As air traffic had become so important with the growth of tourism and freight, Kenya was particularly quick to set up her own airline. East African Airways finally collapsed at the beginning of February 1977. Kenya Airways Ltd. was established as a wholly government-owned company, and Kenya had the 'flag carrier' some prominent Kenyans had long wanted. The East African Airways long-range fleet was grounded by legal problems of ownership and was not available for use by any of the former Partner States. The new airline therefore began operations with leased aircraft, but by the end of 1977 it had purchased three planes for use on international routes, and it was claimed that it had 'taken over a sizeable portion of the business which was formerly handled by the East African Airways Corporation.'[39] Kenya Airways began operating to several European and Asian cities as well as to Indian Ocean and African airports. The airline was unable to obtain permission to over-fly Tanzania *en route* to Zambia.

Air services between Kenya and Tanzania ceased with the collapse of EAA, but international airlines quickly took on the business between Nairobi and Dar es Salaam which had previously been reserved for the national carrier. This traffic was stopped by the Kenya Government in November 1977 and direct air links between Kenya and Tanzania came to an end, though some private charters have been allowed.

EAA did not fail because it was entirely unsuccessful in attracting traffic. The number of passengers carried rose from 344,000 in 1967 to 758,000 in 1976, an increase of 120 per cent, though aircraft kilometres flown increased by only 43 per cent. Cargo and mail carried, measured in ton-kilometres, doubled over the same period. The growth of tourism clearly offers possibilities of commercial success to Kenya Airways, provided it can compete with foreign airlines. There are also possibilities from freight traffic. The growing export of horticultural products could be important, though it is a traffic particularly sensitive to freight charges. It remains to be seen whether Kenya Airways is able to grasp the opportunities more successfully than EAA.

Kenya now has two international airports, equipped to deal with

European flights: Nairobi and Mombasa. Air traffic at Nairobi moved in 1978 to the fourth airport terminal in its relatively brief history. Beginning at the privately owned Wilson airport, it moved to the former RAF base at Eastleigh, and then in the mid-1950s to a new international airport at Embakasi. Despite reconstructions and extensions, the traffic outgrew the old facilities and a great new Embakasi terminal, fully equipped with all the conveniences and inconveniences of modern airport design, was opened to traffic in March 1978. The development of Mombasa airport from a very small affair to an international standard able to handle direct traffic with Europe, took place over the years 1976 to 1978. The new Mombasa airport is an important element in the future of the tourist industry, to a discussion of which we now turn.

(c) TOURISM

Tourism, as everyone must know, is one of Kenya's success stories. *Safari* has become an international word, and contemporary travels are far removed from the big game expeditions of yesteryear. Kenya is now no more remote – and even less 'foreign' – than the Costa Brava. The era of mass tourism arrived in the middle 1960s, and tourism became one of Kenya's leading industries. It is an export industry – in 1977 not much more than one-quarter of hotel 'bednights', to take one index of the size of tourism, were provided by East African residents – and might therefore seem to be immune from the criticisms levelled at import-substituting industry, though it has its own band of critics, and even export industries have an import content. It is not immune from the market changes which affect other export industries, and it would be rash to predict into a future of the distance relevant to the long-lived investments important for tourism – airports and hotels, for instance – the growth rates of the recent past.

The tourist attractions of Kenya are of two distinct kinds: wild life and beach life. The latter has competition from resorts all over the world; competition for the former is mainly from places more distant from the main sources of tourists or less organized to receive them than Kenya. There must be few tourists who do not at least sample both delights, though probably most partake mainly of one or the other. Also of some importance is a group of visitors who doubtless frequently combine pleasure with the business purposes of their visit, including the international conference business.

There is little doubt which of these types of tourism is the growth sector, in terms of numbers at any rate. The contribution to income from tourism is another thing. While hotel bednights in total increased from 1 million in 1965 to 3.6 m. in 1976, bednights at beach hotels increased from only 53,000 to nearly 1.2 m. If a more substantial base,

1968, is taken as 100, the number of bednights in 1976 was 240 in total and 565 for beach hotels. And it is on the beaches that the main expansion of tourist accommodation has taken place. The accommodation available throughout the country increased between 1967 and 1976 by 180 per cent, and in beach hotels by 280 per cent, the beach-hotel proportion of the total rising from 23 to 32 per cent.

Despite the great increase in the number of hotel bednights, the over-ambitious planned targets were not achieved, and there has been an increasing gap between achievement and target. In 1971 the target was hit, but only because an excess of foreign visitors above the target offset the number by which Kenyan and other East African visitors fell below it. In 1973, however, the achievement was below the target also for foreign visitors. In 1977, the number of bednights was only 72 per cent of the target number for foreign visitors, and 81 per cent for East Africans. Occupancy rates continue to be relatively low because of the peakiness of demand. The bed-occupancy rate for Kenya as a whole was 47 per cent in 1965, 55 per cent in 1966, and 51 per cent in 1976, though the rate at beach hotels was 62 per cent.

The number of visitors has not been on an increasing trend, despite the increasing number of hotel bednights. The number of visitors arriving on holiday was at a maximum in 1972, when it was 328,000; after a decline the number was up to 325,000 in 1976 but fell to 261,000 in 1977. Arrivals on business were at a maximum in 1976, but fell off more sharply in 1977, from 65,000 to 40,000. The number of days spent in Kenya in the aggregate increased marginally in 1977, even though there were fewer arrivals, an increase in the aggregate of days spent by holiday-makers offsetting a large decline in the numbers of days spent on business.

The source of Kenya's tourists has been changing. There have been two sets of changes which are best looked at separately. Holiday visitors from Europe and North America increased by over a quarter between 1971 and 1977.[40] The source of the greatest number in 1971 was the United States, which accounted for 29 per cent of the total; in 1977 the United States contributed only 14 per cent of the holiday visitors from Europe and North America. Not only the proportion but the absolute number of US visitors declined: in 1972 there were 58,000 and in 1977 only 29,000. The contribution of Britain also fell from 22 per cent to 17 per cent. In contrast, West Germany became the largest source of visitors, its proportion of all European and North American holiday visitors rising from 19 per cent to 23 per cent. In addition, Switzerland provided 11 per cent of the total in 1977, Italy 10 per cent, France 7 per cent, and the rest of Europe, particularly Scandinavia, provided 33 per cent. These changes underline the sensitivity of tourism to factors beyond Kenya's control. They were largely the result of changes in such things as airline tariffs and foreign-exchange rates, which made a holiday in Kenya cheap from some places and dear from others.

The other notable change has been in the importance of visitors from Tanzania and Uganda. In 1971 the other East African countries were the largest source of visitors. They provided 36 per cent of all holiday visitors. In 1976 the proportion had fallen to 21 per cent and in 1977 to only 10 per cent.[41] In 1977 there were fewer visitors from Tanzania than from Switzerland! As an indication of the change in East African relationships, perhaps temporary, this fact would be hard to beat.

Statistics on the structure of the tourist industry are scanty. It can be thought of as having two main parts: hotels and tour operators. Both are largely within the private sector, though with government financial participation. Private African participation in ownership is as yet minimal. There are hotels owned by Kenyans, not only on a small scale, but they are mostly Kenyans of European origin, though some hotels have recently been acquired by Africans. The major investment in hotels in the last decade or so has been from overseas, and major international chains are represented; Kenya has its Hilton and its Intercontinental. Tour operation is on a smaller scale, but nevertheless there is little participation by Africans in ownership or management.

Various statutory authorities have invested in hotels. The Development Finance Company of Kenya[42] is one of them which had over K£900,000 invested or committed to tourism at the end of 1977. The Kenya Tourist Development Authority (KTDC) is the major instrument of government intervention in the industry. By 1976 the KTDC had invested K£4.2 m. in the industry, and a further K£1.8 m. was invested in 1977. At the end of that year the Corporation held equity investment in 24 projects,[43] in ten of which it was a majority shareholder. The Corporation has an Africanization programme under which it provides soft loans to help the establishment or acquisition of enterprises, and it had invested K£1½ m. in this programme by the end of 1977.

Such direct investments are not the only way in which the government has invested for the benefit of the industry. Some part of total investment in roads and other services must be seen as on behalf of tourism, and in particular there has been a very large investment in airports. The reconstruction of Mombasa airport between 1976 and 1978 at a cost of K£11 m. to handle direct flights with Europe, is fundamental to the future of Coast tourism. The new Nairobi airport terminal, built at a cost of K£28 m., was needed to deal with the tourist trade. Substantial expenditures are also undertaken on the promotion of tourism. The provision of training in hotel work is a further form of government assistance to the industry. A hotel school has been set up just outside Nairobi with aid from Switzerland, and a Catering Training Levy is imposed on hotel and restaurant bills.

It is shown in Chapter 7 that tourism is an important contributor to the surplus on the invisible account of the balance of payments. Estimates of receipts from tourism indicate that they increased from about K£15 m. in 1967 to K£48 m. in 1977. Over the same period, hotel bed-nights of foreign residents multiplied nine times, compared with the rise in receipts from tourism of just over three times. For a shorter period, between 1971 and 1977, receipts and bednights both roughly doubled. But these figures are in current prices, and allowance for the effect of price increases suggests that in real terms income from tourism has not been anything like keeping pace with the growth of tourism. It is easy to conclude that the net benefit from 'mass' or 'package' tourism is small; it is much less easy for the industry to move 'up market'.

There can be no doubt about the desirability of Kenya for the tourist; the desirability of the tourist for Kenya requires more investigation. It might appear obvious that an industry with export earnings at times rivalling those of coffee must be of major benefit to the people of Kenya. But the costs to be set against the benefits are large. It is easy to see that the imports consumed by tourists, either directly or embodied in Kenya-made goods and services, are a cost to be set against the benefits from tourism. What is of greater importance, however, is the fact that the Kenyan resources devoted to tourism would be available to produce something else if they were not used for tourism. Merely to deduct from the expenditure of tourists the obvious offests, such as the import content of goods and services and expatriated profits, to arrive at the benefit would be valid only if Kenyan resources employed in tourism had a zero opportunity cost, that is, if they would be producing nothing if they were not employed in tourism.

One estimate of the value of foreign tourism to Kenya[44] put it at no more than between 5 and 10 per cent of the revenue from tourism in 1967. Higher taxation will have increased the benefit since then. But the estimate is so low particularly because a relatively high opportunity cost is assumed for the resources devoted to tourism. For some resources – capital, for instance – the opportunity cost no doubt is high, because there are many other possibilities for their productive employment. The existence of large-scale unemployment and underemployment suggests that the opportunity cost of labour may be low, and that the employment provided is one of the major benefits of tourism to Kenya.

There are no good statistics of the amount of employment generated by tourism. Its effect is felt in so many different industries – hotels, restaurants, tour firms, car hire, airways, curio shops, night clubs, breweries . . . the list begins to appear endless – that it is very difficult to determine how many jobs would disappear with the disappearance of tourism, or more relevantly, how many would disappear for a given decline in tourism, and how many would be created by a given expansion. It has been estimated[45] that foreign tourism generated about 11,000 jobs in 1966-7, though this estimate excludes some of the more indirect effects on employment, such as employment in the building industry. On that basis, in 1977 perhaps 50,000 jobs were dependent directly and indirectly on the tourist industry. This is a large number of jobs, exceeding 40 per cent of the employment provided in the whole of manufacturing industry. It must be concluded that tourism is of great value to Kenya, though its value is not so overwhelming as some of the advocacy of tourism would imply.

Some deep feelings[46] against the emphasis on promoting tourism in government policy are based on other than economic considerations, though formally they could no doubt be embodied in a cost-benefit analysis. The Government is committed not to 'seek maximum tourist returns at the expense of entrusting too much of the industry to non-citizens, or of permitting too sudden exposure to consumption and spending habits that might damage our cherished cultural traditions.'[47] Nevertheless, the view is sometimes expressed that 'tourism has a corruptive effect on the moral health of the nation and that it is one sure means by which exploitation by foreigners is perpetuated.'[48] There are two different elements in this hostility to tourism which make incompatible bedfellows. First of all there is conservatism, which is strongest, and most threatened, in the Islamic culture of the Coast, which is shocked by the behaviour and attitudes of tourists. This conservative hostility is probably of small importance elsewhere: Nairobi is a cosmopolitan, non-indigenous city in origins and attitudes, and there are few people to be shocked in the game parks. The other element is the radical, tinged with xenophobia, which basically does not like the presence of rich foreigners.

Whatever one thinks of either of these attitudes, it must be accepted that tourism is only one influence, though perhaps the most obtrusive, of a pattern of life they both for different reasons dislike. Those who dislike 'the money ethic' should not blame the influence on tourism, for 'industrial development as a whole is more responsible for social disintegration than is tourism . . . and Kenya's whole ethic of development – and not any particular industry – should be to blame for the adverse social effects.'[49]

It would be wrong to dismiss the possibility of serious social problems being created by mass tourism, but it is implausible that they are yet more than peripheral, observable most of all, perhaps, by such tourists – including journalists – as have themselves an eye for these things. The overwhelming majority of the population of Kenya is untouched and therefore uncorrupted by tourism.

Longer-run plans for tourism include a development at Diani Beach, south of Mombasa, spread over eighteen years and costing K£45–50 m. which was proposed by consultants in 1976. The tourist development would be integrated with the social and economic development of the hinterland area of some 700 sq.km.[50] In the more immediate future, there are serious problems of water supply at the Coast, and more generally the need to develop off-peak tourism so as to raise the hotel-occupancy rate, and to spread tourism outside its present areas of concentration.[51] There are also the radical changes in wild-life tourism made necessary by Tanzania's tourist development policy. In the past some of the major Tanzanian game parks have been viewed by tour operators as an extension of Kenya's tourist facilities. They were commonly visited as part of a tour centred on Kenya.[52] The closure of the Kenya–Tanzania border to road traffic in 1977 brought a dramatic end of this business. Even though the border will presumably in time be open again, it is certain that Tanzania will continue to pursue a self-contained tourist development, and will by one means or another prevent her game parks from again becoming part of a Nairobi-based circuit, with the main benefits from the business accruing to Kenya. Kenya will need to adapt to the changed circumstances by paying further attention to her own resources, and to give particular attention to wild-life conservation, including enforcement of the ban on hunting and strict control of the curio trade, if she is to be able to continue in the long run to attract tourists to her game parks.[53]

CHAPTER 7

EXTERNAL TRADE AND FINANCE

Kenya is an open economy, with exports and imports large in relation to domestic product. Over the years since Independence, although these ratios have varied from year to year they have shown no trend of change. In fact, the ratio of exports of goods and services to monetary GDP at market prices was almost exactly the same in 1977 (43 per cent) as in 1964 (44 per cent). In the intervening years that ratio had never been less than 34 nor higher than 43 per cent, and in all but three years it had been 38 per cent or above. The range of variation has therefore been remarkably small. The ratio of imports of goods and services to monetary GDP at market prices has varied over a wider range, between 36 and 52 per cent, but in all but two years it has been between 37 and 45 per cent, and again there was only one percentage point difference

TABLE 7.1

Exports and Imports of Goods and Services in Relation to GDP at Market Prices

(K£ m.)

	1964	1971	1977
GDP	268	509	1528
Exports	119	182	650
Imports	104	224	584

Source: *Economic Survey*, 1978, and *Statistical Abstract*.

TABLE 7.2

Exports by Destination and Main Commodity

(K£ m.)

	1964	1971	1976	1977
Outside East Africa	47.1	73.2	268.8	428.9
East Africa	25.9	33.9	66.6	61.9
Total	73.0	107.1	335.4	490.8
Coffee	15.4	19.5	93.3	204.4
Tea	6.1	12.2	31.8	71.8
Petroleum products	4.7	15.1	56.9	72.4

Source: *Economic Survey*, 1978, and *Statistical Abstract*.
Note: Exports exclude re-exports.
East Africa means Tanzania and Uganda.

between the ratios for 1964 and 1977.[1] The ratios of exports and imports of goods alone have varied between similarly narrow limits. There has, therefore, been no structural change in the openness of the Kenya economy, though it was shown in Chapter 5 that the import ratio reflects the effect of import-substituting industrialization and of large changes in relative prices.

(a) TRADE

Exports

The value of Kenya's exports in 1977 was six and a half times their value in 1964. The rate of increase over the period, however, had been by no means steady. By 1971 the value had increased by less than 50 per cent, and for several years at a time there was little change. In 1975 exports were barely three times their value in 1964, and it was only two years, 1976 and particularly 1977, that saw very large increases. It was the sharp rise in the price of coffee and tea that was largely responsible for the increased value of exports in those years, and there will have been a fall in value in 1978.

Price changes have been of predominant importance in the increase in export values and quantity increases for exports as a whole have been modest. The published Quantum Index of exports, with base year 1971 = 100, has a value of only 114 in 1977, though in 1973 the index had been up to 121.[2] There have, of course, been changes in different directions and of greatly different magnitudes in the quantity of different products exported, and some of these particular changes are referred to later. The subgroups of the Quantum Index show a dismal performance except for food, oils and fats, and crude materials. The index for other subgroups of products in 1977 was either virtually unchanged from 1971 or smaller. The fall was particularly great for manufactured goods and machinery and transport equipment, the index for the latter group of products falling sharply between 1976 and 1977.

Kenya's exports are highly concentrated by commodity. No particularly sophisticated measures are necessary to show that this is so, when three commodities provide more than half of all exports. Since 1964 the three products have been coffee, tea and petroleum products. Petroleum products became of significance only in 1964 and 1965, after the Mombasa refinery came on stream, but at that time sisal was a large export product, so that even before 1964 more than half of all exports to countries outside East Africa was accounted for by three items. Petroleum products have an important market in Uganda, and a much smaller market in Tanzania, but coffee and tea are exported only to countries outside East Africa, and in this trade the two products made up 64 per cent of total exports in 1967.

TABLE 7.3

Quantum Index of Exports

(1971 = 100)

	1972	1976	1977
All exports	103	110	114
Food	122	142	163
Chemicals	81	70	60
Machinery	76	112	59
Manufactures	79	81	59
Crude materials	110	119	178

Source: *Economic Survey*, 1976 and 1978.
Note: Index on base 1972 = 100 linked to index on base 1971 = 100.
Includes re-exports and exports to Tanzania and Uganda.

TABLE 7.4

Quantum Index of Imports

(1971 = 100)

	1972	1977
All imports	89	85
Food	92	41
Materials	80	130
Machinery	82	90

Source and Note: see Table 7.3.

Given this predominance, no other products come anywhere near in comparable importance. Nevertheless, there are export successes which perhaps are rather less dependent on world market forces entirely outside Kenya's control than coffee and tea. One of these is fruit and vegetables, exports of which increased from just over K£2 m. in 1964 to nearly K£16 m. in 1976. New lines have been opened up, and success has been achieved with airfreighting to European markets of flowers as well as fruit and vegetables, but the big item in this group is canned pineapples, accounting for nearly half the total in 1976. Until 1973 exports of canned pineapple had not reached K£1 m. but in 1976 exports were valued at K£7 m. and in 1977 at K£10½ m. Three other products or groups of products have substantial exports. Between 1964 and 1976 exports to countries outside East Africa of meat and meat products increased from K£2.2 m. to K£8.3 m. of hides and skins from K£1.3 m. to K£8.6 m., and of cement from K£800,000 to K£7.6 m. Of these three, only cement has found a substantial market in Tanzania and Uganda, and for exports to all destinations, including these East

African countries, the value of cement exports rose from K£1.7 m. in 1964 to K£8.6 m. in 1977.

Price increases, it has already been remarked, have been the major reason for the increase in the value of most exports. However, there have also been some large increases in the quantity exported. Tea is the particular success story in this respect. The volume of tea exported rose from 16,500 tons in 1964 to over 70,000 tons in 1977, the large increases occurring from 1972. The predominance of coffee in exports in 1977 was much more the result of the sharp rise in price, but nevertheless, 94,000 tons of coffee were exported in 1977 compared with 42,000 tons in 1964. Over the same period the quantity of canned pineapple exported increased from 10,500 to 45,000 tons, while that of cement roughly doubled, though this figure conceals a great falling off in exports to East Africa, since exports to the rest of the world rose from 174,000 to 601,000 tons. The Mombasa refinery was in its early days at the time of Kenya's Independence, and exports had not been developed. The volume of exports roughly doubled between 1964 and 1967, and then increased very little: they were up by about a quarter on the 1967 volume by 1973, and then fell away following the rise in the price of oil to almost the same figure in 1975 as in 1967, after which they slowly increased to 9 per cent above 1967 volume in 1977.

It has been an aim of policy, set out for instance in the first Development Plan, to diversify Kenya's exports, and in particular to reduce the dependence on coffee. In terms of the share of the total value of exports this aim has evidently not been achieved. Coffee contributed a higher proportion of the total in 1977 than probably ever before. But changes in the share of total value do not provide a test of the achievements of policy, because they are the result of price changes over which Kenya has no control. A collapse in the coffee price would reduce the dependence on coffee and increase the diversity of exports overnight. But Kenya can do without that kind of reduction in dependence. It is just as well that diversification was not achieved by reducing the output of coffee. In a more relevant sense, there has been some diversification, though not much. The much greater increase in the quantum of tea than of coffee exports is one indication of this, as is the increase in quantity of a few other exports. But the disappointing performance in the quantity exported for most manufactures shows that diversification has not gone far.

Something has been said about the export of manufactures in Chapter 5. Before 1977 they had accounted for roughly half total exports, though they were as high as 57 per cent in 1975. But the definition of manufactures, or processed products, includes some products which would not be thought of in the normal way as manufactures at all: dressed hides and skins, for instance, and other processed agricultural products. Others have a very low domestic value added, of which petroleum products is a notable example. One estimate puts the value added in petroleum products in 1970 at only 16 per cent.[3] The importance of petroleum products has been increasing: in 1973 they accounted for a quarter of manufactured exports, and in 1977 for more than a half. Exports of manufactures other than petroleum products have been increasing rather slowly. Between 1970 and 1974 they rather more than doubled, but they were then stagnant, apart from a jump in 1976, and in 1977 they were at virtually the same level as four years earlier. Exports of manufactures including petroleum products were slightly smaller in 1977 than in 1976, and this together with the great increase in non-manufactured exports, reduced the proportion of manufactures in total exports from 49 to 34 per cent. Exports of manufactures were particularly important in Kenya's trade with Tanzania and Uganda, and have been affected by the decline in that trade, though some of the major causes of the decline – not to say collapse in the case of Tanzania – may be too recent fully to be reflected in the statistics.

The most important change in the destination of Kenya's exports, and of great importance, is this decline in the proportion going to Tanzania and Uganda. Although exports to Tanzania and Uganda had been rising in value, even though slowly, as a proportion of total exports they have been on a downward trend since Independence. In 1964 exports to these two neighbouring countries amounted to 35 per cent of all exports. By 1976 the proportion had fallen to 20 per cent, and in 1977 to 13 per cent. In the change between 1976 and 1977, Uganda slightly increased her share of Kenya's exports, whereas Tanzania's share fell from 10 per cent to 2 per cent. As the main agricultural exports do not go to the East African countries, Kenya's exports to them are largely manufactures. In 1973, for instance, manufactures accounted for 90 per cent of Kenya's exports to Tanzania and 84 per cent of her exports to Uganda.[4]

At the time of Independence, intra-East African trade took place within a full customs union which had existed between Kenya, Tanzania, and Uganda since 1937, and from still earlier times between Kenya and Uganda.[5] Imbalances in inter-state trade, which had been consistently in Kenya's favour since 1956, were a source of tension between the three countries and the reason for various attempts to regulate the operation of the common market. The 1967 Treaty for East African Cooperation established an East African Community and introduced a number of measures designed to reduce the imbalances in trade between the Partner States. These measures achieved some modest degree of success, but were insufficient to solve all contentious issues and to remove all differences between the members of the Community. Import licensing in the member countries effectively brought an end to the common market even while it was formally effective, and tensions continued to rise as a result of difficulties in other spheres of co-operation.[6] In 1977 Tanzania closed the border with Kenya and trade between the two countries virtually came to an end, together with the common market and the whole structure of co-operation established by the 1967 Treaty.

Imports

The value of imports multiplied six times between 1964 and 1977, but a large part of this increase was because of price increases. In fact, between 1971 and 1977, although the value of imports rose more than two and a half times, the quantum index shows a fall from 100 to 85. The fall was particularly marked in foodstuffs, where the index value for 1977 is only 41; for materials, in contrast, it is 130.

TABLE 7.5

Imports by Source and Selected Product Groups

(K£ m.)

	1964	1971	1973	1974	1977
Outside East Africa	76.6	184.1	215.2	369.4	529.2
East Africa	11.4	15.9	13.4	14.5	2.2
Total	88.0	200.0	228.6	383.9	531.4
Mineral fuels	9.3	17.7	22.1	81.8	117.1
Machinery	23.2	67.5	70.4	87.4	179.1
Food	12.2	19.1	21.8	25.4	27.5

Source: *Economic Survey* and *Statistical Abstract*.
Note: East Africa means Tanzania and Uganda.
Machinery means Machinery and other Capital Equipment and Transport Equipment (see *Economic Survey*).
Food includes Beverages and Tobacco.

TABLE 7.6

End-use of Imports

(percentages)

	1964	1965	1971	1972	1974	1975
Consumption	27	26	24	22	15	15
Intermediate use	58	61	56	55	72	67
Capital formation	15	13	20	23	13	18

Source: *Statistical Abstract*.

This last figure reflects the change in the composition of imports, with a switch from goods for consumption to intermediate products and investment goods. An analysis of the end-use of imports shows that 27 per cent of imports (by value) were for consumption in 1964, whereas in 1975 it was only 15 per cent. Over that period imports for intermediate use increased from 58 to 67 per cent of the total, and goods for capital formation from 15 to 18 per cent. The distribution of imports between these different end uses fluctuated a good deal from year to year, and it was only after 1971, when the proportion was 24 per cent, that the share of imports going to consumption declined by a substantial amount.

The significance of this change in the composition of imports and its connection with import-substituting industrialization has been considered in Chapter 5. There it was pointed out that the proportion of imports destined for intermediate use seems, in fact, to have changed rather little once the distorting effect of the rise in oil prices is eliminated.

The 1973 World Bank mission saw great significance in the changing composition of imports. They saw it as a reflection of the protection accorded to import-substituting consumer goods industries, which encourages the use of imported rather than domestically produced inputs. The mission's statistics showed that in 1970, although only 28 per cent of consumption was supplied by imports, there was a high reliance on imports for intermediate goods and capital goods, to the extent of 61 per cent in the case of the former and 66 per cent the latter. They viewed with alarm, therefore, the increased import dependency that results from import substitution in consumer-goods industries. Import substitution of this kind does not reduce import dependence, it is argued, but replaces dependence on imported consumer goods by dependence, on imported intermediate and capital goods. One problem of this dependence is that it is difficult to cut imports in a crisis because, as inputs to industry, they are 'essential'.[7] This appears to be saying that it is better to have 'inessential' imports, because they can be cut out when necessary, an argument which does seem slightly odd. It is in any case rather beside the point, because the mission disapprove of controls to influence the balance of payments and recommended a variety of other measures to meet a crisis.[8]

It is, of course, a perfectly sensible view that it is better to cut 'inessential' than 'essential' imports when cuts are necessary. That might reasonably be thought to indicate the desirability of producing 'essentials', like intermediate products and capital goods, at home. However, in the view, of the World Bank mission, the problem of a high dependence on imported intermediate products and capital goods, is not to be tackled by providing protection for the domestic production of such goods. That would be even worse. That would be what the mission call the 'lethal' second stage of import substitution, which taxes all industries using the protected intermediate goods. And the production of intermediate goods under protection does not, as might at first glance be imagined, increase 'domestic input-linkages'. On the contrary, it is likely to reduce them 'either because they are non-tradable and thus more expensive than low-duty tradables, or because they are low-duty tradables and thus unattractive to produce, or because they are high-duty tradables and thus unattractive to use'.[9] Which, all in all, is as fine an example of having it all ways at once as one is likely to come across.

After all this, one may well wonder what pattern of imports would meet with the approval of the mission, as they disapprove both of high imports of intermediate goods and of measures to encourage their local production. The answer, when it comes down to it, is of course the free-trade pattern. Their proposals are for a structure of tariffs and subsidies which would reproduce a situation approximating to free trade. It requires some faith to believe that a vigorous export trade in manufactures, using domestic inputs and labour intensive methods, and all the other desirable features of development, would spring forth in response to a reproduction of the price relationships of free trade. As the mission say, 'the results promised do seem a little too good to be true.'[10]

(b) BALANCE OF PAYMENTS

Some detailed changes in the balance of international payments and in foreign-exchange reserves at particular periods are considered in Chapter 8, when monetary matters are discussed. Here it is proposed to set out the structure of the balance of payments in a more general way and to describe its usual features to the extent that there are usual features of such volatile magnitudes. Policies which affect the balance of payments are discussed in the final part of this chapter.

There is always a deficit in visible trade, though there have been wide fluctuations in the extent to which exports match imports.[11] In 1964 exports were as high as 89 per cent of imports; in 1971 they amounted to only 53 per cent, and in 1977 they were up to 88 per cent. The size of the deficit in visible trade in the balance of payments is exaggerated, however, by the fact that (unlike the common practice of revaluing them fob in calculating the balance of payments) imports are valued cif, including in their value the cost of insurance and freight.

In contrast with the visible balance, the balance of invisibles is always in surplus, though the surplus is correspondingly exaggerated by the inclusion of freight and insurance costs on imports in the figures for visible trade. In consequence, the positive balance of freight and insurance payments is always large from earnings on transit trade to Uganda and Tanzania. There are also large earnings under the item 'Other transportation' from the provision of services to aircraft and shipping, including bunkerage at Mombasa port. The third major item of invisible earnings is tourist expenditures, entered in the account as 'Foreign travel'. This item is also always large and positive on balance, though there are substantial debits to be set against the gross credits on account of expenditure on and by Kenyans abroad, of which expenditure on education is an important component. The total net earnings from these three items together multiplied thirteen times between 1963 and 1977. Freight and insurance increased by only four times, but net earnings from airport and shipping services were multiplied by eighteen, and from Travel, for which receipts and payments almost balanced in 1963, by 140 times.[12] Bunkering at Mombasa increased in 1967 because of the closing of the Suez Canal, and earnings from aircraft and shipping trebled between 1973 and 1974 as a result of the rise in oil prices; the adverse counterpart of these increases, of course, affected the visible balance. The growth of tourism has undoubtedly had an important effect on the invisible balance. The net benefit of tourism to the balance of payments is a more difficult matter, because it is not known by how much the debit items – imports, investment income, etc. – have increased in consequence of the growth of tourism.

The major debit item among the invisible transactions is 'International investment income'. There are inflows under this heading, particularly receipts of interest on the Central Bank's foreign assets, but the total credits in recent years have been no more than 20-30 per cent of the debits. Part of the outflow consists of service payments on government debt, which at one time accounted for around a third of the total, but recently for no more than a fifth. The rest consists of interest and profits on private investments. The size of the actual outflow on this account is exaggerated by the fact that the statistics are recorded gross of reinvestments of profits in Kenya, which are recorded on the other side as an inflow of long-term private capital. The distribution between public and private investment income can vary according to a variety of circumstances. Between 1974 and 1975, for example, a slower rate of economic growth and increased taxation of profits caused a fall in the private outflow, which was roughly balanced by a rise in Central Bank interest payments abroad. The net outflow has both increased and decreased in different years, but the trend has been upward particularly after 1972, and in 1977 the net outflow was six times what it had been in 1963. With the growth of foreign investment and government borrowing the burden of debt service is bound to increase, particularly as the earnings on the Central Bank's foreign assets will not keep pace.

The other major item in the invisible account to be noted is 'Government transfers', which includes the inflow of aid funds, and has fluctuated widely. In 1977, at K£26 m. net, it was the biggest it had ever been, whereas in 1967 the total was only K£1.7 m., and in 1974 K£6.1 m. The total was also unusually high in 1971 and 1972 because of the cancellation of overseas debts.

Although the invisible transactions are always in surplus, the surplus has rarely been large enough to offset the deficit on visible trade. In 1977 the current account as a whole was in surplus for the first time since 1965. The inflow of long-term capital has, however, usually been

TABLE 7.7

Balance of Payments for Sample Years

(K£ m.)

	1965	1969	1971	1973	1974	1977
Imports	97.4	121.3	196.2	219.0	383.9	535.1
Exports	78.0	90.2	104.9	164.5	226.1	470.9
Visible balance	–19.4	–31.1	–91.3	–54.5	–157.8	–64.2
Freight, transport, and travel	17.8	27.3	39.1	39.0	77.0	123.3
Investment income	–9.0	–9.5	–8.8	–35.7	–36.1	–59.5
Government transfers	7.3	7.2	20.9	7.5	6.1	26.0
Invisible balance	19.7	28.2	51.5	7.7	45.8	88.3
Current balance	0.3	–2.9	–39.9	–46.8	–112.0	24.1
Long-term capital	8.1	20.2	15.2	53.1	85.8	90.4
Current and capital balance	8.4	17.3	–24.7	6.3	–26.2	114.5

Source: *Economic Survey* for different years.

TABLE 7.8

Percentage Contributions to Finance of Imports plus Investment Income

(K£ m.)

	1965	1969	1971	1973	1974	1977
Exports	73	69	51	65	54	79
Freight, transport, and travel	17	21	19	15	18	21
Government transfers	7	6	10	3	2	4
Other invisibles	3	2	–	–1	–	–
Capital	8	15	8	21	20	15
Total	108	113	88	103	94	119
Balance	8	13	–12	3	–6	19

Source: Table 7.7.

large enough more than to offset the deficit on current account. In the eleven post-Independence years in which the current account was in deficit, there were only four years, and two of those were the years of the oil crisis, in which the combined current and long-term capital balance was not in surplus.

The main components of the balance of payments for a sample of years are shown in Table 7.7. Table 7.8 shows the contribution of different items to the finance of the total outflow in payments for imports and net investment income, to indicate the relative importance of the items.

Despite the resilience shown by the balance of payments there are no grounds for complacency. Just as it would have been wrong to assume in 1971 that the deficit on current and long-term capital account was the pattern of the future, so it would be even more dangerous to assume that the large surpluses of 1977 could be relied upon to continue. There would be some truth in saying that Kenya was saved from the prices of OPEC by the frosts in Brazil. Certainly, that way of putting it emphasizes the fortuitous nature of many influences on the external accounts. The effects of the exceptionally high prices of coffee and tea were already fading early in 1978. Foreign-exchange reserves which in September 1975, amounted to little more than the value of three-months imports, were equal in value to nearly eight-months imports in September 1977, but with imports rising and reserves falling fast they were down to less than five-and-a-half-months imports in May 1978.

(c) INVESTMENT

Capital has come into Kenya from abroad on both public and private account. In most years, private capital (including reinvestments of profits) accounted for over half the total inflow, though the proportion fell after 1974 to a quarter or a third (see Table 7.9). In the early years of Independence, as in the immediately preceding years, there were large capital outflows, but the flow was reversed in 1965 and 1966, and from 1967 there was no doubt that foreign investors were going into Kenya on a large scale.

TABLE 7.9

Public and Private Shares in Long-term Capital Import

(percentages)

	1965	1969	1971	1973	1974	1977
Public	81	36	−12	35	41	65
Private	19	64	112	65	59	35
Total K£ m.	8.4	20.2	15.2	53.1	85.8	90.4

Source: *Economic Survey* for different years.

Foreign investment has been important for financing the balance of payments and public expenditure, and private foreign investment has been particularly significant in manufacturing and tourism.

It is sometimes suggested that if the outflow of investment income is offset against the inflow of capital it will be seen that a country receiving foreign investment, although becoming increasingly indebted to and dominated by the foreign investor, is not in fact obtaining much supplement to the real resources available to it. According to this argument, foreign investment may appear to bring additional resources to the recipient country, but in reality that is not so, because the resources largely go out again to service the investment. The Kenya balance-of-payments figures show that the ratio of the outflow of net investment income to net capital inflow was 47 per cent for the five years, 1968–72, and 65 per cent for 1973–7, though the ratio would be higher if account were taken of transfer pricing and other practices which lead to an understatement in the figures of the true outflow.[13] However, whatever the magnitudes involved, the basis of the argument is unacceptable. It is, of course, in the first place misleading to mix up current and capital flows, but the error of the argument lies not simply in its neglect of an accounting convention. The important point is its neglect of the effect of the investment on output and income. The capital inflow is undertaken in the expectation that the investment will create the income from which the later outward flow will come. Of course, there can and inevitably will be unsuccessful investments, and the transaction can then involve a loss of real resources: the inflow of resources has been wasted, but the commitment to service the investment remains, though in some forms of private investment the outflow in fact only takes place if the investment is successful. It is also true, of course, that misjudged fiscal incentives to investment can greatly reduce or eliminate the benefit flowing to the recipient country. And firms use various devices, legal or otherwise, some of which are open mainly to multinationals, to minimize their tax liability. But these are reasons to pursue well-designed policies and to select good investments; they are not reasons for rejecting all foreign capital. And this is the point: the logic of setting income outflow against capital inflow implies that no foreign investment which has to be repaid together with interest or dividends can ever benefit the recipient country. Imagine a country in which for a period there is a capital inflow, and then there is no further foreign investment, but there is an outflow to service the past investment. The figures will then show there to be a net outflow of resources, which proves, according to the argument, that the investment has been a burden on the country – however much it has increased the national product. Whatever the costs and benefits of foreign investment in Kenya may have been, no light is thrown on the question by a comparison of capital inflow with the outflow for the service of previous investment.

An extreme version of the argument applied to Kenya is to be found in Leys.[14] In his exposition words lose their meaning,[15] the payment of interest and dividends becomes a form of capital export, and the excess of interest and dividend payments (with the figures boosted to allow for transfer pricing[16] and other practices) over the inflow of capital becomes a measure of the export of capital. The argument is presented as if it is based on the ILO Report, which does not in fact commit the error. The discussion by the ILO mission of the use of transfer pricing and other practices to reduce declared profits is in the proper context of tax minimization, and has nothing whatever to do with capital export.[17]

Objection to the erroneous argument just considered must not, however, be taken to mean that the connection between an inflow of capital and the subsequent outflow of service payments is of no importance. It has already been suggested that debt interest payments will become larger, and foreign-financed government projects will need careful analysis of their costs and benefits if they are not to add to the burden on the balance of payments. The benefits of private investment will depend on the negotiation of the conditions governing the investment. Kenya cannot afford bad projects. The judgement of the World Bank,[18] which remains relevant, was that

> . . . although some of the past investments in Kenya have not really benefited the country, she will continue to need a steady flow of private investment, both to supply the capital and to provide entrepreneurial ability and technical know-how. The issue we see is not whether foreign investment is desirable; rather whether Kenya can continue to attract foreign private investment and whether she can learn to use foreign investment more efficiently for the benefit of the country.

In accordance with its general attitude the World Bank Report argues that 'the grossest defects in the contribution of foreign enterprise to Kenya are the results of trade policy',[19] and that issue is discussed below in the final part of this chapter.

(d) AID[20]

Kenya has been the receipient of much aid in the form of loans, grants and technical assistance. Taking the four years 1973–6 together she was seventh among the countries of sub-Saharan Africa in the 'recorded net flow of resources from DAC countries and multilateral agencies'. Kenya received $US 905 m. over the period, as did the Ivory Coast, compared with Sudan's $US 907 m. and Tanzania's $US 944 m. In the amount of aid Kenya was massively behind Zaire's $US 2,101 m.[21] In the amount of expenditure on technical assistance, Kenya was the fourth largest recipient in sub-Saharan Africa, receiving $US 222 m., compared with the $US 234 m. received by the third-largest receipient, Tanzania.[22]

In the early years of Independence the United Kingdom was overwhelmingly the most important source of aid. In 1964 over 80 per cent of all aid was from Britain; by 1972 the UK accounted for less than a quarter of all disbursements.[23] At the end of 1977, grant and loan commitments amounted to $US 1,453 m., 13.5 per cent of which was from the United Kingdom. The World Bank had assumed the role of largest donor, accounting for about a third of commitments.[24]

An important reason for the predominance of the United Kingdom as a donor in the early years was the importance of the land transfer programme. There were also substantial sums for the other leg of the land-reform programme, the adjudication and registration of African-occupied land. The programme for transferring land from European to African occupation has been discussed in Chapters 2 and 4. The British Government was not the direct agent for the transfer of European-owned farms, but aid funds from Britain financed the Kenya Government's purchase of the farms. The land-transfer programme financed by British aid, which was confined to mixed farms and excluded plantations and ranches, was due to be concluded at the end of March, 1979. Table 7.10 shows the various British capital aid commitments, including the 'Independence settlement'.

TABLE 7.10

British Official Capital Aid Commitments to Kenya since Independence

		£ m.
1964	Independence settlement	
	Land Transfer Programme*	
	Unissued balance of commitment of £21.3 m. as grant and loan	11.0
	Further loan for Land Bank	1.0
	Development grants and loans: unissued balances	4.3
	Development grant 1964/5	1.0
	Development loan 1964/5	2.0
	Pension loans	13.6
	Budgetary grant	1.25
	Special land-purchase-scheme loan	1.275
		34.475
1965/6	General development loan (interest-free, 42% import content)	3.0
	Land Bank loan	1.0
		4.0

1966/70	Land Transfer Programme (interest-free loan)	6.3
	General development loan (interest-free, 60% import content)	8.7
	Land adjudication loan (previously classified under general development)	3.0
		18.0
1970	Land Transfer Programme:	
	Settlement (grant)	2.5
	Agricultural Development Corporation and Agricultural Finance Corporation loan (2% interest)	1.0
	Special scheme grant	0.25
	General development loan (2% interest, 75% import content)	5.0
	Land adjudication/Rural development loan (2% interest)	2.75
		11.5
1973	Land Transfer Programme:	
	Settlement grant	6.0
	Agricultural Finance Corporation loan (2% interest)	1.0
	General development loan (2% interest, 50% import content) content)	10.0
		17.0
1975	Programme Grant	2.5
1976	Land Transfer Programme (Grant)	6.0
	Programme Grant	10.3
	General Development Grant	25.0
		41.3
TOTAL		128.8

Source: G. Holtham and A. Hazlewood, *Aid and Inequality in Kenya*, Table 5, with additional data kindly supplied by the British High Commission, Nairobi.

* In addition between 1963 and 1969 about £1 m. was provided specially for the purchase of farms of compassionate cases outside the settlement areas.

The Kenya Government had expressed the opinion[25] that 'the settlement process was designed more to aid those Europeans who wanted to leave than the Africans who received the land. . . . It is unlikely that Kenya, in accepting the debt burden, has obtained economic benefits of anywhere near the amount of the debt incurred.' However, a detailed analysis, taking into account the costs in the form of lost production and the establishment of a reputation for arbitrary action by the Kenya Government of the alternative of expropriation of the European farmers, reached the conclusion that 'the benefits of [the land-transfer funds] to Kenya greatly outweighed the debt burden.'[26]

Sixty per cent of all grant and loan commitments at the end of 1977 were for three fields of activity: agricultural development, water development, and transport development. Thirty per cent of total commitments was for agriculture; a quarter of the aid for water development was for rural water supplies, while the rest was roughly equally divided between urban water supplies and irrigation; nearly 80 per cent of the aid for transport was for roads.[27]

Technical assistance has been an important form of aid to Kenya. In the middle 1970s about half the technical assistance personnel were from Britain, though the proportion had been very much higher in earlier years. The British personnel fall into three categories: advisers and researchers fully funded by the United Kingdom; 'topped-up' staff employed in Kenya Government departments under the Overseas Service Aid Scheme; and staff employed in statutory authorities and other organizations, such as the University of Nairobi, under the British Expatriates Supplementation Scheme. Table 7.11 shows the number in each category in 1978. Nearly three-quarters of all OSAS staff at that time were employed in Education; the next largest group, though amounting to only 8 per cent of the total, was in Works. Forty per cent of BESS staff were in Nairobi University or Kenyatta University College, and 21 per cent in the railways. The number of operational staff had been reduced – in 1974 there were 846 OSAS staff, 559 of them in Education – but the reduction had been offset by a rise in the advisory staff provided by other donors. There had been thirty-four British advisory and research personnel in 1974; of the fifty in post in 1978, more than half were in Agriculture.

TABLE 7.11

British Technical Assistance Staff at 30 September 1978

Scheme	Number of Staff
Advisers/Researchers	50
OSAS	462
BESS	164

Source: British High Commission, Nairobi.

Aid has had some distorting effects on the Kenya economy and on the process of government. Although it would be wrong to see Kenya as the reluctant practitioner of policies forced on her by the 'leverage' of aid donors, there have been adverse effects of aid. The availability of capital aid requiring a local contribution has led to a neglect of recurrent expenditures which might have been more productive; the need to prepare projects for submission to donors has led to a proliferation of technical assistance personnel provided by donors; there has been an emphasis on the big projects which donors tend to favour; the procedures for the approval of projects have been swamped by the volume of aid and have been circumvented by direct approaches from donors to operational ministries. Technical assistance staff within the government machine may have influenced policies in a direction which would not otherwise have been taken, though the existence and extent of such influence is difficult to assess. Donor influence has probably had more effect on the content of the development plans than on general policies. However, this may be less true of the World Bank than of bilaterial donors, and Kenya is no more immune than other countries from a ukase of the International Monetary Fund.

All in all, despite the adverse effects of aid in some directions, there is no reason to reject the commonsense view that aid has been of benefit to Kenya, has added to available resources, increased the rate of growth, and brought some improvements in the standard of living.

(e) POLICIES

Kenya has come a long way from the days of the simple life in external economic policy, when there was no exchange rate policy, because the currency had an automatic link with sterling, and when the tariff was largely for revenue. The purposive use of the tariff for protection, beginning in the later 1950s, began to become important after the mid-1960s, since when, 'the principal conscious aim of trade policy being import substitution, the main policy instrument has been the tariff.'[28] Later the concept of 'effective protection' reared its head to frown on the simple-minded development doctrine that had been embraced by government. 'I wonder', one commentator primly inquired, 'if Kenya's policy makers realise that their policies are antagonistic to their goals.'[29]

Tariff Protection

The basis of such doubts about the compatibility of Kenya's aims and instruments of policy was the analysis of the effective protection accorded to different productive activities by the tariff. The rate of effective protection given to a productive process is determined by the relationship between the tariff on the imported substitute for its output, and the tariff on its imported inputs. If these two tariff rates are the same, then the rate of effective protection is the same as that of the nominal protection, i.e. the rate of the tariff. If the tariff on the imported inputs is lower than the tariff on the imported substitute for the output, the rate of effective protection will be higher than the nominal rate. In some cases it can be enormously higher. Assume the domestic productive process requires the import of components costing Shs. 90/- for assembly into a product which could be imported for Shs. 100/-. If the minimum price at which domestic assembly is profitable is Shs. 200/-, a tariff of 100 per cent on the imported product would give the market to the domestic producer, so long as the components could be imported duty free. The nominal protection of the product would be 100 per cent, but the effective protection accorded to the domestic assembly activity, which saves only Shs. 10/- at world prices, would be 1,000 per cent.

The example shows that the price increase resulting from the imposition of the tariff is a higher proportion of the value added than it is of the price of the product, when both are valued at world prices. That is hardly a startling conclusion, but conclusions of great importance are claimed to flow from the analysis of effective protection. It certainly makes rates of protection in some cases seem much greater than would appear from the nominal tariff, but 'it uncovers no unexpected additional source of economic waste from protection with which to confront the protectionist.'[30] Nor does a higher rate of effective protection of one activity that another show that the former is the less desirable and is diverting resources into it from more desirable activities: 'the tariff structure can tell one nothing about resource allocation. Among, let us say, fifteen activities ranked by effective protection it is perfectly possible for resources to flow out of the second but into the fifth.'[31]

It is said that the analysis shows that 'the protection system is more "inefficient" the higher the negative correlation between viability and protection.'[32] But the correlation seems simply to indicate that the most protection is given where it is most required to sustain the industry. The rate of effective protection measures the proportional protection accorded the activity, just as the tariff rate measures the proportional rise in the price of the product.[33] But neither says anything about the desirability of the protection, only about the need. Rates of effective protection say something about the relative cost of sustaining the domestic activities, but nothing about the benefits.

It is possible to show, and is indeed obvious, that there is a net loss of foreign exchange if a protected import-substituting activity saves less foreign exchange than the resources attracted into it earned in their old use.[34] But it does not seem that the concept of effective protection is involved in this reasoning.

The concept of effective protection does draw attention to the important fact that the extent to which an activity is protected depends not only on the tariff on its product but also on the tariff on its inputs. The common structure in which tariffs are low on inputs and high on finished goods leads to high rates of effective protection on import substituting activities. But if protection is given to the domestic production of an input previously imported, the protection given to the input-using activity will be reduced. It may even turn out that the input-using activity has a negative effective protection, despite the tariff on its product. As the input–output relationships in an economy are complex, a change in a tariff rate may have consequences which are neither apparent nor intended. Given the piecemeal way in which tariff decisions are commonly made, under the particular pressures for protection that come up at particular times, an irrational and unintended pattern of protection may emerge, which is revealed only by elaborate calculations.

Tariffs can affect the rate of exchange and the international competitiveness of exports. The restriction of imports by a tariff makes balance of payments equilibrium compatible with a higher rate of exchange than would be the case without the tariff. An over-valuation of the domestic currency (under-valuation of foreign exchange) compared with the free-trade valuation makes exports dearer for foreigners. It also makes imports of goods which are least protected by the tariff, which are likely to be inputs into domestic production, cheaper for domestic buyers. If the tariff on imported inputs is low enough they could be cheaper than they would be at the free-trade exchange rate. This is the reasoning behind the contention that protection of import substituting manufacturing both encourages the import of intermediate products and other inputs into manufacturing and discourages the export of manufactures.

The very high rates and the unplanned differences in the rates of effective protection arise because of the non-uniformity of tariff rates. The same tariff on all imports would make the effective and nominal rates of protection identical. One policy recommendation which may be drawn out of the analysis, therefore, is that differences in tariff rates should be narrowed or removed. But if a uniform tariff is applied to all imports, no protection is given to the domestic protection of any of them, and something like free trade with a higher foreign-exchange rate is reproduced. There is certainly a free-trade bias in the effective protection argument, and free trade might be the most logical policy for its proponents to advocate. An alternative recommendation is that industries to be assisted should receive direct subsidies, the subsidies being financed by a uniform tariff on imports combined with a uniform tax on domestic value added.[35]

The effective protection argument was taken up with enthusiasm by observers of the Kenyan scene. It was pursued with evangelistic zeal by the World Bank mission. Although they refer to some of the problems associated with the use of the concept,[36] they had no doubts about its importance and made it a central feature of their report. At times, indeed, their enthusiasm seems to lead the mission into wanting to have it all ways at once. They warmly argue the case for a more uniform tariff. But they also refer to the 'second stage' of import substitution, the production of intermediate and capital goods under protection, as 'so lethal',[37] because it taxes the users of these inputs. Yet the high and variable rates of effective protection occur when such industries are unprotected, and protection of them would result in a more uniform tariff, which the mission advocate. The mission seem to have got the argument rather muddled in their zeal for reform.

An excess of zeal is unfortunate when, for all the theoretical elegance of the argument, the analysis of the facts falls so far behind.[38] The outcome of calculations by Phelps and Wasow[39] has been summarized as showing that 'effective rates of protection range from strongly negative to astronomically high without much hint of rhyme or reason.'[40] The World Bank mission found the calculations to their taste, as the conclusion about the level and variability of effective protection rates provided strong support for their argument. However, enthusiasm was dampened by the discovery that the calculations also showed much agricultural processing to be inefficient, a conclusion which was not to their taste, and which was not believed. In the end, therefore, the mission conclude, somewhat lamely, though realistically, that 'the system is potentially capable of leading to inefficiency' and that 'the precise conclusions concerning average protection and world price profitability can be used only illustratively.'[41] Even that may be claiming too much. The analysis of protection may provide at most a warning but certainly not the basis for a crusade.

The acceptance by the Kenya Government of the criticisms of its protection policy, and what seems to be a somewhat uncertain implementation of a new policy, has been described in Chapter 5, where there is also reference to the quantitative controls which have partly made the tariff redundant as a protective instrument.

East African Integration

This is not the place to recount in any detail the sorry story of the decay of the economic integration of Kenya, Tanzania and Uganda.[42] Reference has been made to the matter in earlier chapters on trade and transport. Kenya's policy towards the common arrangements in East Africa may perhaps be described as proper rather than enthusiastic. Given the fact that Kenya was widely believed to receive the lion's share of the benefits of economic co-operation, even at the expense of the other members, it is possibly surprising that there was less said about East African Unity in Kenya than in Tanzania. It may have been the difference between a commitment to principle and to pragmatism. This is not to say that there were no Kenyans who were alive to the benefits and prospects of economic co-operation, and indeed, there were strong supporters within the Government and the administration. Certainly the pronouncements of President Kenyatta never questioned Kenya's commitment to the Community. Nevertheless, there were prominent

Kenyans who were openly hostile to the association with the neighbouring states, and there was a feeling among ordinary people – enhanced by some of the things that were said about Kenya in the heat of the controversies over the integration arrangements – that it might be best for Kenya to go it alone. There was certainly an impatience with the constraints of co-operation at a time when many Kenyans felt a pride in progress achieved and confidence in the future, despite the fact that at the same time serious problems of unemployment, inequality, and poverty were being canvassed.

Association with the European Economic Community

In common with the other members of the East African Community, Kenya became an associate of the EEC from the beginning of 1971 under the arrangements reached in the Arusha Agreement. Kenya has tariff-free access to the EEC countries and participates in the aid and stabilization arrangements of the Lomé Convention. In addition to aid from the individual member countries of the EEC, Kenya has benefited from European Development Fund finance, to the total of some K£33 m., on approved and proposed projects at the end of 1977, the largest project, accounting for K£12 m., being a contribution to the Tana River reservoir and power station. European Investment Bank approved loans to Kenya totalled about K£13½ m. at the end of 1977. The total included finance for the Development Finance Company of Kenya and the Industrial Development Bank[43] as well as for sugar, cement, and chemical projects. Coffee, tea, sisal, and pyrethrum are among the products covered by the STABEX scheme in principle, but only coffee and tea contribute more than the 7½ per cent minimum share in total exports to qualify for compensation payments. However, levels of prices and outputs are such that Kenya may expect to receive substantial payments in 1980.

Other Regional Associations

Kenya has participated from time to time in discussions on the formation of various regional trade groupings. The negotiations for the association of Zambia, Ethiopia, Somalia, and Burundi with the East African Community may be counted as one example. There were discussions under the aegis of the United Nations Economic Commission for Africa between 1965 and 1967 about the formation of an Economic Community of Eastern Africa, and there have been other discussions on the formation of a wider grouping since the break-up of the Community of Kenya, Tanzania and Uganda. Most regional associations remain, unfortunately, ideas in the minds of officials of the United Nations.

Exchange-Rate Policy

Kenya's first experience of implementing an exchange-rate policy was in 1967 when, in conjunction with the other Partner States of the East African Community, it was decided not to maintain the old rate with sterling at the time of the sterling devaluation. A new par value of just over KShs. 17 instead of KShs. 20 to the £ sterling was fixed. The argument for the policy adopted was that most of Kenya's competitors had not devalued, that manufactured exports were mainly sold in Tanzania and Uganda, which had in any case a fixed rate of exchange with the Kenya shilling, and that Kenya's primary product exports were inelastic in supply, so that a devaluation would not stimulate output. On the other hand, the inflationary effects of a devaluation were feared.[44]

The next issue for the policy-makers arose during the international currency upheaveals of 1971. When the US dollar became inconvertible in August, Kenya and Uganda continued to peg their currency to sterling, whereas Tanzania changed to a US dollar link. At a time when there was free convertibility between the East African currencies this created an unprecedented situation. Transactions between the Partner States were suspended for some days while discussions were carried on, and the outcome was that all three currencies were pegged to the dollar.[45]

The value of the shilling in terms of the dollar was altered during 1973, upwards to KShs. 6.90, so as to maintain a rough parity with Kenya's main trading partners during the world-wide decline in the value of the dollar, but was restored to the old parity of Shs. 7.14 at the beginning of 1974. This rate of exchange was maintained until near the end of October 1975 when the shilling was devalued against the dollar by 14.3 per cent and was pegged to the SDR.[46] The authorities took the view that the instability of the major currencies at that time made it desirable to have a more stable standard than any one currency was likely to provide.[47]

The World Bank mission proposed that the exchange rate should be used as a 'positive and flexible instrument of policy'.[48] It was the view of the mission that the shilling was overvalued, if only because of the effects of protection, though they did not go quite as far as firmly to recommend a devaluation. The change made in 1975 was therefore a further move in the direction of the policies set out in the World Bank report, whether or not it was made for the same reasons. Since then, the temporarily strong balance of payments and the accumulation of reserves suggest that for a time at least the shilling was under-valued. Certainly the Kenya shilling, at par, is greatly under-valued in relation to the 'free market' rates of the Tanzanian and Ugandan shillings, though the paucity of trade with the former of the two countries reduces the relevance of that fact. A revaluation would have helped with the rate of increase in prices, and would have constituted a desirable tax on earnings from the main primary commodity exports during a period of exceptionally high prices, though its effect on other kinds of exports could have been serious. One might conclude that with a need on the one hand to encourage exports of manufactures, and on the other to regulate the income from primary commodities of which Kenya is a small exporter in terms of the world market, a dual exchange rate system would be beneficial. Some of the effect of a dual exchange rate has been achieved by the recently reintroduced export taxes on tea and coffee and the subsidies to manufactured exports, though both taxes and subsidies are small. And with the fall in commodity prices, and the speed with which foreign-exchange reserves were being drawn down in the latter part of 1978, the time for a revaluation to tax commodity exporters would seem to have passed. But a large general devaluation combined with the abolition of protection, which might be suggested by the ethos of the International Monetary Fund and the World Bank as the way to stimulate exports of manufactures, could be highly destructive of both the economy and the social order.

Foreign Investment

The legal context of foreign investment was established in 1964 by the Foreign Investment Protection Act. Under the Act, as amended in 1976, an undertaking can be granted a Certificate which entitles the holder to transfer profits and capital out of Kenya, though each specific transfer requires Central Bank authorization. The Act also reaffirms the constitutional guarantees about compulsory acquisition of property and the payment of compensation, to which there has been a scrupulous adherence. The Government has been generous in approving payments of royalties to overseas patent-holders and to parent companies for overheads, research, and development. These payments can substantially increase the outflow of payments resulting from the foreign investment, and the benefit to the investor, though they have been taxed since 1971.

The fiscal system is designed to encourage investors, and the government advertises that 'an industrialist can write off 120 per cent of his investment against taxable income over a period of a few years',[49] though this statement has become outdated in consequence of a change introduced in the 1975 budget, which restricted the initial investment allowance of 20 per cent to investments in the rural areas or small towns. The view was taken that this allowance, which at the current company tax rate represented a subsidy of 9 per cent for new investments in buildings and machinery, should be retained only to encourage a wider geographical distribution of investment, and not as a general subsidy to the use of capital, encouraging capital intensity. 'In our present balance of payments situation', the Minister of Finance said 'a continuing general subsidy to what is mainly imported capital in addition to all the other investment incentives, is difficult to justify.'[50] In general, tax rates are relatively high and allowances not conspicuously generous, and no provision for 'tax holidays' has ever been mooted. Foreign investment has been encouraged, therefore, by the attempt to establish a reputation for stability and order rather than by the offer of excessively generous financial terms. The importance of the formal and nominal fiscal incentives must be judged, however, in the context of the system of protection under which investments in industry operate.

Probably the most important incentive to foreign investment is in fact the protection which is accorded to many activities, and it has been suggested that 'foreign firms are lodged securely where protection is highest.'[51] A good deal has already been said about protection elsewhere in this chapter and earlier, in Chapter 5. The argument against high protection is particularly strong for foreign investment, much of which is by multinational firms whose protection could not reasonably be justified on 'infant industry' grounds. The profits obtained through protection from sales on the domestic market, together with the provisions for the expatriation of funds, make it possible, indeed provide an incentive for foreign firms 'to expatriate foreign exchange they have neither earned nor saved.'[52]

The practice of 'over-invoicing',[53] entering a high charge for imported purchases from an overseas head office or associated company to minimize tax liability, adds to the expatriation of foreign exchange. The incentive to over-invoice is enhanced when there is local Kenyan participation in the capital of the enterprise, because it is in effect then a way of transferring profits on the local capital to the international company.[54]

Private foreign investors have made great use of local savings. The ease and extent of access to local capital for foreign enterprises has varied from time to time, and bank borrowing had been restricted to an amount equal to between 20 and 60 per cent of the foreign equity. In 1973, however, it was announced that firms engaged in agriculture, manufacturing, and tourism would be allowed over the following two years to borrow locally from the banks up to 100 per cent, so as to encourage increased investment.[55] It may well be wondered whether this relaxation of the restriction on borrowing was wise. But in any case, local funds are available from other sources, including statutory bodies.

The policy of participation in foreign enterprises by statutory bodies, such as ICDC and DFCK, and by individuals, is a plank in Kenya's platform for Africanization, and not lightly to be cast aside. The policy of participation does reveal an ambivalence in Kenya's attitude towards foreign enterprise. Foreign investment is certainly desired, but so is Africanization, and the policy of participation seems to achieve both. It must have seemed preferable to the encouragement of a major switch into manufacturing of resident Asian business concerns. Of course, the provision of some local capital, particularly if it is from a public authority, can be thought of as an investment incentive, and by appearing to increase security may attract foreign investments that would otherwise not be made. However, the insistence on participation comes mainly from the Kenyan side, and is seen as a way of Africanizing ownership and exerting control.[56] It is possible that the costs of this policy outweigh the benefits, and that government assistance with the provision of capital should be confined to Kenyan-owned enterprises.[57]

Even those who do not believe that getting prices 'right' is the answer to most economic problems, and who are not such evangelistic opponents of protection as the World Bank mission, are likely to agree that foreign investment has been too indiscriminately encouraged in the past, and that stringent tests of the desirability of particular investments are necessary.

CHAPTER 8

GOVERNMENT AND THE ECONOMY

The pervasive influence of government on the economy has been apparent in the preceding chapters. But its influence must not be exaggerated. It may still be true that the natural elements, particularly the variability of rainfall, are much more important determinants than government of the welfare of most of the people of Kenya. Nevertheless, it would be foolish not to recognize the enormous importance of government, for good or ill, and some of its main spheres of activity form the subject of this chapter.

(a) FINANCE

Taxation

The yield of taxation increased nearly seven times between 1964/5 and 1976/7.[1] Recurrent expenditure increased only five times in the same period, so that the balance of recurrent revenue and expenditure moved from deficit in the first few years after Independence to a surplus which made a substantial contribution to the finance of government capital expenditure.

At the beginning of the period direct taxes contributed a little over a third of tax revenue. Import duty alone yielded more than all direct taxes, and it was only in 1967/8 that direct taxes began to yield more than import duties. Income tax on persons and companies has accounted for more than 90 per cent of all direct tax revenue, and after 1973/4, when Graduated Personal Tax and export duties had been abolished,[2] for virtually 100 per cent.[3]

The personal income tax is nominally quite progressive, and the progressivity had been increased over time. From the beginning of 1974, the minimum rate on the first £1,200 of chargeable income was 10 per cent and the maximum rate on income in excess of £9,000 was 70 per cent. From 1978 different tax bands were introduced and the maximum rate was reduced to 65 per cent, which was levied on chargeable income over K£9,600, offsetting the increased tax burden which otherwise would have resulted from the rise in money incomes with the rise in the general price level. In the mid-1974 budget the rate of tax on company profits was raised from 40 to 45 per cent and on the profits of branches of foreign companies from 47½ to 52½ per cent. Capital gains tax was introduced in the 1975 budget. In the same budget the scope of the investment allowance was restricted so as to apply only to investments outside Nairobi and Mombasa.

Although there has been some reduction in allowances, there are still generous tax reliefs. In 1973 the sytem of income allowances was replaced by fixed tax reliefs, removing the discrimination in favour of the rich implicit in the old system which relieved the highest-taxed band of income. Personal and children's allowances (on up to four children maintained by the taxpayer) greatly reduced tax liability. From 1978 the children's relief was substituted by a family relief of an amount larger than the maximum available under the old system. The single-person relief was also substantially increased.

The exemption limit, though it was lowered in the 1973 budget, remains high in relation to the general level of incomes in Kenya. In his 1973 Budget Speech the Minister remarked that 'the majority of families were not required to pay income tax until they achieved an income of K£990 p.a. – a figure four times as high as the average family income and probably ten times as high as the income available to the poorest 80 per cent of families.' It might be thought that relief of the lowest incomes from direct taxation through a relatively high exemption limit is appropriate, given the likely regressive incidence of indirect taxes. It has, in fact, been noticed that the high exemption limit for income tax means that 'this major source of Government revenue is derived from the wealthy few'[4] and to that extent is a progressive tax. This does not mean, of course, that the incidence of the tax is progressive within the incomes to which it applies. It has been argued that the tax system is 'regressive over certain income ranges and geared in terms of progressivity to income levels many times higher than those in Kenya'.[5] What this last statement must mean is that for a given taxable income, say K£1,000, the proportion taken in tax is no higher than the proportion that would be taken from an income of that size in Britain, even though an income of a K£1,000 is high in the income distribution in Kenya and low in the UK distribution. The implication that the proportion should be greater in Kenya would be justified only by an extremely relativistic view of income, and an assumed homogeneity of 'life styles' within Kenya which – as is argued in Chapter 9 – does not exist. Without these assumptions, the fact that there are many very poor families is not incompatible with treating those with higher incomes in the same way as people with the same money income would be treated in a rich country.

It is perhaps more to the point to argue that the income tax administration does not sufficiently prevent the avoidance and evasion of tax. Certainly, the increase in the number of persons assessed for tax, other than those from whom tax is collected under PAYE, has been modest.

In 1969 they numbered 34.7 thousand, and in 1975 41.6 thousand, an increase of only a little more than 1,000 a year. And between 1966/7 and 1970/1, although tax-assessed income as a percentage of aggregate income increased from 12 to 20 for employees, for the self-employed it remained constant, at 16, and there was virtually no increase in their aggregate income subjected to tax. Farming, in particular large farms, it seems, managed to avoid paying more tax. Although the marketed output of large farms increased by 14 per cent between 1965 and 1969, tax revenue from agriculture did not rise.[6]

In his 1977 budget speech the Minister of Finance expressed his concern at the extent of tax evasion, and in 1978 he reported that this had been substantially reduced by the efforts of the tax department. In 1978 it was announced that one form of tax avoidance was to be prevented by making it impossible to offset business losses against other forms of taxable income.

The share of direct taxes in total tax revenue increased until 1972/3, when it reached 46.6 per cent. The situation was then radically changed by the introduction of a sales tax. In 1973/4 the yield of direct taxes was down to 36.3 per cent, and the new sales tax alone contributed 20 per cent. By 1976/7 the proportional contribution of direct taxes had recovered somewhat, but only to a fraction over 40 per cent, whereas sales tax contributed a quarter and import duties a fifth of the total. See Table 8.1.

TABLE 8.1

Structure of Tax Revenue

(K£ m.)

	1964/5	1967/8	1972/3	1973/4	1976/7
Direct taxes					
Income tax	13.5	23.0	50.2	56.2	107.5
Other	0.5	1.2	4.4	2.0	0.5
Total	14.0	24.2	54.6	58.2	108.0
Indirect taxes					
Import duty	15.9	20.0	27.0	39.8	52.9
Excise duty	6.2	10.5	16.9	20.9	28.2
Sales tax	–	–	2.7	32.0	65.4
Other	3.7	5.2	16.0	9.6	11.4
Total	25.8	35.7	62.6	102.3	157.9
Total tax revenue	39.8	59.9	117.2	160.5	265.9

Source: *Economic Survey*, annual issues.

Note: 'Other' direct taxes consist of Graduated Personal Tax up to and including 1973/4 and Estate Duties.

'Other' indirect taxes include Stamp Duties, Entertainment Tax, and licences and fees, including those on motoring.

Sales tax, import duties, and excise duties together account for more than 90 per cent of all indirect tax revenue. Import duties have been discussed in other chapters, and it will be expected that most of the revenue is derived from duties on finished manufactures. In fact, the largest revenue from a particular category of imports is from Fuels, which yielded 20 per cent of total import duty revenue in 1977, and as much as 29 per cent in the previous year. The other categories which make a particularly large contribution to revenue are Transport equipment, including motor cars, and Machinery, the two together providing 31 per cent of import duty revenue in 1977.[7]

Excise duties commonly contribute between 15 and 20 per cent of total indirect tax revenue. The largest single source is Beer and spirits (almost all is from beer), which contributed 38 per cent of the total in 1977, which was in fact a decline (though there was a rise in the absolute amount) from the previous year, when its contribution was 44 per cent, and from 47 per cent in 1973. In contrast, the contribution of sugar to total excise revenue has increased from 13 per cent in 1973 to 24 per cent in 1977.[8] The only other major contributor to excise revenue is Cigarettes, which yielded 33 per cent of the total in 1977.

Sales tax was introduced in 1972/3, becoming fully operational in the following year, at a rate of 10 per cent on manufactured goods, locally produced and imported, with a number of exemptions including foods, such as flour and sugar, medicines, and fertilizers. Petrol, beer, and electricity, which had been liable to consumption tax at specific rates from mid-1972, continued to be subject to specific sales taxes. Small manufacturers, with a turnover of less than K£5,000, were exempted from the sales tax. Since its original imposition tax rates have been increased and imposed more heavily on luxuries. The 1974 budget increased the *ad valorem* rate on many luxuries to 15 per cent, as well as the specific rates on beer, cigarettes, and petrol. The 1978 budget increased the specific taxes on fuels and lubricating oils and on beer, and the rate on motor cars and on wines and spirits was put up from 15 to 20 per cent. The turnover figure for exemption from the tax was raised to K£10,000.

The ILO mission came to the conclusion that 'the tax system in Kenya . . . does not have any significant redistributive effect . . . There is therefore a need for a major overhaul of the tax system to improve its equity.'[9] The World Bank agreed that 'the present structure of taxation does not seem to be very progressive.'[10] *African Socialism . . . in Kenya*, the 1965 programme of the government of recently independent Kenya, saw the tax structure as 'a major means for effecting a more equitable distribution of income and wealth'.[11] In fact, several of the specific proposals of that programme have been put into effect. The Graduated

Personal Tax has been abolished, which was the way proposed to exempt people with very low incomes from direct tax. Some basic necessities have been exempted from excise and sales taxes, and some luxuries are heavily taxed. There has also been some diminution in the extent to which tax rates are affected by allowances,[12] and the structure of the income tax has become more progressive. However, the great increase in the revenue from sales tax, which is unlikely to be as progressive as the upper levels of the income tax, and the failure effectively to tax capital gains,[13] suggest that the judgements by the ILO and the World Bank of the tax structure at the beginning of the 1970s may still apply. 'Nor is there any evidence', the World Bank mission found, 'that the expenditure pattern of Government', to which we now turn, 'has gone very far in offsetting income inequalities.'[14]

Expenditure

The statistics show government expenditure divided into three classes: current expenditure; development expenditure; and investment expenditure. Although the allocation of expenditure between these three classes has a considerable element of arbitrariness in it, the division does have a rough and ready economic meaning. Recurrent expenditure includes consumption of goods and services, interest payments, and transfers. Development expenditure is a 'reasonable approximation'[15] to gross capital formation. Investment expenditure, possibly a misleading title, covers the purchase of equity in enterprises and loans, mainly to public corporations.

Total expenditure, the sum of these three classes, increased from K£70½ m. in 1964/5 to just under K£410 m. in 1976/7. Recurrent expenditure increased by five times during the period, and development expenditure by more than eleven times.

TABLE 8.2

Recurrent and Development Expenditure on Selected Government Services

(K£ m.)

	1964/5	1966/7	1968/9	1970/1	1974/5	1976/7
Agriculture	12.7	10.5	13.5	11.4	28.5	(37.5)
Transport	3.4	6.4	9.2	18.7	39.7	47.4
Education	6.8	7.9	11.9	27.6	63.8	80.8
Defence	3.0	5.3	5.6	6.5	19.1	42.9
Debt service	6.4	8.3	8.9	17.7	23.7	36.3
All services	70.5	84.9	105.0	156.8	301.6	409.8

Source: *Economic Survey*, annual issues.
Note: Scope of statistic for agriculture changed in the *Economic Survey* for 1978. The figure above for 1976/7 is the estimate from *Economic Survey*, 1977.

There were several notable changes in the distribution of government expenditure between the different services during the first thirteen financial years after Independence. One is the very great increase in the proportion of total expenditure devoted to education. K£6.8 m. was spent on education in 1964/5, a sum equal to 10 per cent of total government expenditure; by 1976/7 expenditure on education had risen to K£80.8 m., equal to 20 per cent of total expenditure. Although there is not doubt that education is a voracious claimant of government funds, the rise in the proportion devoted to education is to some degree illusory. Between 1969/70 and 1970/1 there was a 58 per cent increase in expenditure on education, which raised the proportion of total government expenditure devoted to this service from 14 to 18 per cent. This increase was primarily the result of the transfer of responsibility for primary education from County Councils to the Central Government; it did not constitute an increased claim on total resources.

That was not the case with the 38 per cent rise in expenditure on education between 1973/4 and 1974/5, which accompanied the introduction from January 1974 of free education in the first four primary-school grades. Primary-school enrolment rose by over 51 per cent in 1974 compared with 8 per cent in 1973, and 5 per cent in 1975. The jump in enrolment in 1974 distorted the usual pattern of entry and wastage, and the increase in the primary-school population was only 0.5 per cent in 1976 and 2.6 per cent in 1977.[16] Surprisingly, the enormous jump in primary-school enrolment in 1974 and the increase of more than a third in expenditure on education did not significantly increase its proportional claim on government funds, taking recurrent and capital expenditures together. The proportion devoted to education rose from 20 per cent in 1973/4 – not much more than the proportion established earlier with the transfer of responsibility from County Councils – by a mere one percentage point; it fell to 19 per cent in the following year and was back to 20 per cent in 1976/7.

There does not seem, therefore, to be strong evidence for any fear that education expenditure has 'got out of hand' and is claiming an 'ever increasing' share of resources.[17] Its claim on resources is certainly large, and it must be remembered that there are large expenditures on education outside the coverage of the official statistics. Expenditures incurred by private assisted and unaided schools are undocumented, but must account for a significant proportion of all expenditure in the field of education,[18] and it was estimated that in 1977–8 the inclusion of private expenditure would raise total expenditure on education from K£92 m. to K£130 m., roughly equal to 8 per cent of GDP.[19] It must also be remembered, however, that expenditures by charitable foundations on education bring, so to speak, their finance with them, and if their activities were stopped[20] the finance would also cease to be available; and expenditure out of taxed income on private education does not seem prima facie to be a less desirable form of consumption expenditure than many others that come to mind. By the spenders it might be seen as investment from a private point of view, as indeed it might be from a social point of view.

Nevertheless, there are worries about the scale of expenditure on education, and its effects. Although the fears that 'demand for education might force the Government recurrent budget completely out of gear'[21] have not yet been justified by events, it is also argued that 'as a proportion of GDP, Kenya's expenditure on education is among the highest in the world',[22] and 'now appears to absorb a disporportionate share of national resources.'[23] It could be countered that there is nothing deplorable for the Government, reflecting the choices of the people, to provide for a large part of public consumption to take the form of educational services. And there is no doubt about the enthusiasm of the people for education. However, the argument is that the enthusiasm for education arises from the belief, apparently justified by experiences of the past but now unjustified, that education is the golden road to riches, that is, to wage employment in the formal sector. The differential in wage levels between the educated and the uneducated is so great that the return from education seems extremely high, and therefore the desire for education is very strong. But the wage levels, the argument runs, are not equilibrium levels at which employment is available, and the expansion of education in fact serves to increase the number of educated unemployed. In the words of the World Bank Report,

> the link between the education system and the labor market is obviously not functioning, and the country urgently needs to question the usefulness of turning out expensively educated young people who cannot be employed. A more disciplined control of secondary and university education, in line with the needs of the labor market, is perhaps the most obvious potential source of savings in education expenditure.[24]

This argument at least is not opposed to universal primary education, though it may be suspected that the abolition of fees, despite its egalitarian effect, would not be wholly congenial.[25] There seems no reason to think it undesirable that the educational standards required for employment should be rising, so that primary education is now the minimum needed for wage employment, even for many unskilled jobs,[26] so long as access to at least the minimum of education is available to all. In these circumstances, primary education should be seen not simply as a selector of the few who are destined to win the prize of further education or a higher-paid job, but as a process for raising the general standard of awareness and ability of the population and increasing the numbers of those who are given the opportunity to compete for the prize.

None of this means that changes in the education system are unnecessary. There is certainly substance in the view that primary education should not be exclusively directed at a preparation for secondary education to which only a minority can in fact reasonably aspire; and it is undoubtedly desirable that post-primary education should be relevant. More technically-oriented education is needed. The quality of education is too variable, particularly in the self-help *Harambee* schools to which 40 per cent of private expenditure is devoted. But it is important to avoid suggesting that unemployment is in some way the result of education, and that less education would (in more than a trivial sense) reduce educated unemployment. It is to be noted that the rate of unemployment falls as the level of education rises. Aspirations created by education and recent history create the surplus of job seekers, particularly school leavers queuing for highly desired jobs, while existing job opportunities are not being taken up.[27] But school leavers are not fixed in their ideas and aspirations, and there is a good deal of evidence in Kenya and other countries in Africa that they soon adjust to the realities of the changing situation.[28]

A second change in the distribution of expenditure in the different government services is the rise in the proportion devoted to defence. There was a significant rise during the first few years of Independence. Before Independence virtually the whole cost of defence was borne by Britain, and these costs had to be assumed by Kenya. More or less at the same time, a security problem in the North Eastern Province required an increase in defence expenditure. By 1966/7 expenditure on defence was thirty times what it has been in the last full financial year before Independence, and as a proportion of total government expenditure had increased from little more than a quarter of 1 per cent to 6 per cent. The hope was then expressed that agreements with the Somali Republic would allow a levelling off in defence costs in the coming years.[29] This hope proved to be justified, and the defence share in total expenditure did not rise and was even reduced – in 1970/1 it was down to 4 per cent. However, security deteriorated again after the mid-1970s, and defence expenditure was increased sharply in 1976/7. It rose from 6 to 10 per cent of total expenditure, and was expected to rise to 15.5 per cent in 1977/8.[30] Expenditure at this level constitutes a considerable burden on a country whose Government is committed to a policy of 'helping the "working poor" in agriculture',[31] and although doubtless a small proportion as compared with that incurred by the regimes in power in many less fortunate countries, it is a radical departure from the distribution of resources that had been usual in Kenya.

The third kind of services the expenditure on which it is necessary to examine are the economic services, and in particular agriculture. Together, these services constitute the largest claimant on government funds, absorbing nearly one-third of total expenditure in 1976/7.[32] This proportion has been pretty constant over the years: in 1962/3, before Independence, it was 30 per cent, it dipped to 28 per cent in 1965/6, and was up to 33 per cent in 1968/9.

In contrast to the relative constancy of the proportion spent on economic services in total is the declining proportion devoted to agriculture. The highest proportion spent on agriculture was 66 per cent in 1963/4; by 1970/1 the proportion was down to 22. Even the absolute amount spent on agriculture declined: in 1963/4 it was K£13.5 m., in 1966/7 K£10.5 m., and in 1970/1 K£11.4 m.

The total expenditure classified as on agricultural and veterinary services is a very mixed bag, and is affected significantly by changes in particular expenditures. Until the later 1960s it was much affected by the changing level of expenditure under the land-settlement programme. These were large in relation to the total: in 1963/4 and 1964/5 they accounted for more than half the total agricultural and veterinary expenditure. They then fell off sharply. In 1964/5 they amounted to K£6.82 m. and in 1967/8 to K£2.07 m. Expenditure other than on the settlement programme increased in absolute terms after 1963/4. But these expenditures include subsidies, such as the K£2 m. to meet losses on maize exports in 1968,[33] the amount of which fluctuates widely. To what extent such subsidies can in any case be counted as expenditure to foster the development of agriculture is a moot point. Guaranteed prices for the product may be necessary if there is to be innovation, such as the adoption of high-yielding hybrid maize. But maize is not an economic export crop, and it is not desirable to encourage production in excess of need for current consumption and storage. So the extent to which expenditures have been devoted to improving agricultural productivity, particularly among the least productive, where they are needed most, is difficult to disentangle from the total expenditure figures. In any case, it seems clear that agriculture has not been of obviously increasing importance in the allocation of government expenditure, at any rate up to 1974.

The same cannot be said for transport and communications. Expenditure on roads and other items of transport and communications accounted for 17 per cent of total expenditure on economic services in 1964/5, and rose in importance to a maximum of 44 per cent in 1972/3.

It does not immediately follow as a matter of logic that the importance of agriculture in the economy of Kenya requires a correspondingly large allocation of government expenditures. In principle, it could be that other sectors had a greater need for the services of government, and that for instance the inadequacy of the transport system was retarding economic growth as a whole. And an improvement in transport might be the most effective contribution to agricultural development, if production were inhibited by marketing difficulties arising from poor roads. Nevertheless, it is difficult not to feel that agricultural services were neglected in the 1960s and early 1970s. The pattern may have changed after the middle of the decade.[34] There are indications that the claim of transport diminished relatively, and that of agriculture and water supply increased. If so, the change is no doubt 'partly explained by the Government's current emphasis on helping the "working poor" in agriculture, and in extending water supplies in rural areas'.[35] But it is difficult to find in the statistics any justification for the claim that 'in recent years the expansion of expenditure on economic and community services has been particularly marked',[36] if the test is their share in total government expenditure.

The final category of expenditure to be examined is debt service, an item so prominent – disastrously prominent, it might be said – in the budgetary problem of many developing countries. Total debt-servicing charges, internal and external, which amounted to K£5.21 m. in the fiscal year 1963/4, had risen to K£36.29 m. by 1976/7. Of this total K£21.52 m. was internal, against which can be offset interest and loan repayment receipts of nearly K£10 m., reducing the net budgetary burden of the internal debt to less than K£12 m., or under 3 per cent of total government exenditure.

The burden of external debt is of a different character from that of the internal debt, but in Kenya it shares the characteristic of being small. The size of the external debt-service payments can be judged against three criteria: in relation to government expenditure, GDP, and the value of exports of goods and services. In relation to all three of these magnitudes it is small. In 1976/7 the service charge of K£14.8 m. on the external debt amounted to less than 4 per cent of government expenditure, to 1 per cent of monetary GDP, and to 2.3 per cent of the value of exports of goods and services.[37]

However, it would be wrong to create the impression that debt charges are and will be of no significance. There was heavy borrowing in the middle 1970s, particularly in 1973, 1975, and 1976, the full effect of which on service charges was delayed by grace periods on capital repayment. It was estimated that the service charges on the external debt outstanding at the beginning of 1976 would rise from K£12 m. to K£28 m. by 1980, and to a maximum of K£31 m. in 1985, before it began to decline consequent upon repayments.[38] The proportion of debt service to GDP was expected to rise fairly rapidly between 1978 and the middle 1980s, as a result of continuing substantial expenditures on purchases of equipment. It was forecast that the ratio of the external debt service charge to the value of exports of goods and services would rise to between 6.5 and 7 per cent by 1983.[39]

The Finance of Public Investment

Over the period since Independence, a quite remarkably high part of the Government's requirement for capital finance has been met from a surplus on recurrent account. In the first three fiscal years, 1964/5 to 1966/7, the recurrent account was in deficit. The deficit in the first of these three years amounted to 40 per cent of the finance required on capital account, and in the second of the years it was as high as 44 per cent. Thereafter the deficit declined, and the account moved into surplus in 1967/8. Since then, the surplus has contributed less than 20 per cent of the requirement in only two years, and in one year its contribution was over 40 per cent. The size of the capital finance requirement and the contribution to the recurrent surplus and other sources are set out for a selection of years in Table 8.3.

TABLE 8.3

Finance of Public Investment

	1964/5	1967/8	1974/5	1975/6	1976/7
Development Expenditure	7.5	12.2	62.0	74.3	86.0
Loans etc.	6.1	7.4	32.2	52.1	38.7
Total Finance Requirement	13.6	19.6	94.2	126.4	124.7
Source of finance as percentage of total requirement:					
Recurrent Surplus	–40	15	20	18	28
External loans and grants	150	49	36	40	32
Domestic Borrowing					
Long Term	7	42	16	42	20
Short Term	–1	4	7	26	24
Change in Balances	–16	–10	20	–26	–4

Source: *Economic Survey*, 1978, Table 6.1, and corresponding Table in earlier issues.
Note: Change in Balance, minus equals increase.

In most years the largest contribution to finance for government capital expenditure (defined to include both Development Expenditure and Investment Expenditure in the official terminology) has been external loans and grants. This external finance was discussed in Chapter 7. At its smallest in relation to the financial requirements it contributed 26 per cent; in 1964/5 its contribution was 150 per cent, so that in effect it contributed to the recurrent finances on a massive scale, as well as increasing cash balances. (See Table 8.3).

Although external grants and loans have commonly been the largest source of finance, the importance of domestic borrowing increased sharply from a very low level in the first two years after Independence. Within the total of domestic borrowing, the contribution of short-term borrowing has fluctuated widely, between a negative figure of 4 per cent and a positive 33 per cent.

These various sources of finance have sometimes been deficient, but more often they have been in excess of what was needed. Cash balances have been drawn down in four of the thirteen years 1964/5 to 1976/7, but in the other years they have increased, on two occasions to the extent of a quarter of the total financial requirement of the year.

The total of long-term debt rose from K£86 m. at the middle of 1964 to almost K£401 m. in 1976, and K£442 m. in 1977. The rise in domestic borrowing has led to a rise in the locally issued proportion of the total long-term debt from 21 per cent in 1964 to 48 per cent in 1977. Most of the domestic debt is in fact held by public authorities, the largest holder being the National Social Security Fund, which held 40 per cent at mid-1976, while various other public authorities, including local government, the Central Government itself, and the Post Office Savings Bank, held 20 per cent. In addition, the Central Bank held 24 per cent of the locally issued debt at this date. The commercial banks held a further 5 per cent. The extent to which an increasing volume and proportion of the public debt has come to be held by the banks, Central and commercial together, has caused comment, as it has been seen as an indication of inflationary finance.[40] So far as commercial bank lending to the Government is concerned, in 1977/8 the banks were required to purchase additional government stock, it being pointed out that 'unlike treasury bills, purchases of Government stock by commercial banks do not count as a component of liquidity base, and as such they do tend to have a deflationary effect . . .'[41] There was a sharp increase in borrowing from the commercial banks in 1970, when the debt they held rose from K£2.3 m. to K£8.0 m. There was a further rise in 1973 to K£10.8 m., but there followed a decline in commercial bank holdings to K£8.7 m. at mid-1977.

The Central Bank's holding of government debt remained constant at the amount taken over from the East African Currency Board until 1972, when there was an insignificant rise from K£3.5 m. to K£3.7 m.; the holding increased again to K£4.2 m. in 1973. In the following years it increased to K£8.3 m. in 1974, declined to K£7.2 m. in 1975, and then sharply increased to K£36.3 m. in 1976, with a further rise in 1977 to K£37.7 m. In 1975 the Central Bank's holding of government stock amounted to 12 per cent of the total locally issued;[42] at mid-1977 the holding amounted to 24 per cent. The increase in the Central Bank's holding accounted for 62 per cent of the total increase in locally issued debt, and is reflected in the fact that the proportion of the total financial requirement contributed by local long-term borrowing rose from 16 per cent in 1974/5 to 42 per cent in 1975/6.

The short-term borrowing by the government also needs examination. It has already been mentioned that the scale of short-term borrowing has been erratic. As a contributor to the Government's financial requirement on capital account, it was at a maximum of 33 per cent in 1970/1, and it was again high, at 26 per cent, in 1975/6, the year when long-term borrowing was also particularly high, mainly because of a sharp rise in borrowing from the Central Bank. But the Central Bank was not a contributor of short-term funds in that year, nor has it been a consistent or in any year a particularly large contributor. The major source of short-term funds, which have been large only in 1970/1 and 1975-7, has been the sale of Treasury Bills to the commercial banks. The forecast, representing a policy intention, for 1977/8 was to avoid short-term borrowing through the sale of Treasury Bills, and to increase long-term borrowing.

The extent of borrowing from the banking system to provide capital finance needs to be qualified, however, by reference to a fact already mentioned: in most years finance has been provided from the various sources in excess of needs, so that the Government's cash balance has increased. This was notably the case in 1975/6, a year to which we have already referred as one in which there was large-scale domestic borrowing, including large borrowing long-term from the Central Bank. Total domestic borrowing in that year, long-term and short, amounted to 68 per cent of the financial requirement, but the cash balance increased by 25 per cent, in effect reducing the domestic borrowing to 42 per cent. However, even so, the level of domestic borrowing remained high, and in the forecast for 1977/8 the contribution of the banking system was put at nearly 60 per cent. It could be that the Central Bank will come to play a larger part in the finance of investment than it has played during the first decade and a half of Independence.

(b) MONEY

The Central Bank of Kenya was opened by President Kenyatta on 14 September 1966, with the expression of sentiments of impeccable respectability in monetary matters of which Mr Montagu Norman would have been proud. It was no gangster government, and it was to be no gangster bank. There was to be no rival to the Government Printer set up in the Central Bank of Kenya.

Until the new bank opened its doors, Kenya had, and could have, no monetary policy. Its currency was issued by the East African

Currency Board, which operated as the money-issuing authority for all the East African territories. Together with other currency boards, this colonial institution, which had existed since 1919 with headquarters in London until 1960 when they were transferred to Nairobi, had been subjected to criticism as being unnecessarily restrictive, and as transferring funds out of East Africa for investment mainly in Britain.[43] The Board, operating through the commercial banks, issued East African shillings at a fixed rate in exchange for sterling (EAShs. 20 ≐ £1). Its assets were held mainly in United Kingdom securities, and its currency issue had in effect to be 'fully backed' by foreign exchange. The Board had no discretion in its currency-issuing role, though it had limited discretion over the investment of its reserves, so long as it did not invest in securities of the territory of which it was the currency authority. This was the position until 1955 when some relaxation of the strict rules was permitted making possible the holding of a small part of the reserves in the securities of the East African countries. In the beginning the limit to the holding of such securities was set at £10 m., but the limit was subsequently raised in 1957 to £20 m., in 1963 to £25 m., and finally in 1964 to £35 m. In addition, the Board was authorized from 1960 to issue up to £5 m. of currency to meet seasonal demand for crop finance, and the amount was increased to £10 m. in 1962. Also from 1960, the Board began to hold balances for the commercial banks and to influence local interest rates, though it had no significant control over credit.[44]

The currency 'backed' by local securities was simply a fiduciary issue with a prescribed maximum. Kenya did not in fact take full advantage of the opportunity offered by the change in the Currency Board rules, and had utilized only 35 per cent of its fiduciary entitlement at the middle of 1965.[45] The new rules by no means converted the Currency Board into a central bank, though there had been debate on the question of whether in 'open' economies in which the level of income was largely determined by the value of exports, and fluctuated with it, a central bank would in practice be able to do much more than the new-style Currency Board. Possibly the consensus was that although the primary fluctuations in income which were the direct result of changes in export earnings, could not be controlled by monetary measures, a central bank could attempt to offset the exaggeration of the primary fluctuations by secondary expansions financed by bank credit, for which there would be a demand when the economy was booming, and for which there would be a supply of funds as the banks would be highly liquid because of the export boom. It could also attempt to maintain incomes by expansionary measures when there was a fall in foreign earnings, though there was an asymmetry between booms and slumps because attempts to offset contractionist influences would be severely limited by the effect on foreign-exchange reserves, as well as by a low demand for credit in a deflationary situation. It was also suggested that a central bank could be beneficial in extending the 'monetization' of the economy, expanding the money supply in step with the growth of the monetary economy, in a way that was not open to the currency board.

As the currency board operated for the whole of East Africa, and as there had been talk of a political federation of Kenya, Tanganyika (as it then was), and Uganda, there were attempts to devise schemes for an East African central bank.[46] These academic and official speculations were brought to an end in early 1965 when Tanzania announced her intention to establish her own central bank and to withdraw from the currency union. This decision was quickly followed by the other countries, and the Central Bank of Kenya Act received Presidential Assent in March, 1966.

It was a common characteristic of British banks operating in less-developed countries, that they found little scope for the local utilisation of funds. The funds they collected locally were to a large extent remitted to Britain for investment. The banks, therefore, operating according to their accepted banking criteria were a second means, in addition to the Currency Board, of transferring savings from the less to the more developed country. This practice was reflected in banking statistics as a low ratio of local earning-assets to total assets, and its counterpart, a high reserve ratio.[47]

In 1938 the local assets ratio was only 0.4, so that the reserve ratio was 0.6. During the war the unavailability of imports produced balance of payments surpluses for Kenya, and at the same time there was little scope for the expansion of bank credit. As a result the banks became even more liquid: in 1945 the local asset ratio was a mere 0.13, and the reserve ratio in consequence was 0.87. An extreme version of the standard 'colonial' banking situation existed.

Things were soon to change, however. Opportunities for the local lending of funds appeared, and the potential for credit expansion existing in the highly liquid state of the banking system was rapidly exploited. By 1955 the local earning assets ratio was up to 0.78, but the growth did not stop there. A new element entered the situation: there was a capital flight following the Lancaster House conference on the political future of Kenya at the end of 1959. In 1960, although there was an increase in advances of £4.5 m., deposits fell by £6.6 m., indicating an outflow of funds of £11.1 m. The usual position in which the local branches were in credit with head office was reversed, and they came to draw funds from abroad for utilization locally: in 1960 the local assets ratio was 1.10. In the last year before the establishment of the Central

Bank, 1965, the ratio had fallen below unity, but only just, to 0.97.

When the Central Bank started operations, therefore, the excess liquidity, which was the basis for much of the criticism of the old system, no longer existed. The Currency Board had invested in local securities, and the commercial banks had reduced their excess liquidity virtually to zero. Whatever the Bank would be able to achieve, it would not be a large expansion of domestic investment to draw down excessive funds held abroad.

The Act establishing the Central Bank of Kenya requires the bank to 'use its best endeavours to maintain a reserve of external assets at an aggregate amount of not less than the value of four months imports', which at the time meant a reserve of not less than about £30 m.[48] 1965 and 1966 were years of surplus on the combined current and long-term capital account balance of payments. At the end of 1966 Kenya's foreign-exchange reserves totalled nearly £42 m., an amount comfortably exceeding the value of four months' imports.

When the Central Bank was established there were nine commercial banks operating in Kenya, all of them branches of overseas banks, and business was dominated by the three United Kingdom banks. Since that date the banking system has developed and become less wholly expatriate. In 1968 two new banks, the Cooperative Bank of Kenya and the government-owned National Bank of Kenya, were established, and one – the Ottoman Bank – was taken over by National and Grindlays. At the end of 1970 agreement was reached on major Government participation in National and Grindlays Bank. The bank was split into an international bank in which the Government took a 40 per cent share, and the local branch system of the bank, renamed the Kenya Commercial Bank, in which Government took a 60 per cent share.

The operation of the monetary system since the establishment of the Central Bank may be conveniently examined by looking at four periods of change in important variables.[49] The first is the sharp fall in foreign-exchange reserves in the last three months of 1967, the second is the 1971 foreign-exchange 'crisis', the third the increase in oil prices at the end of 1973, and the fourth the commodity price boom of 1976–7.

At the end of September 1967 Kenya's foreign assets totalled K£45.1 m. By the end of the year they had fallen to K£31.6 m., and in January 1968 they were down to K£30.2 m. After that the total value of foreign assets increased, and was back to more than K£44 m. in January 1969.

In November 1967 sterling, to which the East African currency had been tied since 1920, was devalued and after three days of consultations the East African countries decided to break the link and not to follow sterling down. The immediate effect of the decision to allow the Kenya shilling, in common with the other East African currencies, to appreciate in terms of sterling was a loss in the Kenya shilling value of Kenya's sterling assets. The sterling assets held by the Central Bank fell in value by K£3.5 m. for this reason, but there was in addition an outflow of foreign exchange of K£10 m., the two causes together accounting for the decline in foreign-exchange reserves of K£13.5 m. during the last quarter of the year. This fall in reserves of 30 per cent during the quarter brought the total to below the four months' imports requirement.

The outflow of foreign exchange during the last quarter of 1967 was speculative. It did not, the Bank argued, provide evidence of 'overheating in the economy'; it was the result of expectations that Kenya would before long follow sterling down, so that there was a rush to pay off sterling debts while the favourable rate of exchange continued to hold. These redemptions of debt and the speeding up of foreign settlements were in part financed by a sharp expansion of advances to the private sector, which rose from a little under K£58 m. in October to a peak of K£68.8 m. in January 1968. They were also financed by running down deposits, which fell by K£2.9 m. between October and January, despite the large increase in advances. Bank liquidity declined with the expansion in advances: the cash ratio of the commercial banks fell from 15 per cent in October to 6.5 per cent at the end of January 1968; balances with the Central Bank fell from K£9.7 m. to K£2.2 m.; and the net balance with banks abroad changed from a credit of K£2.6 m. to a debit of the same size.

The reason for the fall in the reserves made the situation largely self-correcting. As it became clear that a devaluation of the shilling was not imminent the pressure to switch from overseas borrowing, such as suppliers credit, to local borrowing subsided. The commercial banks adopted a more restrictive credit policy, in consequence of their loss of liquidity and of their unwillingness to rely for long on borrowing from their overseas offices to support credit expansion in Kenya.

The powers of the Central Bank were exerted cautiously. The Bank provided a forward cover of sterling transations, thus reducing the incentive for quick settlement of sterling debts, as debtors had a guarantee that the Kenya shilling value of the debt would be unaffected by a devaluation. No attempt was made to limit borrowing from abroad by the banks, which was substantial, because it was realized that the banks would not themselves wish to be exposed to the exchange risk. But inter-bank lending within Kenya was prohibited, so that banks with greater liquidity could not support credit expansion by banks with low liquidity. For the rest, while requesting the banks to refuse credit for speeding up payments for imports, the policy was largely passive, allowing the fall in bank liquidity to have its effect, though special arrangements were made to prevent the shortage of liquidity from affecting the financing of crop movements during the season.

From the beginning of 1968, foreign-exchange reserves accumulated rapidly. In every quarter, except one (second quarter of 1970), the reserves increased. By the end of the first quarter of 1971 they had nearly trebled since January 1968 and totalled K£89.1 m. Thereafter they declined to the low figure of K£62.34 m. in November, recovering slightly to K£62.76 m. by the end of the year. Recovery continued, and the total was up to K£72.61 m. in December 1972.[50]

Over this period of decline and recovery in the foreign-exchange reserves, other monetary magnitudes changed in the following ways. Central Government borrowing from the banking system, which amounted to K£6.6 m. at the end of the first quarter of the year, fluctuated during the succeeding months and totalled K£8.3 m. at the end of October; in November it jumped to almost K£18 m. From the end of the first quarter of the year, the liquid assets of the commercial banks declined, whereas deposits increased, so that the liquidity ratio fell from 30.5 per cent in March to 15.6 per cent at the end of the year. Bank advances to the private sector increased by K£29.5 m. or 36 per cent over the year, and by 26 per cent from the end of the first quarter. During 1972, in contrast, advances had risen by less than 1 per cent, and by the end of that year the liquidity ratio had risen to 22.7 per cent.

The increase in central government borrowing from the banking system reflects the deficit financing embarked upon during the 1970/1 fiscal year. Up to that time most government borrowing cannot properly be considered as deficit financing. Long-term borrowing from the National Social Security Fund was of genuine – even though 'forced' – saving; the requirement imposed on the commercial banks to maintain a minimum level of capital reserves in Kenya, and the transfer of the assets of public-sector pension funds from overseas into Kenya Government securities, involved genuine – if 'forced' and once-for-all – capital inflows. Short-term borrowing had been small, and was partly offset by a cash reserve. In 1970–1, however, the Government borrowed K£10 m. on Treasury Bills and a further K£5 m. from the Central Bank. Although this deficit financing would have reduced the reserves, it would not have resulted in a crisis. The reserves were high, and had a long way to fall before they approached the level of four months' imports. And as the figures quoted above show, the Government's indebtedness to the banking system did not rise sharply until November, whereas the reserves began to fall in April.

There was therefore an additional and earlier-operating cause of the fall in foreign-exchange reserves after the end of the first quarter of 1967. This was, of course, the increase in commercial-bank lending to the private sector which is reflected in the increase in advances and the fall in liquidity. It has been persuasively argued[51] that these movements were the result of a large reinvestment in stocks. There was a run-down in stocks in 1968, following uncertainties created by the policy of Kenyanization which had begun to be implemented, and a low level of stocks was maintained until restocking began in 1970 and continued on a large scale in 1971, when business confidence recovered. The counterpart of this low investment in stocks was a low demand for credit and high commercial-bank liquidity, which permitted a ready expansion of credit when demand for it increased to finance restocking.

The restocking boom was itself enough to produce the decline in bank liquidity and the fall in reserves to near the four months' imports level, and had done so almost before the effect of the deficit financing was felt. But the deficit financing on top of the restocking boom, in addition to its direct effect could, by increasing the cash of the banks and permitting a multiple expansion of credit, result in the reserves running out. Hence the crisis measures which were taken, despite the fact that the reserves did not actually fall below the minimum desired level.

Measures were taken by both the Bank and the Government. Import restrictions were imposed which, although regretted by the Minister of Finance in his 1972 Budget Speech as 'they can distort the pattern of production . . . and lead to high domestic costs', were deemed essential because 'an axe with an immediate effect to safeguard the foreign exchange reserves was . . . imperative.' Higher import duties also were introduced. The Central Bank imposed restrictions on credit for certain imports, and exchange control was tightened on travel allowances and certain remittances. Hire-purchase conditions were tightened, though the restrictions seem to have been ineffective.[52] For a short time a minimum cash balance was prescribed for the commercial banks in addition to the 12½ per cent liquidity ratio. In substitution for this control measure, guidelines to the banks were put forward, which included a restriction on the expansion of lending to 12 per cent. It was claimed that 'all these measures have had an effect.'[53]

But in addition, the extent of deficit financing was much reduced.[54] The loss of reserves was certainly arrested and reversed. The Central Bank concluded from the episode 'that there is a danger of over much reliance on the banking system by the Central Government.'[55]

In the middle of 1973 the foreign-exchange reserves had reached a record level of over K£100 m., almost twice the four months' imports target. Because of the large external reserves, the credit controls and controls on imports imposed in July 1971 were relaxed in July 1973, and there was a rapid expansion in credit to the private sector. By the end of the quarter, advances had risen by 10 per cent, and by the end of the year by 28 per cent, an expansion which is in sharp contrast with the 4 per cent increase in advances to the private sector for the whole year to June 1973, which was only one-third of the target for the growth of credit. The liquidity ratio of the banks fell from 30 per cent to 25½ per cent. The foreign-exchange reserves fell quite sharply in step with the expansion of credit and by the end of the year had fallen by 19 per cent from the mid-year peak. A new and major influence then began to operate: the rise in oil prices.

The impact on Kenya's imports of the rise in oil prices did not have its main effect until the second quarter of 1974. In the first quarter, imports of mineral fuels and lubricants were 42 per cent up in value on the previous year; in the second quarter they were nearly seven times greater than in the second quarter of 1973; in the third quarter they were nearly three times, and in the fourth four and a half times greater than in the corresponding quarters of 1973. For the year as a whole, fuel imports were nearly four times greater than in 1973, and total imports were greater by three-quarters. At the end of September 1974 foreign-exchange reserves were only 63 per cent of their level in the middle of 1973 and were well below the four months' imports level, which they had fallen to in June. Advances had continued to rise and the liquidity ratio of the banks as a whole had fallen below 20 per cent, and some were near or at the 15 per cent prescribed minimum.

Measures to check the deterioration in the balance of payments reflected in the loss of foreign exchange were introduced in the middle of 1974. In the first place, credit to the private sector, which had expanded by 56 per cent between June 1973 and June 1974, was to be restricted to a growth of 12 per cent between June 1974 and June 1975. Within this total increase, the needs of agriculture, small African-owned business, and for the finance of industrial raw materials were to be fully met, so that the restriction was aimed primarily at personal and commercial credit demands. Secondly, the 15 per cent liquidity ratio, which applied to commercial banks, was extended to other financial institutions. In addition, interest rates were raised. Finally, capital inflows from abroad were encouraged by a number of measures, including a stricter control on local borrowing by companies with more than 15 per cent non-resident equity ownership.

External reserves continued to fall after these measures were introduced, but had recovered to above the June 1974 level by the end of March. Difficulties with the reserves were not over, however, and they did not finally rise above the statutory minimum until after the middle of 1976, when a new feature had again entered the picture. Commercial-bank liquidity increased a little, and the liquidity ratio was up to 22½ per cent in the first quarter of 1975, though it declined to 21 per cent in the next two quarters, and to 19 per cent in the last. The guidelines for credit priorities were followed by the banks, which increased their lending to agriculture and manufacturing and reduced their advances for trade. But the 12 per cent limit on advances was not in fact restrictive, as advances rose by less than 10 per cent in the year 1974/5. At the time of the imposition of the controls in the middle of 1974, the Bank feared that a shortage of liquidity caused by the large deficit in the balance of payments might prevent the banks from meeting the needs of the priority sectors for credit, and 'in order to forestall the expected liquidity shortage, banks were invited to make use of credit facilities from the Central Bank with effect from August, 1974.'[56] Between August and December advances rose by a further 4 per cent, which was equal to the permitted rate on an annual basis, and at the end of the year the banks were in debt to the Central Bank for nearly K£12 m. In the first six months of 1975, however, advances rose by only a little over 1½ per cent, and at the end of June the banks' indebtedness to the Central Bank was only K£1½ m. The Bank noted the inherent weakness of credit controls, which had not escaped the notice of those who in earlier times had wondered how much more a central bank could do than the Currency Board, that although 'they work very effectively when directed towards restraining the rate of growth in bank credit',[57] they are weak when required to stimulate expansion. It is possible to provide a horse with water, but difficult to make him drink. It seems probable that the horse was not thirsty, that there was a lack of demand for credit, because of the general depression in the economy (rather than the other way round, as some statements of the Bank appear to suggest). The high price of imports together with a drop in agricultural production from a failure of the rains, caused a sharp decline in the rate of economic growth. In 1973 monetary GDP at constant prices increased by 7 per cent; in 1974 the increase was 4 per cent and in 1975 just over 1 per cent. The Central Bank correctly concluded:[58] 'It was apparent that monetary and fiscal policy alone were unlikely to be sufficiently effective to achieve the dual aims of encouraging the domestic economy to continue to expand at a satisfactory rate, and of reducing the deficit on the current account of the balance of payments to more manageable proportions.'

The powers of the Bank in an expansionary climate were soon, it seemed, to be put to the test. The price of coffee started to rise from the middle of 1975: a year later it had risen by 182 per cent and was continuing upward. At its peak in April 1977 the price was more than six and a half times what it had been in the middle of 1975. The price of tea began to increase a year later than that of coffee, and the increase was less marked and less continuous, but nevertheless at its peak in May 1977 the price of tea was more than three and a half times what it had been a year earlier. The effect of this price boom on the value of Kenya's exports was very great. In 1974 the value of exports was almost the same as it had been in the previous year; in 1975 it increased by 45 per cent, and in 1977 it was more than twice what it had been in 1974. There was a correspondingly large effect on the balance of payments. The balance of the current plus long-term capital accounts moved from a deficit of K£15 m. in 1975 to a surplus of K£36 m. in 1976 and of K£115 m. in 1977. Even the current account alone was in surplus in the latter year.

With the changes in the balance of payments the external reserves increased rapidly during 1976, and by the middle of 1977 they were more than three times their level of eighteen months earlier. Commercial-bank private advances increased by no more than 35 per cent over the eighteen months. The sluggish growth of credit caused the Bank to offer encouragement to further lending by a reduction in its minimum lending and rediscount rates at the end of 1976, though one might doubt if this was much more than a gesture. Perhaps likely to be more effective was the relaxation of the constraints on local borrowing by foreign companies engaged in agriculture, manufacturing, and tourism. They had been restricted to local borrowing of between 20 and 60 per cent of investment, and from April 1977 they were allowed to increase their local borrowing up to a maximum of 100 per cent of their investments.

The commercial banks' liquidity ratio rose from 19 per cent in the last quarter of 1975 to 37 per cent in the third quarter of 1977. The demand for credit, therefore, did not keep pace with the Bank's ability to supply, and it might seem that concern with 'the problem of excess liquidity' should not have been with its inflationary potential but with the lost opportunities for economic expansion. The measures to liberalize credit would have been an appropriate reflection of such a view. So after all, the export boom of 1976–7 did not provide a test of the Bank's ability to constrain a domestic expansion when liquidity was rising fast for external reasons. To paraphrase Roy Campbell, 'They had the snaffle and the curb all right, but there was no bloody horse.'

The liberalization of borrowing conditions from the end of 1976 took place 'at a time when credit to the private sector was sluggish while liquidity was rising sharply and the balance of payments was running in surplus.'[59] But private advances had been expanding consistently since August 1976, and they continued to increase. In June

1978 they were just about double what they had been at the end of 1975. The horse may have arrived late at the starting post, but it was running strongly. The liquid assets of the commercial banks declined pretty consistently from month to month after September 1977, and the banks' liquidity ratio had fallen to 22 per cent by the middle of 1978. The excess of liquid assets over the minimum statutory requirement, which had been 19.5 per cent of deposit liabilities in August 1977, was down to 1.9 per cent.

The Bank took the view that the rate at which advances were expanding was too high and restrictive measures were introduced from the beginning of 1978, including an increase in the legal minimum liquidity ratio from 18 to 20 per cent, and a tighter definition of allowable liquid assets. By the middle of the year there had been no slackening, but rather an acceleration in the expansion of advances, and alarm was being expressed in the second half of 1978 at the rate at which the foreign exchange reserves were running down.

The operations of the Central Bank must be seen in terms of the aims of monetary policy. 'The main aim of monetary policy [to quote the Governor of the Bank] is to maintain the stability of the country's money and thereby contribute to the economic development of the country.'[60] At greater length it has been explained that the objectives are 'to maintain sound money and control the rate of inflation, to check the rapid deterioration in the balance of payments, and to protect the key productive sectors of the economy – namely, agriculture, manufacturing, exports and small African businesses.'[61] But in addition to the objectives, the operations of the Central Bank must be seen in the context of the tremendous changes in the world economy during the years since it opened its doors for business. For one thing, the whole system of world exchange rates has been transformed. Rather plaintively, perhaps, the Bank noted that in 1975, when the exchange rate of the shilling was related to the Special Drawing Rights of the IMF, 'this was the third time that the shilling had been pegged to a different monetary unit since the establishment of the Central Bank.'[62] Then there was the 'oil crisis' and the later upsurge of coffee and tea prices. However well managed and competently and imaginatively directed, the Bank could not but seem to be a straw on the waters, blown hither and thither by the force of such storms. In the four incidents described above, it cannot be said that monetary measures were particularly important. In the first, the 1967 speculative movement in reserves, the situation was largely self-correcting. The 1971 'crisis' also contained a self-correcting speculative element, as well as the deficit financing which the Bank can rail against, but cannot prohibit. It could hardly be expected that monetary policy could counteract the 'oil crisis', and the Bank remarked:[63] that 'any attribution of the decline in the deficit in 1975 solely or even mainly to the effectiveness of the Central Bank's monetary and credit policies would overstate the effect of its actions, since 1975 was a year of depressed domestic activity.' Finally, and surprisingly, it seems to have had no need to restrain a boom in credit-financed investment in 1976 and until late in 1977, so as to prevent a multiplication of the export boom, because again the demand for credit was relatively slack. And when the expansion in the demand for credit did get under way, restrictive measures were not quickly effective.

Nor can it be said, unfortunately, that the influence of the Bank has been entirely successful in achieving its priorities for the distribution of credit between the different economic sectors. Certainly, in 1974/5 credit for commerce was reduced while for agriculture and other priority sectors it increased. But year after year the Bank has had to report disappointment at the extent to which the commercial banks have supplied credit to agriculture, although such credit was always exempt from the restrictions that were from time to time imposed on lending. The difficulty in expanding bank credit for agriculture comes from both the supply and demand sides. It was the common argument that under traditional land tenure the farmer had no suitable security for a loan. Registration of title removed this difficulty, but enough of the traditional attitude to land remains for farmers to be unwilling to risk its loss by pledging it against a loan. On the supply side, the banks which have an extensive network of branches are reluctant to incur the high costs of administering agricultural credit, when there are other banks which restrict their activities to the cheap and lucrative business available in Nairobi.

In 1975/6 the Bank set a target for the commercial banks' lending to agriculture of 17 per cent of their deposit liabilities, to be reached by the middle of 1976. At that date the proportion was in fact 12 per cent, though it had been 15 per cent at the beginning of the year, and was only 6 per cent in 1971. In June 1977, lending to agriculture was only 11 per cent of deposit liabilities, and the Bank was complaining about the slow progress towards the achievement of the target and the fact that despite the banks being excessively liquid only four of the banks operating in Kenya had reached the 17 per cent target.[64] A year later credit to agriculture had risen to 14.7 per cent of deposit liabilities, but still only 4 of the 14 banks operating in the country had achieved the 17 per cent target.[65]

The Central Bank has not been used as a printing press to finance government expenditures on a massive scale. There have been times, as we have seen, when deficit finance has contributed to a loss of foreign exchange, and from the middle 1970s the government has been relying more on bank finance. This development was forseen in the 1974 Development Plan, where it was argued that it would not necessarily be inflationary because of economic growth and the need increasingly to monetize the non-monetary economy. Any danger of inflation, the Plan stated, would not be met by price controls but by 'traditional instruments of monetary and fiscal policy' and the 'vigorous application of monetary policy'.[66] The Central Bank has warned in various *Annual Reports* of the dangers of government's borrowing from the banking system. 'There are dangers inherent in excessive expansion of Government sector spending and its heavy reliance on the banking system for its financing', the 1976 *Report* stated, and referred to 'excessive growth in lending to the Government', though it also pointed out that in the year in question the borrowing had in fact taken place 'in the context of deficient aggregate demand in the domestic economy and did not, therefore, create undue pressures on either domestic prices or foreign reserves.'[67]

It can only be concluded from this survey, that monetary policy has been no more than a modest contributor to whatever success there has been in achieving the stated aims of monetary policy.

It would be wrong to end, however, without acknowledging the valuable and successful operations of the Bank in various other fields of activity, notably the management of the currency issue and of exchange control. The Bank has been active in international monetary affairs. It has worked in harmony with the commercial banks, and has helped to achieve a situation in which 'though still largely consisting of foreign banks Kenya's commercial banking system can be considered as a national system in the sense that it is guided by the conditions in and interests of Kenya.'[68] But experience since it began operations had confirmed the truth of D.H. Robertson's dictum that 'the real economic evils of society – inadequate production and inequitable distribution – lie too deep for any purely monetary ointment to cure'[69] and even that the more superficial economic strains and disharmonies are often too strong to be overcome by the weapons wielded by a central bank.

(c) AUTHORITIES, BOARDS, AND CORPORATIONS

Kenya is a great place for statutory authorities. It always was. The settler community in colonial days was adept at enlisting Government in support of its economic interests, and the statutory authority was a common means. Later, many of these authorities came to deal also with Africans. The 1963 IBRD report on the economic development of Kenya included a ten-page list of boards and committees concerned with agriculture alone. They include the Kenya Dairy Board (KDB), the

Kenya Meat Commission (KMC), the Pyrethrum Board, the Wheat Board, and many others. It is no wonder that the IBRD mission remarked that 'few underdeveloped countries can compare with Kenya in the magnitude of the organizational arrangements which have been provided by Government to further agricultural development and marketing',[70] and statutory authorities were not confined to agriculture. With adaptations, the various authorities continue to operate,[71] and new ones have been created since Independence. The work of some of them has been referred to in earlier chapters. In this chapter a brief description is given of the functions and character of a sample of these organizations.

The *Industrial and Commercial Development Corporation* (ICDC) is the successor of the Industrial Development Corporation (IDC) which was established by an Ordinance of 1954, which itself succeeded the war-time East African Industrial Management Board.

The ICDC, financed by government and bank loans, was seen as the main vehicle for government participation in industry, and as a major instrument for the Africanization of manufacturing and commerce. Sessional Paper No. 10 of 1965 saw ICDC performing wide-ranging functions.[72] Africanization was to be partly through the support of small businesses which were unable to obtain commercial bank credit, and businesses taken over from non-citizens, and partly through the acquisition of equity in larger firms for subsequent transfer to individual Africans. One analysis of ICDC assistance to small business concluded that primarily it had helped successful business men to consolidate their success rather than playing an initiating and creative role. There were long delays in the processing of applications for assistance, and ICDC had a preference for providing loans for equipment, whereas often the greater need was for working capital.[73]

The reason for government participation through ICDC in large enterprises – the first string of the ICDC's bow – was in part to attract capital, and in part to control it. It would not be only in marginally profitable enterprises that an overseas investor might be encouraged by government participation; even in profitable projects the participation of government might be thought to reduce risks and to make it easier to obtain protection. For the ICDC it was essential for financial reasons to participate in profitable projects because the other string to the bow, the finance of small business, was unlikely to be profitable, and default has in fact been a persistent problem. ICDC has the difficulty of pursuing not wholly compatible goals, so that the need to foster the development of small business pulls one way and the need to make profits and participate in larger scale industry pulls the other.

The difficulty of reconciling the different goals has been diminished, or perhaps concealed by the establishment of subsidiaries and agencies in which the ICDC participates. The Development Finance Company of Kenya (DFCK) was set up to deal with large-scale finance; Kenya Industrial Estates Ltd. was established as a subsidiary of ICDC to provide opportunities for small industry. For small-scale trading the ICDC operates through a Commercial Loans Revolving Fund Scheme. It is also concerned with commerce through its subsidiary, the Kenya National Trading Corporation.

The need to engage in highly profitable activities leads to the somewhat curious practice of ICDC's investing in long-established multinationals. For instance, at the end of 1977 the ICDC and the ICDC Investment Company[74] acquired the shares in East African Industries which were held by the Commonwealth Development Corporation, increasing their total holding in the company to 45.2 per cent. Unilever had been the majority shareholder and manager of the company since 1953. In recording the increase in its investment ICDC pointed out that East African Industries was 'a highly profitable and well managed industrial undertaking that provides a first-class investment'.[75] Although this was undoubtedly true, and although the investment could be viewed as Kenyanization, it might be thought that the developmental purposes of ICDC would be better served by investments which were catalysts, attracting additional capital which would not otherwise become available, rather than by providing funds for already well-established enterprises.

Another noticeable feature of the public participation in industrial and commercial activities is the interlocking nature of some of the investments as a result of the ubiquity of ICDC finance in 'parastatal' organizations. For instance, the ICDC shareholding in Sokoro Fibreboards Ltd. is 29.91 per cent, but in addition there is a 12.76 shareholding by DFCK, and ICDC is a 25 per cent contributor to the capital of that organization. Tiger Shoes is another enterprise with both ICDC and DFCK participation. Similarly, ICDC holds a third of the shares of Yuken Textiles Industry Ltd.; the Industrial Development Bank holds another third, and 26 per cent of IDB's capital is held by ICDC (and the remainder by other government institutions).

In 1977 the assets employed by ICDC totalled nearly K£31 m., of which 45 per cent was in loans and advances, 27 per cent in equity and 24 per cent in subsidiary companies. The Kenya Government was the source of 65 per cent of the funds employed in equity and loans, 14 per cent came from the Corporation's capital and reserves, 11 per cent from bank loans and the rest mainly from the governments of Germany and Sweden.[76]

Kenya Industrial Estates Ltd. is an ICDC subsidiary concerned with establishing and operating industrial estates for small manufacturers, so as to provide opportunities for Africans in industry. On the estates, factory buildings are available for renting and there are associated administrative and technical services. Machinery and equipment are provided with 100 per cent credit and with technical and managerial assistance. In 1977 fifty-four units on the Nairobi estate had been taken up, as had twenty-five of the twenty-seven units at Nakuru, sixteen of the twenty-five at Kisumu, and five at Mombasa. An estate had also been established at Eldoret.[77] Products include textiles, furniture, plastic goods, footwear, and metal products. The ILO mission judged the estates to be an aspect of the general import substitution policy and to be dependent on protection. The capital per job provided was much higher than with other small producers, and many tenants on the estates were short of working capital and lacking supporting technical and advisory services.[78] It is clear from the figures that the number of Kenyan businesses that can be accommodated on the estates is relatively small. Some, indeed, go on to bigger things: Tiger Shoe Co. Ltd., operating on the Nairobi estate, received a loan of Shs. 2.5 m. from the DFCK in May 1976 to provide itself with its own building in the industrial area.[79] Others may remain too small to take advantage of economies of scale and to compete with imports or local multinational products. And an estate isolated from the main shopping centres is not ideal for activities, such as bakery, dry cleaning, furniture making, where direct retailing of part of the output is important.[80] There is a view, therefore, that potential donors for the estates programme should consider carefully whether 'the same effort might not more usefully be dispersed among a larger number of entrepreneurs, spread over a wider geographical area.'[81]

However, there is a more optimistic view of the activities of Kenya Industrial Estates than this. In fact there is a widespread distribution of the estates over the country which is one valuable feature of the programme, and KIE has an important role in introducing Africans to industry and providing training. It is true that the main urban estates do not cater for the smallest of enterprises. At the beginning an enterprise qualified as small-scale for the purposes of KIE when its investment in machinery and equipment was less than Shs. 1.5 m. This limit was raised in 1976-7 to Shs. 3.5 m., to take account of increased costs of equipment, and there is a proposal to raise the limit further to Shs. 5 m. But in addition to the main estates KIE has a programme for the establishment in smaller locations of nine Rural Industrial Development Centres. Of the Shs. 43.2 m. expended by KIE on buildings and works up to the middle of 1977, Shs. 10.7 m. were on RIDCs, so it can be seen that they are more than a nominal part of KIE's activities. Most of the Centres planned are in Western, Eastern, and Coast Provinces, so they will contribute to the wider geographical distribution of industrial activity. These Centres provide for very small-scale producers and assistance with simple buildings and services is to be provided from the European Economic Communities' aid programme.

At the end of 1976–7, when KIE completed its first ten years, it ceased to be a wholly owned subsidiary of ICDC and began to operate directly under the Ministry of Commerce and Industry. The programme continues to expand and a substantial injection of funds from the World Bank is expected.

The *Industrial Development Bank* (IDB) was set up by ICDC in 1973 with 49 per cent ownership by the Ministry of Finance and Planning and 51 per cent by ICDC. Loans have been obtained from the World Bank and other agencies, and a major reason for the establishment of the IDB was to provide a vehicle for the investment of World Bank funds. IDB's concern is with medium and large enterprises, in much the same way as the next organization to be described, the DFCK.

The *Development Finance Company of Kenya* (DFCK) was incorporated in 1963 with capital subscribed equally by Kenya, through the ICDC, the United Kingdom, through the Commonwealth Development Corporation, Germany, and Holland. The paid-up capital is K£2 m. and the shareholders have provided an additional K£5 m. in loans. Loans have also been received from other agencies, including the European Investment Bank. The DFCK participates with private investors in large enterprises, mainly industrial, including agricultural processing, but also in hotel development. It is interested only in investments which are expected to be profitable and in investments of not less than K£20,000. It is the intention to regenerate the DFCK's cash in the future by sales to the public from its investment portfolio. However, a substantial part of its participation is in fact in the form of loans, not equity: at the end of 1977 its investments totalled K£7.1 m., of which 31 per cent was in equity. The DFCK at that time had invested in 56 enterprises; 22 per cent of its investment was in textiles, 12 per cent in metal products, and roughly 10 per cent each in tourism, engineering and agricultural processing, food and beverages. The rest was in chemicals, wood, vehicles, paper, and leather products. It has been said of the DFCK that 'for every KSh 20 million invested, it has induced over KSh 140 million of private investment, most of it foreign',[82] but this statement involves a big and unverified assumption that without the DFCK contribution none of the investments would have been made.

It has been suggested that the size of the minimum investment rules out African business men, and that the Company is really a validating agency, helping entrepreneurs to court official favour.[83] Certainly, the

DFCK seemed designed to look abroad for its entrepreneurs, and most of its investment is in foreign firms and local European-owned firms, but it does have investments in African-owned companies. The Tiger Shoe Company is one that has been mentioned already; another is the Chui Soap Factory Ltd., to which DFCK has lent Shs. 2.8 m. DFCK is also embarking on a new kind of enterprise in the form of a small industries scheme intended to assist African business men in rural areas, and is receiving Shs. 3.5 m. from the Netherlands Government for this purpose.[84]

The *Kenya National Trading Corporation* (KNTC) was established in 1966 as a mechanism for transferring trade from non-citizens to Africans. The Corporation was given a statutory monopoly of the first stage in the distribution of specified products; the later stages were to be carried out by distributors appointed as agents by the KNTC. When the KNTC began operating it handled only sugar, but by 1974 over fifty products, including cement, salt, vegetable oil, and certain textiles, were confined to the KNTC. Two products were of major importance: sugar which accounted for 66 per cent of total turnover in1972/3 and domestic sales of cement, which accounted for 21 per cent.

The KNTC worked in the context of the Trade Licensing Act, 1968, which prohibited non-citizens from trading in specified commodities, except in designated 'general business areas' in the main towns. Trade licences were withdrawn from non-citizens even in areas where they were otherwise free to trade, where this could be done without disrupting the distribution of the product. The basis for monopoly gains by those appointed as agents was immense, but the pressure to appoint agents was such that they became numerous enough to eliminate large profits for many, and inefficiency and inexperience took their toll. By 1969 the KNTC had bad debts to the tune of K£800,000 and there was a high failure rate among distributors. It was reported that 10 per cent of KNTC-appointed distributors had disappeared by the end of 1970 and between 10 and 20 per cent had gone bankrupt.[85]

Heavy losses during its early years caused the Corporation to abandon credit trading and to require cash payment. The loss of credit was an extremely serious matter for the distributors, who needed cash to pay KNTC while extending credit to retailers. The ILO mission's terse judgement was that 'Government participation in wholesale trade through the Kenya National Trading Corporation should in principle facilitate regular supplies of commodities to retailers. However, this does not seem to happen at present.'[86]

Nor did the operations of the KNTC seem to be creating either an energetic African trading class or an active state trading corporation. It has been alleged that some distributors were in fact only 'front men' for non-citizens, and not themselves performing a necessary service.[87] The proliferation of distributors and the insertion of sub-agents in the chain of distribution may have been largely parasitic growths. And the KNTC itself became more and more a commission agent, simply approving applications from its agents to import goods, and taking a commission, instead of directly trading by buying and selling on its own account. The 1974-8 Development Plan noted this tendency. It announced the Government's intention that the KNTC should relinquish control of small items which African traders were now capable of handling themselves, and should be 'reorganised and strengthened, so that it may acquire a capacity to operate as an authentic state-trading corporation.'[88]

It is in agriculture that statutory authorities really proliferate, there being nineteen in all. They can be classified into four groups: (a) finance boards; (b) development boards; (c) commercial boards; (d) regulatory boards.[89] The work of the *Maize and Produce Board* (MPB), successor to the Maize Marketing Board set up in 1959, has been discussed at some length in Chapter 4. It is classed as a commercial board, and potentially it probably affects the lives of more Kenyans more directly than any other of the statutory authorities. The Board has powers under the Maize Marketing Ordinance to 'regulate, control and improve maize supply and marketing'. Although the Board has the legal monopoly of buying and selling maize, and movements of maize over quite short distances require a permit if they are to be legal, there is widespread unofficial marketing, in addition of course to farmers' own consumption, and it has been suggested that in 1966 only about 10 per cent of the maize crop was handled by the Board.[90]

The *Agricultural Finance Corporation* (AFC), established in 1963 and reconstituted in 1969, when it took over the Land and Agricultural Bank, has been concerned primarily with providing credit for large farms. In 1972 its loans to 2,500 large-scale farmers and ranchers amounted to K£12 m., and to 14,500 small-scale farmers to only £2.5 m. Its coverage of the large farms was virtually universal, whereas it provided credit for little more than one per cent of smallholders. The Corporation administers the Guaranteed Minimum Return programme for wheat and maize, which is also relevant to larger farmers, because a minimum of 6 hectares under either of the crops is required for participation.[91] The Corporation had provided loans for the purchase of large farms by syndicates and co-operatives, a programme which continued until 1977,[92] and it had a major concern with the rehabilitation of large farms which had been purchased by Africans with little capital and no experience of large-scale farming.[93] Large loans to large farmers, it was argued were easier to administer and easier to charge with the full administrative costs of lending. It must not be deduced from this argument, however, that there were no problems of recovery of loan charges from large farmers. The need for rehabilitation suggests the opposite, though it was said that loan repayments were satisfactory – the proportion of repayments made to those due increased from 62 per cent in 1968 to 78 per cent in 1972 – 'considering the many problems which they faced'.[94]

The branch and sub-branch offices of the AFC provide a reasonable coverage of the main agricultural and range areas, but its administration is highly centralized, despite recent moves towards decentralization, with decisions being taken at head office. Its administration is cumbersome for small loans, causing long delays, and it has little contact with small farmers. It is therefore deprived of a source of knowledge in deciding on loan applications, and of local sanctions on payments and supervision possibilities, which may make the difference between success and failure in a small-farmer credit scheme. There is a very limited range of purposes for which loans have been made to small farmers, and 70 per cent are for the purchase of high grade dairy cattle and related investments.[95]

The *Kenya Tea Development Authority* (KTDA) is the body responsible for the impressive expansion of small-holder tea production. The small-holder share of tea acreage increased from 6 per cent in 1960 to 44 per cent in 1970. KTDA is a statutory body with full regulatory and financial powers, and has obtained finance from IDA, CDC, and other international sources of investment finance. The Authority has organized the production, processing and marketing of small-holder tea in conformity with a phased plan of factory development. The collection of picked tea is arranged so that it arrives at the factory speedily, and the Authority has constructed the roads necessary to make this possible. It is intended that eventually the ownership of the factories will be transferred to the small-holders concerned, and the growers are represented on committees concerned with the industry. Nevertheless, it is said that there are complaints about the pricing system of the Authority and its paternalism, and it does indeed present an overwhelming presence in the areas in which it operates.[96]

The *Kenya Meat Commission* (KMC) was set up in 1950 and empowered to operate abattoirs and to process meat and meat products. It undertakes slaughtering, chilling and freezing of meat, and canning. It has a legal monopoly of exports and in the urban markets within Kenya. It does not control slaughtering in the rural areas. In addition to operating its own abattoirs the KMC licences others to slaughter specified numbers of cattle for the urban market. The canning plant for low-grade meat is operated with technical assistance from a multinational specialist firm, and most of the output is exported. In 1975 only 20 per cent of production of all kinds was for the local market, whereas 60 per cent was exported as canned meat and 20 per cent chilled or frozen. In 1970 the local market took 15.6 thousand tons, equal to 56 per cent of total output, but by 1975 local sales were down to 3.2 thousand tons.[97]

Although the KMC has a nominal monopoly of the urban trade there is substantial illegal competition, and it was estimated that in 1967 the KMC's share of the Nairobi market was no more than 60 per cent. The decline in KMC output has been partly because of competition for supplies of cattle. KMC has faced increasing competition from a growing number of private rural abattoirs, and its purchases have been hindered by a producer-price structure which was both too low and did not sufficiently discriminate between quality of cattle. Prices were raised, and a futher increase announced in January 1978 was expected to improve the situation. The difficulties of the KMC have, however, also been attributed to inefficiency. Although the IBRD mission in 1963 declared the KMC to be 'operating very efficiently',[98] that has not been the judgement of some more recent observers.[99]

The *Kenya Dairy Board* (KDB) was set up in 1958 to exercise control over the dairy industry. In practice the Board has been able to exert very little control over the industry, which is dominated by the near-monopolistic Kenya Cooperative Creameries, a private producer-controlled organization engaged in distribution and processing.[100]

(d) PLANNING

The influence of planning has been implicit in much of the discussion in earlier chapters. Here it is proposed to describe in a general way the Kenyan approach to development planning and to review the series of published plans.

Planning was begun in colonial times with the ten-year development plan, for the period 1946–55, which was required to obtain finance under the Colonial Development and Welfare Act. After this plan the Kenya Government adopted a series of three-year development programmes, which continued until the eve of Independence in 1963. The 'colonial plans' which were a feature of the colonial territories generally in the early post-war period, were criticized at the time as mere 'shopping lists' of government projects, as contrasted with 'real' planning. There is a great deal in this characterization of the post-war colonial plans, Kenya's included, but it is less clear that such a list of projects is not necessarily the core of any development plan, colonial or not, outside a 'centrally planned economy' in which the authorities possess powers (or believe they possess powers) to enforce their decisions on all facets of economic life.

The Government of Independent Kenya had no illusions that it possessed such powers, and its analysis of the aims and possibilities of planning were realistic. The planning exercises undertaken in Kenya since 1963 have been enormously more sophisticated than the preceding plans and programmes, and their sophistication of analysis has increased over time, but their core consists of government expenditure projects and of policies for influencing the course of economic development where it is determined by decisions which the authorities cannot directly control.

The successive development plans are impressive documents, distinguished by a thorough and competent analysis of the economy, involving forecasts, the setting of targets, and the estimation of the effects of government policies and expenditures on the various economic sectors. As the revised First Development Plan put the matter:[101]

> A comprehensive development plan is a blueprint for the social and economic development of the nation as a whole. It describes the impact of the planned development efforts on all aspects of the social and economic life of the nation . . . the Plan is comprehensive in the sense that it both projects the summary impact of social and economic changes to 1970 in a target rate of economic growth for the economy as a whole, and shows what these changes require in terms of scarce resources such as capital, skilled manpower and foreign exchange, as well as how the planned growth itself will supply a significant part of these resources.

The 'planned development efforts' consist to an important extent of 'targets' for achievement during the period of the Plan. The question of whether a target is a plan or a forecast is a nice one, and depends ultimately on the degree of control the authorities can exercise over the achievement of the particular target. The plan document recognizes that 'realization of Plan targets depends on factors which are subject to varying degrees of Government control and predictability.' There are some factors entirely outside the control of Kenyans, and in which changes are difficult to predict, including 'climatic conditions, the incidence of plant disease . . . and the development of market conditions and prices abroad' – an unfortunately percipient statement, as the third development plan had been largely drawn up just as the 1973 increase in the price of oil became effective. The behaviour of the domestic private sector, the Plan document argues, though not really subject to control, can be predicted within reasonable limits. Finally, the programmes which the government intend to carry out itself, are under its direct control. So private sector targets, in fact, are forecasts, and it is only the government projects that can properly be called planned expenditure targets.

The policy of planning was given an executive instrument by the establishment in 1964 of the Ministry of Economic Planning and Development. Planning units were also set up in other ministries. Later the MEPD was merged into the Ministry of Finance to form the Ministry of Finance and Planning which is now responsible for development and the formulation of the development plans.

The philosophy behind the development plans and policies of Kenya was set out in Sessional Paper No. 10 of 1965, *African Socialism and its Application to Planning in Kenya.* It has been suggested that African Socialism is a 'verbal pretence',[102] and that Kenya is committed to a capitalist mode of production. Certainly, it is abundantly clear that 'African Socialism in Kenya does not imply a commitment to indiscriminate nationalization',[103] and in 1964 the President declared that 'nationalization will not serve to advance the cause of African Socialism.' Indeed, economic policies have been little encumbered with much in the way of overt ideology, and have been essentially pragmatic. To foster the entrepreneurial society and to increase the role of Africans within it is, perhaps, the most summary form in which the general aims of policy can be expressed. It was all well stated in the *Development Plan, 1974-1978*:[104]

> It is frankly recognised by the Government that the economic philosophy most suitable for the country is an eclectic one. The forms of prevailing productive organization must include an increasing role for the Government, expansion of the cooperative form of organization, encouragement and active promotion of self-help schemes and respect for private ownership, coupled with a growing domestic share in that ownership. Essentially, this is a prescription for a 'mixed' economy. Private enterprise has received active encouragement; at the same time the Government has involved itself in all sectors of the economy to promote development as well as Kenyanization.

It must not be thought, however, that the implementation of policies and plans within the framework of this broad approach is simply a matter of bureaucratic management. It is true that government is to an important extent by the civil service, but there has been another ingredient of the 'style' of government in Kenya. The initiative of the civil service, particularly in economic policies, has been far-reaching, but it reached only so far and could not be exercised without thought for the possibility of Presidential intervention. Major policy changes have been made from time to time by Presidential announcement, without apparently much foreknowledge by civil servants, or even ministers. The desirability of careful preparation and planning of major innovations was not allowed to stand in the way of 'the felt necessities of the times' – the President's feel for the political realities. In this manner the price paid to farmers for milk was increased, creating financial problems for

Kenya Cooperative Creameries, which had to buy at the higher price, and making it necessary to raise other produce prices to prevent an excessive switch to grazing; so the prices paid to maize, wheat, and pyrethrum farmers were raised, although a policy of reducing producer-prices was contained in the Development Plan. Similarly, free primary education was introduced, and in a different field of policy *Kiswahili* was declared to be the national language.

The first post-Independence plan for Kenya, *Development Plan 1964–1970*, appeared in June, 1964. A revised version, prepared in less haste and with more resources, *Development Plan, 1966–1970*, was published two years later. Preparation of the 1964 Plan was inhibited by the lack of clearly specified objectives for which the planners could plan – the lack of a specific 'welfare function'. It was drawn up before many important objectives and related policies had been decided. It has been said that 'the ambiguity of the welfare function at that time coupled with the shortage of time and planning staff meant that a detailed plan could not legitimately be written.'[105] The 1966 version was much longer and more detailed, correcting defects of the 1964 document. Sessional Paper No. 10 had been published by then, providing a guide for the planners. Successive plan documents have been increasingly specific, and the initial priorities have been adapted to reflect more fully worked out and developing objectives.

The Plan for 1966–70 put forward a target annual growth rate of 6 per cent at constant prices, based on detailed analysis and predictions for the various sectors of the economy.[106] It forecast a total investment during the Plan period of K£360 m., and a rise in monetary GDP of K£109 m. by 1970. Public-sector-development expenditure was to total K£144 m., of which the Central Government would spend K£92 m. The inflow of foreign capital was expected to finance two-thirds of Central Government investment, 40 per cent of private investment, and one-half of investment in total, and to provide a substantial margin over the forecast balance of payments deficit. Although the target rate of growth was lower in the original than in the revised version of the Plan, even the latter has been described as 'cautious', realistic rather than ambitious, and too modest to inspire a greatly increased national effort.[107]

The main emphasis of the Plan was on agriculture. The agricultural plans were seen as well prepared and realistic, but inegalitarian, focusing on the high-potential areas and the progressive farmers within them. A large part of total expenditure – K£14 m. out of the total K£38 m. to be spent on agriculture – would be for land transfer and settlement. The famine-prone, marginal agricultural areas received no specific attention.[108]

The argument for agricultural priority is interesting. The approach to development favoured by the Government was 'to start with people in the circumstances in which they now live and with the traditions and knowledge to which they are already accustomed and to build on this knowledge an increasingly more modern economy', and hence the principal emphasis was placed 'on the development and modernization of agriculture on which most of the people depend for their livelihood'.[109]

The document rehearses the arguments for industrialization based on the idea of the low opportunity cost of surplus labour in agriculture, and finds them unconvincing. Industry was to have its place, but its development would be a consequence of expansion in agriculture and other sectors. One commentator felt that with its relatively well-developed industrial, commercial, and financial sectors 'the base for a "great leap forward" in industrial development already exists in Kenya' and that 'the case for development in Kenya through industrialization has not received the priority it deserves'.[110]

The emphasis on the activities 'on which most of the people depend for their livelihood' meant that the Plan would bring no structural transformation of the economy. In terms of the relative importance of the different economic sectors this was true. However, in another sense the Plan involved a radical transformation, because if from one point of view its main emphasis was on agriculture, from another it was on Africanization. A large part of the Plan is concerned with increasing the role of Africans in agriculture and in commerce and industry. In fact, the Plan can be seen as primarily concerned with establishing the infrastructure for development, not simply physical infrastructure of roads and buildings, but primarily the organizational infrastructure for African participation in development. The Plan document contains a long list of measures, from the extension of formal education and training to the provision of housing finance and the establishment of the National Trading Corporation, 'designed to ensure that the people of Kenya will have every opportunity to participate in the development of the nation'.[111] It must be said, however, that some of the measures might reasonably be thought to be more conducive to these aims than others, and for example, as will be realized from what was said in an earlier section of this chapter, that the DFCK would assist the participation of 'the people of Kenya' only in a rather restricted sense, at any rate until the inauguration of its small-industries scheme.

The *Development Plan 1970–1974* claimed to be more ambitious than anything attempted before, and to be practicable because of the success of the previous Plan. Its aim was for the economy to be 60 per cent larger in 1974 than it had been in 1967. To achieve the overall aims of the Plan an annual growth rate of 6.7 per cent was needed, which it was thought could be achieved on the basis of the high growth rates already experienced in the recent past. Central Government expenditure was to be K£720 m. during the Plan period, an increase of nearly 70 per cent over the K£430 m. spent in the preceding five years. Internal finance would provide 87 per cent of the total.

The immediate aim of development policy, the document stated, was more prosperity and better living conditions in the agricultural and range areas. There were two reasons, which can also be found in the previous Plan, put forward for the emphasis on rural development. The reason which seems to be given most weight is the basic nature of agriculture in the economy, and the dependence of all other sectors on it. Without a prosperous agriculture there would be a low demand for the products of industry, for the services of transport, and for all other outputs. Agriculture had set the pace for the growth of the whole economy, and national economic growth and prosperity depended on a prosperous and growing agriculture, and particularly on marketed agricultural production. The second reason given for the continuing emphasis on rural development is the fact that it will ensure the wide distribution of the benefits of growth. Within the total programme for agriculture, less was now to be spent on land transfer and land settlement – 22 per cent of total agricultural expenditure. Land adjudication and registration would take a further 16 per cent, and there is an acceptance of the need for more agricultural credit, from both of which kinds of expenditure it has been argued by some observers there is no clear evidence of benefit.

One assessment of the Plan concluded that although it appeared to be a recipe for success along the lines which had worked in the past, and although the majority of the people would share in the benefits of growth, there would be a growing number who would be left out of it. This would be the problem of the future. There was also too little attention paid to the question of population, because the success of the whole development policy could be frustrated if there were not a substantial reduction in the rate of population growth.[112]

The *Development Plan, 1974–1978* gave much greater prominence than earlier Plans to the wide distribution of the benefits of economic growth. The ILO report had been published and the Kenya Government had issued its Sessional Paper stating its policy towards the ILO recommendations.[113] Employment and equality were topics very much in the air. In his Introduction to the Plan the change of emphasis was clearly set out by the President:

> This new Development Plan . . . continues to lay emphasis on overall growth of the economy . . . But the forward thrust of the economy can no longer be regarded as the only objective of our nation. Rather, it is a

means of attaining other goals . . . These include full participation of our people in the economy, greater employment opportunities, and a more equitable distribution of resources and income.

The Plan adopted the strategy of 'redistribution through growth' which had been the theme of the ILO Report, and stated that improved income distribution and greater employment were the primary objectives, for the achievement of which faster economic growth was the means.[114]

There is a great deal in the Plan for 1974-8 to please the critics of the earlier Plans. The doubts expressed relate not to the Plan, but to its means. It has been argued that the means were inadequate to achieve the ends, and that the Plan gave insufficient attention to the possibility that some measures were mutually incompatible.[115]

Taxation was seen as a major instrument for improving equity. The Plan stated that the better-off would contribute proportionately more through taxation, but it contained no measures for increasing the progressivity of the tax system in addition to those, such as the abolition of graduated personal tax and the application of sales tax to goods consumed by the affluent, which were introduced in 1973. And there was no consideration of the possible inconsistency between a redistribution of income and the rate of saving and investment upon which the growth targets of the Plan depended.

Within the programme for agriculture – which continued, as in the earlier Plans, to receive priority – there was acknowledgment of the concentration in the past on assistance to the progressive farmers and to the areas of high potential, and a statement of the intention to avoid this bias in the future. But a rather optimistic view was taken of the possibility of directing agricultural extension to those who need it most without 'significantly increased funds or numbers of staff',[116] and no consideration was given to the possibility that those who need most help are the most difficult to help, so that the beneficial effects of the extension services on production might for a time diminish.

The measures to be taken to assist the medium- and low-potential areas were not very clearly specified and remained expressed in rather general terms. As for any broader concern for regional inequalities, which have been reinforced by the pattern of government expenditure in the past, if such a concern existed in government it was not reflected in the policies and programmes set out in the Plan.

The Plan appeared to herald the end of the 'large farm myth', if that is not too optimistic a reading. The view established as orthodoxy long ago, in colonial times, for obvious reasons, that while smallholders scratched the soil for a living, it was in the large farms that serious, productive farming was carried on, at last seemed to have been abandoned in the face of the evidence:[117]

The evidence available suggests that most farm products can be produced very successfully on small-scale farms. In the long run, therefore, a considerable amount of land currently used for large-scale farms will be sub-divided. Large-scale farms will be retained intact only to the extent necessary to ensure sufficient supplies of those products which can be best produced on a large-scale basis. These products include wheat, hybrid maize seed and breeding herds of livestock.

This prediction of the future division of most large farms appeared consistent with the opinion, stated elsewhere in the Plan, that '350,000 new agricultural smallholdings must be created'[118] in order to achieve the employment goals of the Plan. However, it has been calculated that the settlement of this number of small-holders would require between 1.2 m. and 4.3 m. hectares of land, depending on the size of small-holding established, whereas the total area in large farms was only 2.7 m. hectares, and many nominally large farms were in any case already run by co-operatives or 'companies' with many members. It did not seem, therefore, that the subdivision of large farms could provide the land needed for settlement. The Plan itself, in this connection, referred to the intention to 'redefine the size of all cooperative and low-density settlement schemes'.[119] It was likely that the necessary land could not be found without extending cultivation further into the marginal lands and by increasing the density of settlement in the small-holder areas. Both required an attention to the development of appropriate cultivation practices which was given insufficient weight in the Plan.

The Plan, accepting the arguments that have been described in earlier Chapters,[120] recognized the desirability of getting prices, if not 'right' then at least 'better'. Tariffs were to be made more uniform. The use of labour-intensive technology was to be encouraged by holding down wages and increasing the cost of capital through sales tax on capital goods and higher duties on imported capital goods. The Plan was clear that a policy of holding down wages could not be allowed to enrich capitalists at the expense of workers. Nevertheless, a lowering of the price of labour relative to that of capital could well both increase employment and reduce the share of wages, possibly increasing income inequality.

Finally, it is necessary to return to the matter already raised in connection with the 1970–4 Plan: the growth of population. The Plan accepted all the arguments for the enormous importance of achieving a lower rate of growth, but proposed little more than a continuation of existing family-planning programmes which had been ineffective: the growth rate had continued to increase.

These comments may seem unduly carping when directed at what is a technically impressive document. That so many critical comments are possible underlines the fact that planning on the scale and of the comprehensiveness attempted in Kenya is a very complex exercise. Leaving aside any political constraints on developing the full implications of policies and on implementation, simply to take account of all the interrelationships and ramifications in the economy as a whole is extremely difficult. It is hardly surprising that the planners were not wholly successful.

Earlier chapters have shown that some of the problems raised in this examination of the 1974-8 Plan were not resolved during the period of the Plan. However, it was not these problems which had the most immediate and devastating effect, it was the rise in oil prices, because 'the bulk of the present plan was prepared before the magnitude of this emergency was known.'[121]

In concluding this examination of Kenya's development plans it must be said that planning, for all the weaknesses and errors that may be detected, is a serious exercise in Kenya. The Plans are not simply window dressing for local consumption. Nor are they, what is not unknown, purely externally oriented documents, drawn up solely to satisfy the requirements of aid donors by technical assistance staff supplied by the aid donors.

CHAPTER 9

INEQUALITY, POVERTY, AND PROGRESS

It has for long been a cliché of development economics that growth is not enough. In writings on Kenya attention has been focussed particularly on inequality and widespread poverty as detracting from the virtues of a high rate of economic growth.

Inequality

Kenya as a home of inequality has become a commonplace of the literature. With vast priviledge for the few and deepest poverty for the many, the reader is given the impression of the creation during the Kenyatta Era of a contemporary *ancien régime*, with so to speak a Versailles on the Equator at the President's home, Gatundu. But the evidence can be differently read. There are several dimensions of inequality with which it is necessary to deal.

Regional Inequality

The greatest regional inequalities are the work of nature. One need look no further than the 307 mm rainfall in North Eastern Province and the 1084 mm in Central Province to find a major cause of the inequalities between the two.[1] Nevertheless, the work of man can diminish or enhance the inequalities of nature, and a process of cumulative causation can operate. The purpose of this discussion, however, is rather to describe the inequalities than to explain them.

Statistics are, of course, the work of man, as is the delineation of boundaries. The Provincial boundaries do not conform to 'natural' zones, but they do have an economic, social, and political rationale – the tribal association was analysed in Chapter 1 – which makes it useful to render comparisons in terms of them.[2] Although the term 'inequality' carries pejorative overtones, except perhaps to mathematicians, it is a pity that it should be so, because the existence of Provincial inequalities in Kenya does not necessarily imply that they all should – let alone could – be diminished. Some inequalities are simply differences.

Table 9.1 shows the Provincial distribution of various characteristics of economic and social relevance in relation to the distribution of population. If a Province had the same share in one of the items shown in Rows 2-12 as it had of the population, it would have a zero value for that item. If it is 'over-endowed', having a larger share than its share of population, the entry has a positive sign; if it is 'under-endowed' the entry has a negative sign.

TABLE 9.1

Provincial Characteristics: Percentage Distribution of Population and Difference (+/–) between Percentage Distribution of Characteristic and Percentage Distribution of Population

(Kenya = 0)

	Province							
	Central	Coast	Eastern	Nairobi	North Eastern	Nyanza	Rift Valley	Western
1. Population	15.3	8.6	17.4	4.4	2.2	19.4	20.4	12.3
2. Land area: total	–13.0	+6.0	+10.0	–4.3	+20.1	–17.2	+9.3	–10.9
3. Land of high potential	–1.9	–3.1	–10.0	–4.2	–2.2	–1.4	+24.2	–1.4
4. Land of low potential	–13.4	+4.5	+9.8	–4.3	+22.2	–17.0	+9.1	–10.9
5. Large farms by area	–2.7	–5.3	–5.8	–3.4	–2.2	–18.4	+49.8	–12.1
6. Coffee small-holders by no.	+21.8	–8.4	+21.2	–4.4	–2.2	+0.6	–19.3	–9.3
7. Tea small-holders by no.	+18.5	–8.6	+19.0	–4.4	–2.2	–3.4	–12.7	–6.1
8. Wage employment	+0.3	+3.8	–9.6	+22.5	–1.6	–12.0	+4.9	–8.1
9. School enrolment, primary	+4.4	–3.1	+1.4	–1.5	–1.9	–0.4	–2.1	+3.1
10. School enrolment, secondary	+8.5	–2.7	–1.3	+5.6	–2.0	–3.0	–8.1	+3.0

A comparison of the first two lines of Table 9.1 indicates the variations between Provinces in population density. Nyanza Province has 19.4 per cent of the population of Kenya but only 2.2 per cent of the country's land area.[3] In contrast, North Eastern Province has only 2.2 per cent of the population but 22.3 per cent of the land of Kenya. Differences in population density are partly the result of tribal exclusiveness which restricts movement into an area by members of other tribes. It must not be presumed, however, that a Province with a large area in relation to its population is necessarily well endowed with economic resources relative to the number of its inhabitants. Row 3 of the Table shows that North Eastern Province, although it contains 2.2 per cent of the population has no land of high potential whatever, and nearly a quarter of all Kenya's low potential land. Central and Nyanza Provinces, however, make up for their relative deficiency in land by having an unusually large proportion of land of high potential; in fact, they each have a percentage of Kenya's total supply of high potential land not far short of their share of the population, as also does Western Province.

Line 5 of the Table reveals another characteristic of the Provincial distribution of economic resources: the distribution of large farms. Just over 70 per cent of the large farm area is in a single province, the Rift Valley. There are no large farms in North Eastern Province, and only a small area in Nyanza and Western Province. The indicators of the distribution of small-farm coffee and tea in Rows 6 and 7 reveal the importance of Central and Eastern Provinces for the small-holder production of these crops. It is hardly surprising that Nairobi is greatly 'over-endowed' with wage employment, but the deficiency of employment in relation to population in Eastern, Nyanza, and Western Provinces is to be noted. Central Province has virtually its 'fair' share of employment, shown by an entry in the Table close to zero.

The two indicators of educational status need to be read with care. There is no reason to think, despite its negative entry, that Nairobi is relatively under-endowed with primary education. The fact is that Nairobi has a low proportion of its population of primary-school age. The 1969 Census showed that in Kenya as a whole 48.4 per cent of the population was under age fifteen, whereas in Nairobi the percentage was only 34.6.[4] The secondary-school enrolment, certainly for Nairobi and probably also for elsewhere, is affected by the fact that pupils do not always pursue their secondary education in their own Province.

Table 9.2 takes a different approach to the measurement of Provincial differences in the availability of services. Though not the sole determinant, of course, population density has an important affect on accessibility. Access to all services is greatly below the national average in the Eastern Province, which is of large area in relation to its population, and above average in the relatively densely populated Western Province. The population density in the North Eastern Province is so low as to make such a comparison of accessibility meaningless.

TABLE 9.2

Accessibility to Services in Rural Areas

(percentage above +/below −national average)

Service	Central	Coast	Eastern	Province Nyanza	Rift Valley	Western
(a)						
Drinking water (dry season)	+15.1	−39.9	−15.7	−3.7	−3.2	+20.0
Primary school	−0.6	−23.1	−7.4	+4.1	−25.6	+20.2
Health centre	−3.2	+6.3	−19.5	−47.8	+107.8	+62.9
Market	+33.5	+0.1	−50.4	+2.1	+27.0	+13.9
Post Office	+6.8	+51.4	−82.2	−27.3	+129.6	+87.5
Bus route	+0.3	+43.1	−53.2	+46.6	−44.1	+6.6
(b)						
Drinking water (dry season)	+1.5	−12.2	−7.9	+3.5	+3.1	+3.3
Primary school	0	−3.5	−2.7	+2.6	−4.4	+2.3
Health centre	+24.1	−11.3	−38.2	+17.7	−15.2	+3.3
Market	+8.1	−41.2	−24.3	+21.6	+0.1	+1.8
Post Office	+41.8	+39.3	−49.1	−2.9	−7.2	+10.2
Bus route	+11.6	+17.9	−28.0	+16.7	−34.9	+5.9

Note: The measure of accessibility is the percentage of households within 1 mile of the service for part (a) and within 4 miles for part (b) of the Table.
Source: *Integrated Rural Survey 1974–75*, Table 6.14.

The relative position of the Provinces when the measure of accessibility is 4 miles compared with when it is 1 mile is to be noted. Western Province retains its above-average, and Eastern Province its below-average, accessibility to all services. The relative position is worsened for Rift Valley and Coast Provinces, whereas the position of Central Province is marginally improved. Particularly notable is the improvement in the position of Nyanza Province which, in terms of a distance of 4 miles, has above average accessibility to all services except a Post Office.

The average accessibility around which the position of the Provinces vary deserves a reference. On average for Kenya as a whole, nearly three-quarters of the population covered by the Integrated Rural Survey has dry-season drinking water within a mile, and more than 90 per cent has it within 2 miles. It is available within 2 miles to virtually the whole of the small-holder population of Central and Western Provinces, with Nyanza and Rift Valley Provinces not far behind. In Coast Province, in contrast, no more than 66 per cent has access to dry-season drinking water within 2 miles. For Kenya as a whole, a primary school is within 2 miles of 83 per cent, and within 8 miles of virtually the whole population. Nearly 80 per cent of the population is within 8 miles of a health centre, 94 per cent within 8 miles of a market, and more than 70 per cent within that distance of a Post Office. A bus route is within 2 miles of 55 per cent of the population, but a *matatu* taxi route is within that distance for 70 per cent, suggesting the benefits that have resulted from the removal of the former constraints on this type of service.

TABLE 9.3

Income and Consumption of Small-holder Households by Province

(percentage of national average)

	Central	Coast	Eastern	Nyanza	Rift Valley	Western
Income:						
Farm operating surplus	102	40	92	134	148	57
Non-farm operating surplus	92	177	139	103	86	36
Other income	147	154	89	62	98	97
Total income	116	91	95	107	125	68
Consumption:						
Own produce	118	52	129	81	130	69
Purchased	137	115	109	70	81	89
Total	130	91	117	74	99	81

Source: *Integrated Rural Survey, 1974-75*, Tables 8.4 and 8.12.

Table 9.3 shows by Province the variation from the national average in various components of household income and consumption. There are problems with the figures for both. The income figures are affected by recordings of negative income, partly because of large negative changes in the value of livestock as a result of drought and partly 'caused by holders not revealing the full extent of their income'. Also 'the consumption of own produce is likely to be underestimated since there are considerable practical difficulties in recording produce which may have been consumed by household members.'[5] The very great difference in the position of Nyanza in household income and in consumption, implying a rate of saving very much above the national average is surprising.[6] Several elements of the Table are of particular interest, such as the differences in the availability of 'other income' from employment and gifts, and in own-produced and purchased consumption.

Poverty can be caused in some years by inadequate rainfall, and relieved in years when the rains are good, as in parts of Eastern Province. In other areas, as in much of Nyanza and Western Provinces, irregularity of rainfall is not a problem, and persistent poverty may result from a lack of involvement in the monetary agricultural economy and few opportunities for off-farm employment. Poverty is found together with underdeveloped agricultural potential, and could be alleviated by a fuller use of agricultural resources, as the Mumias sugar scheme has demonstrated.[7]

This discussion has been in terms of Provinces, and the differences between Provinces are indeed a matter of great importance. But also of importance, though less open to statistical demonstration, are the differences and inequalities within Provinces. The Provinces, particularly some of them, are vast regions over the area of which there are enormous variations in natural and man-made circumstances. It must not be thought that the Provinces are in any way economically homogeneous entities.

Inequality between Town and Country

There can be no question that there are great inequalities between town and country in Kenya – in what nation are there not? Statistical representations of the inequality, however, can be too simple-minded, and in their concern for the statistical trees miss certain important features of the wood. This is so with one analysis[8] which concludes from data on the 'total distribution' of income that the urban 12 per cent of the population receives 30 per cent of total income, that the 80 per cent engaged in agriculture receives only 47 per cent of total income,[9] and that average agricultural incomes are only 41 per cent of average urban incomes.

The income estimates used in that analysis are derived from small farmers' consumption (used as a proxy for income) of various purchased items and own-produced food. They include nothing for housing. On small farms the homes are largely home-made, even though some purchased materials are used, so that the services of housing are part of subsistence or own-produced income, and are additional to the income as defined above. They are no less important for that, and it is quite misleading to compare the income of a rural household as estimated with that of an urban household without making allowance for the expenditure required of the latter on rent, which has a weight of 22.9 per cent in the urban low-income price index. It is also misleading to take no account of the fact that rural food prices are generally lower than urban prices.[10] It may be a reasonable procedure when estimating rural household consumption, to value own-produced food at local, rural prices. But it is quite another matter when making rural–urban comparisons, when it is essential, if the result is to have any meaning, to value the quantities consumed in country and town at the same set of prices.

The comparison will be additionally misleading if no account is taken of expenditure in the town on services which are 'disutility off-setting' rather than benefit conferring, such as at least part of expenditure on transport. Expenditure on transport has a weight of 3.8 per cent in the urban low-income price index and allowance should be made in comparisons of rural and urban incomes for expenditure required of town workers on travel which is unnecessary for farmers who live on their small-holding.

When the calculations are adjusted to take account of these considerations it turns out that the urban population receives not 30 per cent, but 23 per cent, and agriculturalists not 47 but 60 per cent of total income. And agricultural incomes are not 41 but 69 per cent of average urban incomes, even though a high proportion of the highest-paid jobs in business and Government are naturally enough located in the towns, particularly Nairobi. It is not suggested that these are 'the right' figures, for other adjustments working in either direction may be necessary.[11] They are reproduced merely to show that the urban-rural comparison is complex and open to more than one answer. In addition to the statistical complications there are also conceptual difficulties in the way of such a comparison and of a 'complete picture of income distribution'.

Changes in the ratio of prices received by farmers for their produce to the prices paid by farmers for consumer goods and production inputs, may be taken as an indication of changes in the rural–urban terms of trade. This index moved against agriculture from 1972 to 1975, and then moved sharply the other way. The improvement was mainly because of the high prices for coffee and tea, but the exclusion of exports from the index would still leave the terms of trade in 1977 slightly more favourable to agriculture than in 1972. This improvement results from improved producer prices for cereals, sugar cane, and milk.[12] On the other side, the position of the urban community has certainly deteriorated. Although the Industrial Court has been affective in remedying specific abuses, wage rates have been held down and real wages have fallen, and in 1977 were at about the same level as in 1974-5.[13]

In the light of all this, the apparent differential between urban wages and rural incomes is not all that it seems. Nevertheless, the idea that urban wage earners are a privileged minority remains a piece of conventional wisdom which is examined in a wider context later in this chapter.

There are obviously great differences between the rural and urban areas in the provision of services of one kind or another. Some urban services are designed to counter undesirable characteristics of urban life, particularly the risk of disease. Transport is required to marshall the urban labour force in a way that is unnecessary in rural life. However, the extent to which rural people sometimes have to travel in the absence of public transport should not be forgotten, and the availability of piped water to urban dwellers, though it may be necessary to prevent disease, is a benefit of enormous worth. One of the major costs of rural life, a cost which falls almost exclusively on women and children, is the effort required to carry water for domestic use over long distances. There can be no doubt that this is a major rural–urban inequality affecting the standard of life. The inequality is being diminished, however, and although a statistical demonstration is impossible, it will become increasingly possible with the accumulation of data from rural surveys. In summary, the availability of services certainly provides an advantage to urban over rural dwellers, but the net benefit is nothing like so great as the gross, a large part of urban services being essential in the circumstances of urban life.

The system of industrial protection, about which a good deal has been said already, is relevant to urban rural inequality because it mainly protects activities in the towns. The subsidization of manufacturing through protection implies the taxation of other productive activities, notably agriculture. Industrial protection, therefore, has the effect of increasing urban incomes at the expense of rural, though foreign participation in industry results also in transfers abroad. It has been said that the effects of protection are 'to benefit the foreign capitalist most, then the local capitalist, then the wage earner in manufacturing, all at the expense of agricultural producers.'[14] No sophisticated analysis is needed to make it clear that protection imposes losses and redistributions of income. In a rational system they are accepted when it is judged that the benefits of the structural changes in the economy resulting from protection – the enlargement of manufacturing – outweigh the costs. That protection imposes burdens on the rural areas where the great mass of the poor are to be found is a reason for looking hard at the costs as well as the benefits of industrial protection, though the fact that there is a large element of own-produced consumption in rural areas and substantial money transfers from the towns diminishes the adverse impact of the protective system.[15] And it needs to be remembered that manufacturing, a substantial part of which is concerned with agricultural processing, creates a demand for the products of the rural areas.

An important feature of the relation between country and town is migration of people. Although all sorts and conditions of people migrate, the migrants from the countryside to the town tend to be young, male, and educated, or at least literate. Migration may be influenced by that 'idiocy of rural life' to which Marx and Engels scornfully referred, and this may be a reason for the readiness of the more educated to move to town. However, a survey in Nairobi indicated that 'bright lights' reasons were influential with only a small proportion of migrants. Moreover, Kenyans have a strong attachment to the land, and there is a substantial reverse flow of older migrants.[16]

It is generally accepted that the major motives for migration are economic, with economic forces both pushing and pulling. The landless do not predominate among the migrants, however, and often those who are landless have expectations of an inheritance.[17] The prospect of an urban job is a strong attraction for migrants. Formal models have been produced in which the rate of migration is a function of the probability of obtaining employment in the town and of the gap between urban and rural wages. In such a model, an increase in urban employment will itself increase urban unemployment. This is a gloomy prognostication, but perhaps not so gloomy as at first appears. It must be presumed that with a rise in urban employment those who obtain employment are better off, as are those who choose to come in from the countryside, often living with relatives or friends, to replace them in the ranks of the unemployed. The latter are better off, if only because they are buoyed up by the possibility of obtaining an urban job, and the greatest poverty is not always to be found among such unemployed migrants. Nevertheless, complacency about the frustrations and hardships facing unemployed urban immigrants would be very wrong. A survey of Nairobi immigrants showed that over 10 per cent was still unemployed three years after they arrived.

The effect of migration on urban-rural inequality is mixed. To see it simply as an equalising equilibrating movement is obviously inadequate. The rural areas suffer from the loss of the more educated, energetic, and able-bodied, but they gain from the remittances sent home by the migrants. In the towns migration puts strains on the available services and leads to severe housing problems.

In conclusion, a tentative comment may be made on the question of whether there is 'urban bias' in Kenya, though any answer implies an imported value judgement. It is difficult to detect such a bias during the 1977 tea and coffee boom when rural producers were not insulated from its benefits and the imposition of export taxes can be said to have been both too little and too late. The situation is quite different from that in countries where marketing boards siphon off a high proportion of export income before it reaches the producers. Taxation of farmers has been relatively light. Savings have been transferred from the rural areas for investment in the towns, but voluntarily. It seems likely that the decision to permit and to foster the development of the economic and social structure of Kenya in its present way, including its focus on tourism and on foreign investment, made inevitable the attention given to the main towns, particularly Nairobi. Relatively few resources have been devoted in the towns to structures of conspicuous consumption and the demonstration of power. There are few monuments. Despite the new offices for government departments, built in the last few years, the most elaborate buildings in Nairobi are for business, not government, which perhaps says something not entirely denigrating about the outlook of the Kenya people and their rulers.

It could, indeed, be argued that too few resources have been devoted to one kind of urban development: low-income housing. Kenya is not unique in the wide gap that sometimes appears between the professed concern for the well-being of the *wananchi*, the common people, and the treatment meeted out to them when their interests conflict with more powerful interests. The more powerful interests are not always solely pecuniary, and sometimes reflect the power of ideas. The idea of what is proper, healthy, neat, or orderly in a modern nation has been inherited from colonial days and perhaps reinforced by the feeling that Kenya must present a modern face to the world. It seems to be the local authorities which are particularly infected by the virus of a good appearance, though it may be simply that they have the most direct concern with and power over the phenomenon which particularly offends the eye conditioned by these ideas: that world-wide manifestation of development and under-development, the shanty town.

Official action against insanitary accommodation goes back to the earliest colonial days. In 1899, when a case of plague was found in the bazaar, the railway Divisional Engineer reported that, with the concurrence of the railway surgeon, 'I gave the natives and Indians who inhabited it an hour's notice to clear out and on my own responsibility promptly burned the whole place to the ground.'[18] There was a curious echo of this incident in April 1978, when during a cholera scare it was reported that the medical authorities had ordered the removal of a large number of people from a squatter settlement and the demolition of their houses. The outcry led to an explanation that it was all a misunderstanding. Although nothing was done on that occasion, there is a wealth of evidence of continuity of policy in the insistence on inappropriate technology and inappropriate standards. In 1945 the Native Affairs Committee agreed that tea hawkers should be allowed only if they had 'a properly equipped "coffee stall" similar to those used in London'.[19] In 1975 at Homa Bay traders' stalls were demolished, leaving 'more than 200 traders and their families . . . homeless and unemployed'.[20] 'Just the other day', in September 1977, 'the City *askaris* dragged out a pregnant woman in labour from one of the shanty houses in Nairobi, demolished her cardboard shanty house and she had to give birth in the open during a chilly night.'[21] 'It was the Day of Destruction. Dawn broke and with grinding efficiency a herd of municipal bulldozers moved in on the villages. Within hours 4,000 people were homeless as settlement after settlement was reduced to dust and rubble.'[22] These are no isolated incidents, and very many similar reports could be cited.

Mathare Valley, Nairobi, is a notable example of what has been called a Self-Help City.[23] When official attitudes have been not openly hostile they have been indifferent. The rubbish that collects in shanty towns is undoubtedly a health hazard, but the solution 'to clear the rubbish rather than the shanties, was not officially considered until Mathare Valley settlements had been in existence for eight years, when a form of refuse collection was instituted.'[24] A further health hazard arises from the use of impure water, but at Mathare Valley the residents had laid pipes 'to within a yard of the city's water supply, but the city for years had refused to allow the connection to be made.'[25] From official comments 'one may be forgiven from drawing the conclusion that the gravest crime that a squatter settlement could commit was to be visible.'[26]

The problem of the shanty town with its 'informal housing' and its close connection with marginal trading and other economic activities such as illegal brewing, is part of the general phenomenon of the informal sector. Following the ILO Report, official hostility to the informal sector was relaxed and its economic importance acknowledged.[27] The most immediately apparent manifestation of the change in attitude was in passenger transport, with the bestowal of official approval on the *matatu.*[28] In other spheres, and particularly in the behaviour of local authorities, the new attitude has not always been in evidence. It may be that new attitudes do not quickly filter down to the lowest levels of the official hierarchy, but the need for a new approach was recognised as long ago as 1969, when Nairobi City Council approved 'a programme of improvability' for the Mathare Valley.[29] Certainly it is true that 'vast numbers of people will not be able to afford rents for modern standard housing' and there is great need 'for them to be housed with increasing dignity, instead of against the background of a deteriorating environment, economic exploitation and public degradation.'[30] 'Site and service' housing schemes being carried out in Mathare Valley and in nearby Kawangware, in conjunction with the World Bank and the European Economic Community, seem designed to achieve that end and to bring progress to where it has long been needed. But until such progress is apparent it might be difficult to persuade the residents of the Self-Help City that policy has been biased in their favour.

It is in fact arguable that the very concept of urban bias is irrelevant to Kenya where everyone still has links with the country, and many countrymen are townsmen at some stage of their life. Except in Mombasa, which is an ancient city, urbanization is so recent and attachment to the 'home area' is so strong that few would claim Nairobi or any other town as 'the place I come from'. Farming families have non-farm incomes, often from the towns, and many who appear 'as "pure" farmers are more likely to be men at the end of their "occupational chains" who have retired or returned to farming, or even perhaps men who are still "waiting" to make yet another change into trade, or business, or employment.'[31] Altogether, it seems that reality in Kenya, with the various interrelationships between town and country, is too complex to be captured by a catch-phrase like urban bias.

The Inequality of Women

If life for the poor in Kenya is hard, it is particularly hard for poor women.[32] Although there are women prominent in the professions and in public and commercial life, and women are active in their local communities, Kenya remains a male-dominated society. Yet a large part of the work is done by women. Apart from the few who have escaped into a different life, women constitute 'a silent majority of the most overworked and underpaid of agricultural workers in Kenya'.[33] The division of labour in small-scale farming gives women a major economic role. In the life of rural women the national accountant's usual distinction between productive and non-productive activity is particularly irrelevant. In a way, of course, it is simply the familiar point about the domestic services of housewives writ large. But productive activities merge with family activities not usually counted as economic, and no joke about the effect on the national income of a man's marrying his housekeeper can convey the importance to the economy of rural Kenya of women's work in such tasks as cultivating food crops, cutting firewood, and carrying water.[34]

The burden on women is increased by the migration of men to paid employment, or to the search for paid employment, away from their home areas. Tasks performed by men in the traditional division of labour, such as land clearing, have then to be assumed by women, and added to their other activities. The 1969 Census figures indicate that there could have been as many as 400,000 rural households where the husband was away and the maintenance of the household and the farm was the responsibility of the woman.[35] In such households in particular, and in the rural areas in general, there is no unemployment problem for women, no problem of under-utilized labour, but rather a life of unremitting toil.[36]

In contrast, in wage employment and modern sector self-employment, women find few opportunites.

> . . . a higher proportion of rural women than men are involved in agricultural production while . . . females are very under-represented in wage

labour employment. Women's difficulties in finding jobs in urban centres have resulted in higher rates of female unemployment and possibly deterred many women from migrating to urban areas with their husbands. . . . The ability and willingness of women to provide sustained labour inputs into farming enable men to seek wage employment in rural areas or in urban centres to supplement the family income.[37]

Women accounted for only 15 per cent of the total in wage employment in 1975. The proportion of women among the modern sector self-employed was 22 per cent.[38]

Even outside the rural economy it would be unreasonable to expect to find Kenya meeting the highest standards of contemporary feminism, which so many, if not all other countries fall so far below. A preference in families for spending money on the education of boys rather than girls is hardly surprising, if regrettable. It is not by any means that girls are deprived of education entirely, but that their educational careers are short. In 1975, girls made up 47 per cent of the pupils enrolled in Grade I of primary school, but only 39 per cent of these enrolled in Grade VII. Girls accounted for only 37 per cent of the pupils in secondary schools in 1976, though the proportion has been rising and three years earlier it had been no more than 33 per cent. That women have in fact made great strides in education is something to admire. The abolition of fees for some grades of primary education may increase the enrolment of girls, but it is likely to be some time before women are 'level-pegging' with men in all forms and levels of education. There are regional differences in the participation of women in education, and it is particularly low in pastoral areas and where Islam is predominant.

The evidence suggests that girls also come second to boys in access to nutrition. In a survey designed to measure the incidence of 'protein energy malnutrition' among a sample of children aged between 1 and 4 years, 'male children generally appeared to enjoy a healthier nutritional status than their female counterparts'.[39] It was found in the survey that females had lower weight-for-age values than their brothers in the same age range, regardless of which was older, but that the gap was more pronounced when the girl was the younger of the pair.

One reason for the inequality of women is the double burden they carry of work and motherhood.

. . . most women spend much of their adult lives in a continuous cycle of pregnancy, child birth and child dependency. Repeated pregnancies and prolonged lactation often leave women in a physically weakened state. . . . The burden of the high dependency ratio (half the small farm population is below 15 years of age) is particularly heavy on the female adult population who have to provide constant care for the very young as well as to undertake much of the agricultural work to feed the family.[40]

The spread of family planning, in addition to the possible benefits for the national economy which are discussed below, might be seen as an important potential contributor to the welfare of women. But the Government's programme has had only modest success: the rate of 'acceptance' is low and of 'drop-out' high. The available information indicates that 'better educated females are more likely to have fewer children and to utilise family planning to time and space their pregnancies. They are also more able to raise healthy children who will survive to adulthood.'[41]

The Vagrancy Act, under which people are returned from the towns to their home areas, bears particularly on women. Although directed at prostitution[42] (which is not illegal) its use can limit the scope for female participation in all informal sector economic activities, as well as in formal sector job-seeking. Its justification, that vagrants in towns should seek their living in their home areas, is based on the myth of an access to land which in reality no longer exists.

An intriguing manifestation of an attitude to women was the decision of Parliament in 1969 to repeal the Affiliation Act. This decision deprived the mothers of illegitimate children of the possibility of securing maintenance from the fathers. In Parliament[43] it was argued that illegitimacy was an alien concept in African society, so that the law was an otiose colonial hangover, an argument which ignored the fact that traditional society with its *mores* no longer ruled. It was also argued that women abused the law, securing maintenance from several men for the same child, an argument which, one commentator has observed, is like saying that 'since robberies are too numerous, the law against robbery ought to be repealed.'[44]

In the words of *Women in Kenya*:[45] 'The foregoing analysis is of importance with respect to its implications for Kenya's rural development policy. A comprehensive rural development programme needs to incorporate prospects for improving the quality of rural women's lives. This implies reducing their workloads as well as increasing their productivity.' For all the progress in Kenya, it is still not fully recognized that 'the hard core of the development problem is constituted by women. Women are the most unequal among unequals.'[46]

Racial Inequality

Legally and constitutionally a distinction is drawn not between races but between citizens and non-citizens. Yet Africanization is a primary aim, even if it is sometimes called Kenyanization, and it may be thought that this is a well justified policy of 'reverse discrimination'. Economy and society in colonial Kenya were based on racial distinctions, and both by law and practice were fundamentally discriminatory: the reservation of the White Highlands, restrictions on the acquisition of agricultural land by Asians, separateness in education, and so on. Only in the last few years before Independence were the discriminations relaxed. The result was that in newly Independent Kenya, discrimination against Africans was no longer lawful, but the 'commanding heights' of the economy were in the hands of non-Africans. This was so not only in ownership of productive resources – in 1960 fewer than 4,000 White farmers owned four-fifths of the land which had a reasonable and reliable rainfall – but also in the wages of those in employment. In 1961, although formal discrimination in salary scales had been abolished, the average annual earnings of the 22,000 Europeans in employment were over £1,350, compared with just over £500 for the 38,000 Asians and about £75 for the 530,000 Africans. The Europeans, constituting less than 4 per cent of total employment, received a third of the total wage bill.[47]

These inequalities in wages would not be so very different fifteen years later. Although the data are now not available by race, the conclusion pretty well follows from the distribution of employment of different types between citizens and non-citizens. It is not to be expected that Europeans would come to Kenya in large numbers for employment as unskilled labourers, nor that non-citizens would be permitted to take up employment for which there were well qualified Kenyans (although there have been complaints that this principle is sometimes breached, and from time to time there are reports of foreigners discovered in unauthorized employment).

It could be deduced, therefore, that non-citizens would be found predominantly in employments requiring higher qualifications or experience and better-paid. In 1975, 58 per cent of non-citizen employment was in such occupations. If teachers are added, who are the largest non-citizens group and of great value to Kenya, the proportion becomes 71 per cent. Non-citizens as a proportion of total employees accounted for a mere 2½ per cent, but in the higher-paid managerial and professional occupations they constituted nearly 20 per cent, and almost all Europeans would be in such occupations, though there is some employment of wives of non-citizen Europeans in secretarial and clerical jobs. Citizens of European and Asian descent will also be found disproportionately to their numbers in the higher grades of employment. There are also wealthy European and Asian citizens in business, including farming. All this, in a way, is little changed from colonial days.

There have been, however, radical changes in two main respects. One is the discrimination in favour of Africans and particularly against Asians which has been discussed in connection with the Africanisation of commerce.[48] The Asian role in the economy has been greatly diminished, absolutely as well as relatively (casual observation in Nairobi misleads), by the removal of non-citizen business and the generally discouraging, sometimes even hostile, attitude to Asian enterprise.[49]

A large part of small-scale production, and a large part of the supply of skilled services were supplied by Asians, and 'by providing cheap and efficient services the Asians played a vital role in the economy at large.'[50] The Asian *fundi* was as characteristic of the colonial economy as the Asian trader. The ILO mission were alarmed at the effect on the supply of repair and maintenance services of the uncertainties facing the Asian community and the inadequate facilities for training Africans.[51]

The second radical change is that the ranks of the wealthy have been recruiting, as they did not before Independence, from the African population. In that respect racial inequalities have been reduced, both in terms of income and property and in social activities. African interest in the golf course and the turf is a post-Independence phenomenon. But that narrowing of racial inequalities has as a counterpart the growth of personal inequality, to which we now turn.

Inequality of Persons

It is the growth of personal inequality, in income and property ownership, that has been most discussed. Put crudely, the argument is that the racial inequalities of colonial Kenya have been replaced by even greater inequalities within the African community, and that these have been growing as a result of the policies of Government, and even more of the actions of those with power. There can be no doubt that 'some Kenyans are more equal than others', but the measurement of the degree of inequality, the assessment of the extent to which it is increasing, and the interpretation of what such an increase means, are not straightforward matters.

A balanced statement of the view crudely summarized above is to be found in the ILO Report:[52]

It is . . . possible to identify broad groups of persons who have benefited substantially from the rapid growth of the economy since independence. There is first of all the small group of Kenyans who have filled the high level jobs previously held by expatriates. Secondly, a much bigger group of persons have benefited from the transfer of land from European farmers to African settlers. Thirdly, new opportunities have arisen for Kenyan traders, builders, transporters, and small-scale manufacturing, repair and service firms. Finally, there is the relatively large group of employees in the modern, urban sector who have been able to secure increases of 6–8 per cent a year in their real incomes since independence.

The group of persons who have failed to derive much benefit from the growth generated since independence includes the great majority of smallholders, employees in the rural sector, the urban working poor, and the urban and rural unemployed.

Most of the assertions about income distribution in Kenya appear to lean heavily on Table 25 of the ILO Report, which is reproduced below (see Table 9.4). Care must be taken when reading some statements about income distribution, because it is not always made crystal clear what they are purporting to measure.

TABLE 9.4

Household Income Distribution, 1968–70

Income (K£ p.a.)	Number of households (thousands)
0–20	330
21–60	1,140
61–120	330
121–200	240
201–600	220
601–1,000	50
1,001–over	30
Total	2,340

Source: ILO, *Employment Incomes and Equality*, 1972, Table 25.

The distribution of some parts of money income has the firmest statistical and conceptual foundation. But figures of that kind do not contribute all that much to the Great Debate on inequality, statements about which are often couched in terms of the fact that 'a shorthand typist in Government . . . can earn . . . 8 to 12 times the average income of 80 per cent of the rural population.'[53] Data on money income, and particularly on wage income, cannot bear very directly on that, because the rural poor depend in varying degrees on self-employment and non-monetary income. That the difficulty of comparing unlikes has not however deterred comparers has been mentioned already in the discussion of rural–urban inequalities.

Even data on money incomes have been seriously misinterpreted. One author, purporting to measure inequality by the 'ratio of remuneration of employees to total income in the monetary economy',[54] argues that 'in a relatively poor country like Kenya a lower wage-share will indicate a more unequal general distribution of income if, as we would expect, profit and rent recipients have higher average income than wage recipients.' The analysis is worthless because the author apparently believes that non-wage-money incomes consist of 'profit and rent'. In reality, a large part of non-wage incomes ('operating surplus' in the terminology of the national accounts) in agriculture consists of a return to family labour. If operating surplus were all profit and rent, there would be exploitation indeed: in 1976 this item accounted for 82 per cent, and in 1977 for 88 per cent of GDP generated in agriculture.[55]

Several publications of the World Bank contain data on income distribution in Kenya. The study entitled *Kenya: Into the Second Decade* appears to take all its figures on the subject from the ILO Report, but it is unclear to what extent this is also the primary source for *Redistribution with Growth*[56] and for *Size and Distribution of Income: A Compilation of Data.*[57] These publications show that roughly speaking 20 per cent of the population receives nearly 70 per cent of the total income. This distribution refers, as does the ILO Report, to both monetary and non-monetary or subsistence income.

The ILO Report is scrupulously fair in setting out the limitations of its data:[58]

> A comprehensive analysis of income distribution in Kenya is unfortunately precluded by lack of adequate data. There are parts of the population, especially wage earners in the formal sector, for whom the existing data yield a reasonably complete and accurate picture of income distribution, but for other parts only fragmentary data of limited reliability are available. Nevertheless, we have attempted on the basis of the existing information, supplemented by additional research, to build up a rough picture of income distribution in Kenya.

The trouble is that results, when so clearly set out as in Table 25 of the ILO Report (see above, Table 9.4), inevitably carry more weight than the qualifications attached to them, even perhaps with the authors themselves, let alone with the users, interpreters and propagandists of the results. Certainly, the confidence with which statements are made about inequality is unjustified by the nature of the statistics.

According to Table 25 of the ILO Report, 1,140,000 households in 1968–70 had an annual income of between K£20 and K£60, while 330,000 had not more than K£20. These are pretty startling figures – but they can hardly be taken at their face value. The data ask us to believe that there were many thousands of Kenyans living in households which received less than K£20 a year, or less than K£4–K£5 per person a year, and this is total, not just money income. Such figures cannot conceivably indicate the reality they purport to reflect.

The difficulties of international comparisons of national income have for long been recognized. The argument can be expressed most graphically as follows:[59]

> Something is very wrong with these statistics [of national income in

terms of US dollars]. For instance, if the figure of $40 for Ethiopia means what it appears to mean, namely that Ethiopians are consuming per year an amount of goods and services no larger than could be bought in the United States for $40, then most Ethiopians are so poor that they could not possibly survive, let alone increase their numbers.

This logic can be carried further, taking the hint that 'the absurdities that arise when national incomes are compared in money terms cast suspicion on procedures for comparing incomes among regions or trades within a country.'[60] Disraeli wrote of England in the 1840s as Two Nations,[61] and this is a useful characterization of the developing countries today, including Kenya, even though the borderline between the nations is blurred and many individuals stand with a foot on each side. If the terms can be used without misunderstanding and as convenient labels, one might refer to the 'traditional nation' and the 'modern nation'. It is fairly safe to assume that there is a welfare gain for those who move from the former to the latter,[62] but the gain is nothing like as great as the increase in income required to sustain the new way of life, and the strictures on the international comparisons of average income per head apply equally to that between members of the Two Nations within a single state.

Consider the implications of denying that intranational comparisons are as invalid as international comparisons. If Kenyans in the rural areas can survive on household incomes of less than $US 1 per week (which is the rate of exchange equivalent of K£20 p.a.), and if the internal comparisons are valid, those at the upper end of the distribution might seem in comparison to be rich beyond the dreams of avarice. There are some in Kenya who may well be in that position – but not those on a family income of K£1,000 a year (which is the minimum of the top 'bracket' of the ILO table). A family income in the 'modern nation' of K£1,000 does not, by any means, allow a lavish way of life, even though it is fifty or more times that at the lower end of the distribution.

It must not be thought that the literature on the economy of Kenya in which emphasis is placed on inequality fails to notice the conceptual difficulties and statistical inadequacies of the income measures. The ILO Report itself refers to (i) the underestimation of the subsistence component of income; (ii) the supplementary subsistence income often received by wage employees on large farms; and (iii) the fact that 'the cost of living, not to mention the differences in styles of living and intensity of work, varies a good deal between urban and rural areas. In particular, the cost of housing and food, which absorb a large proportion of the incomes of poor people, is a good deal higher in urban areas' (p. 80). If considerations such as these were given full weight it is difficult to see how one fashionable piece of doctrine could be treated with the seriousness that is lavished on it. This is the doctrine referred to in the discussion of urban-rural inequality, that wage-earners in the formal sector are to be identified with the rich. The point is not usually stated as bluntly as that – more often there is a reference to the 'privileged' who are in wage employment.[63] However, the meaning is clear, and does indeed follow from the data on income distribution. Table 9.4, when taken at its face value, does indeed show no more than 13 per cent of all Kenya households with an annual income of more than K£200,[64] and only 3 per cent with an income over K£600. Indeed, therefore, the typist with a salary of K£489-690, and the skilled wage-earner with K£216-452,[65] are among the middle class and the rich. But as the Duke of Wellington, at the height of his fame, replied to the person who approached him with 'Mr Smith, I believe?': 'Sir, if you believe that, you will believe anything.' That the typist and wage-earner are in any significant sense among the rich could be believed only by someone without experience of the way they live or with his nose firmly buried in the figures.[66]

The reasons why the comparative income figures are so poor a reflection of reality are complex. One view is that the estimates use the wrong price relationships, and once these are adjusted comparisons can properly be made. There is no doubt that this provides part of the explanation, but it was remarked in Chapter 3 that it is not the whole story. It is difficult to think that the International Comparisons Project's calculations have entirely overcome the incomparability.[67] It is true that when measured in 'international dollars' the Kenya GDP per head is greater than when converted into US dollars at the going rate of exchange – but the ratio of the former to the latter is only 1.9:1. To conclude that for the very poor the income for a family in 1968–70 was not less than $US 1 a week, but only less than $US 1.9, does not suggest that the comparison is now entirely without difficulty.

Another group of explanations are those mentioned above, such as the understatement of the value of subsistence production, the understatement of transfers in rural incomes,[68] and the different requirements for expenditure on housing, travel, and other things in town and country. Another way to put this last point is to say that national accounting procedures do not distinguish the 'disutility compensating' and the 'benefit conferring' components of income, the balance between which is affected by different environments within a single country.

A more radical approach is to deny the assumption that wants of different sections of society – of the 'Two Nations' – are the same. All the comparisons make sense, whether in terms of US dollars or of international dollars, only if they are comparing the different degrees to which in different circumstances the same wants are being satisfied. It cannot be assumed that they are the same simply because people in the poor countries adopt the rich-nation patterns of consumption whenever they are able to do so.[69] That would be to neglect the fact that appetite grows with eating. The wants are created by their satisfaction rather than the other way round.[70] Care must be taken not to push this argument too far, otherwise tautology results. The demonstration effect of high consumption standards of which they become aware, but cannot attain, reduces the welfare of the poor by expanding their wants.[71] But the effect is at most partial. The man in the street, if he is sensible, does not allow his welfare to be much reduced by his knowledge that Rolls Royces exist.

A poem of the 1930s satirized those who seek 'to show the poor by mathematics' that

> Wealth and poverty are merely
> Mental pictures, so that clearly
> Every tramp's a landlord really
> In mind's events.

This is a cutting criticism of the argument that national income per head comparisons mislead because wants are not everywhere the same. But it is not the suggestion that inequality is imaginary, only that reality is inexplicable on the assumption of a similarity of wants.[72] It may be a convenient – nay, essential – assumption for 'comparers' that wants are everywhere the same, so they have the relatively straightfoward problem of measuring the differing degrees to which different people are able to satisfy them. It may be a nice liberal assumption, and very likely ought to guide some aspects of policy – that of aid donors, for instance. But it cannot be accepted as an assumption which reflects reality. If it did, it may be wondered how the poor in the developing countries – on US cents 3 a day in Kenya – survive, let alone multiply – at 3.5 per cent a year in Kenya!

The danger of the emphasis on inequality, as measured by the income figures, is that it risks throwing the baby out with the bath water. The concern for inequality in developing countries, at any rate in Africa, may in part be traced back to René Dumont's remark that 'a lifetime's work of a peasant equals one and a half months work of a Deputy.' But it was shown above that, according to the data, it is not only legislators who have incomes many times those of most citizens of their country. The difference between 'the peasants' and the rest according to the statistical measures is so great that people in a very modest way of life are classified among the middle class and the rich. In short, the comparison of incomes as in Table 9.4 misleads because it is not sufficiently discriminating. It exaggerates the differences between the poor and the 'rich', and ignores those concealed within the highest income group in the table.

The concept of inequality is itself applied with insufficient discrimination. It is applied to two very different phenomena. In one, the contrast between the labouring poor and the rich (though they are by no means all idle) is not a caricature. There are great inequalities of this kind in Kenya, of that there is no doubt, which are not effectively attacked by taxation, as the Minister of Finance is wont to complain.[73]

Inequality of this kind has arisen in various ways. Some Keyans now receive large salaries from employments which have been Africanized or which have been created by the development of multinational enterprises. Senior civil servants might reasonably be counted among the rich, though civil-servants salaries are low in comparison with those in Britain.

In business of one kind and another, great fortunes have been made by a few, by no means always in the way fortunes are made in the academic model of a competitive economy. Observers who have had no chance to succumb to temptation can afford to adopt a high moral attitude. But corruption, though immensely distasteful, is not necessarily an impediment to economic growth, as eighteenth-century England demonstrates, and may in effect bring back the price mechanism to a world of controls, while the incidence of the cost may not wholly be on the poor. Corruption has strong official disapproval, and soon after he succeeded to the Presidency President Moi denounced 'money hunger' and demanded that leaders should ensure 'they obtained their wealth in a proper way.' He pointed out that 'one can accumulate enough wealth to buy a golden bed, but one cannot buy sound sleep.'[74]

The distribution of income might be expected to be closely related to the ownership of land, but it is not a simple, causal relationship. It would probably be less true to say that 'some people are rich because they own large farms' than to say 'some people own large farms because they are rich'. There is no long-established class of large landowners (except for the remaining Europeans). The accumulation of wealth since the early 1960s has been mainly the consequence of an earlier access to education, providing the opportunity for salaried employment in business and administration, and of whatever in different cases has determined the ability to achieve political influence. Having acquired wealth, the wealthy – often with the help of bank loans – have acquired land, though doubtless the process is often cumulative, and there are worrying indications of increasing concentration of land holding.

The existence and growth of this first kind of inequality, whether it results from illegitimate activities or not, are proper subjects for concern, and are open to the standard arguments about inequality. But there is a second kind of inequality created by economic developments in Kenya which cannot properly be approached in the same way. This is the inequality created when some of the poor, but only some, become less poor. They are able, for one reason or another, to grasp opportunities which occur, or to receive the benefits of government programmes. Those who were fortunate enough to become out-growers on the Mumias sugar scheme are an example. They are in danger of being classed among the rich.[75]

If what has been said already is not enough to show that such improvements in income really are seen by some observers as evidence of (presumably undesirable) inequality, the following remarks may be noted.[76] 'The new elite . . . includes . . . clerical workers and skilled labourers, and smallholders . . . they have all gained by the post-independence strategy . . .' '. . . strategy has been directed to a considerable extent at the first two categories in the table . . . [whose] real income has risen substantially.' The categories referred to contain households with incomes of £120 a year and upwards, so that they include just the sort of households whose improved position creates the second kind of inequality.

It seems that the creation of inequalities of this second kind would be difficult to avoid in Kenya. If resources are insufficient for gains to be made by all at the same time, the growth of inequality is inevitable. An over-emphasis on equality would seek to deprive the 'rich', including in reality the very modestly circumstanced, of consumption possibilities the diffusion of which is the very stuff of economic progress. Are these to be denied to some because their achievement would increase inequality? The question is important because improved levels of living cannot be spread like butter, thickly over part of the slice or as thinly as is necessary to cover the whole. Many improvements – such as that great contributor to female emancipation, rural domestic water supply – can only be provided in discrete steps. When it is provided for some it increases inequality. Policies to prevent the creation of inequalities of this kind, to prevent some from achieving a new way of life, may only succeed in producing an equality of poverty.

Poverty

The most important issue in the discussion of poverty is not, in fact, the question of inequality, with which it has become too much entwined, but the question of absolute levels of income and consumption.

Kenya is a poor country, without any doubt, and millions of its inhabitants are poor, some desperately poor.[77] For most life is hard. Some studies have suggested that a high proportion of the rural population is below a 'poverty line'. One[78] comes to the conclusion that 39 per cent of Kenya's small farm households fall below the poverty line, and in Nyanza and Western Provinces it is more than 50 per cent. For Kenya as a whole, 36 per cent fall below a 'minimum food requirements' line, and more than half the Nyanza population fall below even that level. However, there are a number of considerations which suggest that, although such calculations may be useful in drawing attention to the problem of poverty and its varying regional impact, their conclusions purporting to show the size of the problem cannot be taken seriously.

In the first place, the calculation is based on average household size, without account being taken of the possibility that households with an income that would be below the poverty level for a household of average size are in fact smaller than the average.[79] If every person had the same income, but some people lived in large and some in small households, a distribution of households by income would show some to be poor and some rich, and some would fall below a poverty income drawn with respect to an average-size household. The existence of households in poverty would then be entirely a statistical illusion, because everyone has the same income. Of course, in reality that is nothing like the whole story. But there are clear indications of a positive relation between household income and household size,[80] so there would almost certainly be fewer households below the poverty line if proper account were taken in the calculation of variations in household size.

It is also difficult to reconcile the conclusion that more than half the Nyanza population is unable to obtain the 'minimum daily caloric requirement' with the food-production information available.[81] As the poverty line, and the distribution of households around it, is based essentially on a calculation of calories required and available, in this study for the ILO, a comparison can be made on the same basis with production per head. Five crops[82] provide in Nyanza a total income per head in terms of calories which is well above the prescribed poverty line – 45 per cent above it, in fact. Of course, this is on average, and the unequal distribution of income will mean that some have much less than the average. The finding of the study quoted, that more than half the Nyanza population was below the poverty line, was based on the fact that the median value of consumption[83] was below that line. The median value is said to be 81 per cent of the mean, and on this basis the median value of income per head in terms of calories from the five crops is still well above the poverty line – 18 per cent above it, in fact. And there are, of course, other sources of income than these five crops, though the data on the production of these alone seem to contradict the figures of the extent of poverty.

In any case, there are substantial difficulties facing this dietary approach to the definition of poverty.[84] Man does not live by calories alone, and it seems that he can also live without enough of them. What meaning is to be attached to a 'minimum daily caloric requirement' when half the population does not receive it, and yet population continues to increase? It may be that in some groups, perhaps among pastoralists in marginal areas, malnutrition is reducing fertility, but it seems implausible that such an effect is widespread in Nyanza.[85] Is all the population growth in Nyanza to be attributed to the less than 50 per cent who are above the 'minimum daily caloric requirement'? Of course, poverty may manifest itself in chronic ill health, high infant mortality, and in other ways. The possibilities justify the careful collection and analysis of evidence, of which there has been no more than a beginning. The nutrition survey of a sample of rural children between the ages of 1 and 4 found a low incidence of severe 'protein energy malnutrition' (PEM) but that mild and moderate PEM were widespread.[86] The incidence of this form of malnutrition seemed to be associated with weaning habits – children weaned both early and late were particularly affected – and any connection with 'poverty' as measured by the availability of calories per head would clearly require much detailed investigation to establish. And that is the point. The issue is far too complex – and far too serious – to be the subject of confident statements based on inadequate methodology applied to incomplete evidence.

Despite the findings of such poverty-line inquiries, therefore, it should not for a moment be imagined that Kenya is a land of widespread starvation and chronic hunger. Diets are inadequate for many, but hunger is not a primary manifestation of Kenya's poverty. Most people grow most of their own food, particularly maize. Over the last twenty years there have been times of national shortage, and at times there have been local shortages when maize was in surplus in other areas. At other times there have been large surpluses, so large recently that the marketing system has been unable to handle them.[87] In these circumstances it is implausible that a third of the total rural population, and more than half in so populous a Province as Nyanza, should not have enough maize to eat. Nor should it be thought that inequality is such that hungry millions are beating on the doors of the granaries, while some latter-day Marie Antoinette instructs them to eat cake. Kenya, in reality, is not like that.

The 1972 ILO mission reached the conclusion that[88] 'hybrid maize is almost certainly the most significant innovation for raising the living standards of the poorest farmers. Yet a survey in Central Province showed that only 31 per cent of farmers were growing hybrid, few of the poorest among them.' A few years later things had changed. The

Integrated Rural Survey[89] conducted in 1974-5 indicated that in Central Province 67 per cent of small-holders were growing some hybrid maize, in Western Province it was 73 per cent, and in the Rift Valley 92 per cent. The national average was pulled down to 50 per cent by the low proportions in other Provinces: Coast 19, Eastern 30, and Nyanza 36. The area under hybrid maize in Kenya as a whole amounted to 30 per cent of the area under local and hybrid maize combined. In Central Province the percentage was 28, in Western Province 71, and in the Rift Valley 81.

The distribution of hybrid maize growers by size of holding is published only for Kenya as a whole. Although it is indeed cultivated on a particularly high proportion of large holdings – over 70 per cent of holdings of 5 hectares and more – it is cultivated on as much as 44 per cent of the holdings of less than 2 hectares. The proportion of all holdings cultivating hybrid maize contained in the two smallest classes of holding, less than ½ hectare and 0.5-0.9 hectare, is almost the same as the proportion of holdings of those sizes in the total of holdings. Holdings of less than ½ hectare constitute 13.9 per cent of all holdings and 12.2 per cent of holdings growing hybrid maize; for holdings of 0.5-0.9 hectare the corresponding percentages are 17.9 and 15.6. Hybrid maize is certainly not confined to the larger farmers, and by 1974-5 could fairly be claimed to be making a significant contribution to 'raising the living standards of the poorer farmers'. In the succeeding years the use of hybrid maize must have further increased as its cultivation had been encouraged by a higher producer price.[90]

The problem of hunger is not, however, to be dismissed, but it is primarily a problem for marginal zones and marginal years. Life may be on the edge but it is not perpetually over it. It has been remarked more than once that Kenya is still in the grip of nature. In many areas, when the rains fail, or disease or pests strike, people go hungry, as they sometimes do before the harvest. The hunger of the marginal zones is particularly disturbing because it is likely to increase. There has been a large migration, particularly of the landless, from the high potential areas into the marginal lands. The growth rate of population in some drier parts of Eastern and Coast Provinces has been up to ten times the national average.[91] These lands are marginal particularly because of low rainfall, and together with lower rainfall on average goes a greater variability of rainfall. Into this unfavourable environment techniques of cultivation are transferred from the high-potential areas without adaptation to the circumstances, and this can cause deterioration in the productivity of the land. An increasing population of cultivators is in danger in time of coming into conflict with the migratory pastoralists who inhabit these areas. Pastoralism itself is often unable to sustain the existing, let alone provide a rising standard of living. The incidence of hunger, and the prospects of serious food shortages, are to be found therefore particularly in the marginal low potential zones, and their avoidance in ways of raising the productivity of these lands.

Turning to a more general view of poverty, the interesting issue is not simply how many people are poor, but how the extent of poverty is changing. Are people getting richer or poorer, and whichever it is, how many? There are no statistics to provide easy, direct, and convincing answers to these questions. Obviously of great relevance is the way that small-holder agriculture has been developing, because on that the vast majority of the poor are dependent. There has been a very large growth, both absolutely and relatively, in the contribution of the small farms to monetary agriculture. Although their share in gross marketed output has not increased since the late 1960s, it is more than one-half, whereas in 1963 it was little over one-third. The small farms doubled their output of coffee between 1964 and 1975, their area under tea between 1971 and 1975, and the value of their gross marketed production between 1970 and 1975. Their output of cash crops has continued to increase. These figures of the growth of small-holder monetary agriculture should be seen against the background of a subsistence economy in which, until the Swynnerton Plan of 1954, the main thrust of official policy towards the small farms was to discourage and inhibit the extension of cash cropping. It should also be recalled that many farms which are nominally large are in fact being operated as small-holdings.

Figures of small-holder agriculture may not be a totally satisfactory proxy for the income and standard of living of the mass of the people, particularly for the landless, but it seems plausible that there is a fairly close connection. There are different impressions about the spread of the benefits of small-holder development from settlement and from increases in marketed production. The ILO mission thought that nearly a quarter of a million small farmers, or one-fifth of the total had gained substantially, and another fifth to a less marked degree, whereas the rest had benefited marginally, if at all. But another view is that the majority of small farmers have benefited to a significant extent. It has been objected that studies of small areas have shown the benefits to be very unequally distributed, with little going to the poor. The evidence is inadequate for firm generalizations, but it is difficult to believe that only the rich have benefited from the great expansion of small-holder agriculture when 90 per cent of small-holdings are of less than 5 hectares, and only little more than 3 per cent are of 8 hectares and over.[92]

Progress

So much about Kenya has been written by inverted Coués, with their incantation that 'day by day and in every way it's getting worse and worse', that there is a danger of over-reaction. Kenya may not have been a 'Progressive' country, but during the fifteen years of the Kenyatta Era it made some progress. 'Signs of progress abound.'[93] There have been enough examples in the preceding pages, and little more need be said. The number of pupils in primary schools almost trebled between 1965 and 1977;[94] the number of hospital beds almost doubled over the period. Good roads have been brought nearer to large numbers of people, and domestic water supplies have been and are continuing to be made available to more and more people in the rural areas. There are even signs of progress in the provision of housing for the urban poor. The teeth of taxation have been sharpened, even if evasion is serious and many still escape its bite. Above all, there has been the great expansion in the incomes of small farmers. Progress was greatly assisted by the buyers of coffee and tea, though hindered by the sellers of oil. It was also greatly helped by the opportunities for Africanization in employment and the take-over of the White Highlands. The scope for progress could be narrower in the future, and progress still has a long way to go. It would be wrong by quoting the progress that has been made to give the impression that all is for the best in the best of all possible Kenyas. Far from it.

Kenya is still a very poor country, and there are great inequalities. Despite commitments to the reduction of inequality and the improvement of the welfare of the 'working poor', which is said to be the theme of the Development Plan for the period after 1978, many would argue that policies have been directed to help those who have already helped themselves.[95] A few have certainly 'helped themselves' in an unrestrained manner. With a less prejorative meaning of that term in mind, it was suggested in the discussion on inequality that to some extent the limitation of resources makes a focus on those who have already made progress inevitable. Agricultural extension and other assistance has been directed towards 'progressive farmers' in the high potential areas. In other words, the benefits have gone to those it has been easiest to benefit, and those, including pastoralists, less able to help themselves and more difficult to help, because of the quality of their location or for other reasons, have been left behind. But they cannot permanently be left behind if Kenya is to continue to progress. Nor can women.

This book has been concerned with the economy of Kenya during what we have called the Kenyatta Era, and it is not proposed to conclude by indulging in an exercise in 'futurology'. Nevertheless, it is worth setting the scene for the future in the form of Table 9.5,[96] which indicates the dimension of the 'employment' problem at the end of the century, if population is in fact expanding and continues to expand at what is said to be its present rate. Even if non-agricultural wage employment continues to increase at a rate to confound the pessimists, it seems likely that the numbers engaged in small-scale farming will have to rise roughly by 75 per cent during the last quarter of the present century. With the scope for further division of large farms greatly diminished, with migration already under way into the marginal lands, with most small farms already exceedingly small,[97] and with an increase in land consolidation, absentee ownership, and the use of less labour-intensive methods, that outlook does not seem bright.

TABLE 9.5

Labour Force and Economic Activity, 1976 and 1999

(millions)

		1976	1999
I.	Potential Labour Force	6.28	12.65
II.	Economic activity		
	(a) Modern sector, non-agricultural	0.73	3.47
	(b) Urban informal sector	0.12	0.25
	(c) Large-scale agriculture	0.28	0.23
	(d) Small-scale farming and other rural work	4.31	7.49
	(e) Pastoralists	0.39	0.50
	(f) Residual: Unemployment	0.45	0.71
	(g) Total (a) to (f)	6.28	12.65

Note: Labour force *equals* population aged 15–59 *minus* those in full-time education. Projection for 1999 from age distribution and age-specific mortality rates in 1969 Census, vol. iv.
Modern sector, non-agricultural projection on rate of increase achieved 1973–6.
Large-scale agricultural employment declining as subdivision continues or farms become co-operatives.
Unemployment includes housewives in urban areas not economically active.
Source: Based on calculations by Mr T.R.C. Curtin by kind permission.

The pressure of population is already being felt in the over-cultivation of marginal lands, and in cultivation up to the edges of river banks, resulting in loss not only of fertility but of the soil itself, and leading to silting of dams and damage to marine life. Population pressure has also been instrumental in the destruction of wild life and natural forest – though illegal export of animal trophies (against which strong action is now being taken) and the legal export of vast quantities of charcoal to the Middle East has probably been more responsible for the damage. It is not only the extreme 'environmentalist' who can see the dangers.

One might have expected to find that 'a spectre is haunting Kenya, the spectre of Population', but it is not so. Although 'population increases relentlessly',[98] and despite official acceptance of the importance of family planning, large families still have a central place in the Kenyan ethos, and the pressure for a population policy comes largely from outside agencies.[99] Even the target of official population policy is to achieve no more than a reduction in the rate of increase to the very high figure of 3 per cent a year.[100]

A more optimistic view would see the rate of population increase falling from its exceedingly high level in the 1960s, and early 1970s, and would expect the 1979 census to demonstrate the fact. In any case, the Malthusian spectre has been so often exorcised, and might it not be once again? There is plenty of land, of a sort, if ways can be found to farm it. The stultifying effects on industry of protection and the multinationals might not turn out to be so great or permanent as the theorists and ideologues seem able to demonstrate. The possibilities are numerous.

But whatever the future holds in store, it can safely be said that Jomo Kenyatta left Kenya a very different place from what he found it.

NOTES

CHAPTER 1

1. *Kii Nyaa,* the mountain with streaks (of snow).
2. Kenya became a Republic one year later.
3. In the UK the corresponding figure is less than one-quarter.
4. This is the percentage of the population in the age group 15–59. In the group 15–49 there is 42 per cent of the total population, which is in fact larger than the corresponding figure for Britain, because Kenya has a very much smaller number of old people. In Kenya, less than 10 per cent of the population is aged 50 and over, compared with 30 per cent in Britain. For age 60 and over the figures are 5 per cent in Kenya and 20 per cent in Britain.
5. On the higher growth assumption mentioned above, the number of children of school age in the year 2000 would be almost as large as the present total population.
6. Negley Farson, *Behind God's Back.*
7. Estimates of the population by race have not been published for the years after the 1969 census.
8. In addition to Africans, Asians, and Europeans, the statistics distinguish 'Arabs', of which there were 39,000 in 1969, and 'Others', of which there were 4,000.
9. See John R. Nellis, 'The Ethnic Composition of Leading Kenyan Government Positions', The Scandinavian Institute of African Studies, Research Report No.24, Uppsala, 1974, pp.19–20.

CHAPTER 2

1. This chapter is a revised version of Chapter 1 of *Aid and Inequality in Kenya*, by G. Holtham and A. Hazlewood, Croom Helm and Overseas Development Institute, London, 1975.
2. This is the title of Elspeth Huxley's 1935 biography of Lord Delamere, one of the founders of European settlement in Kenya. In explaining her title the author wrote that it was not a statement of fact but the expression of Lord Delamere's ideal 'to establish a permanent British settlement in the highlands of East Africa', and that the question of whether 'Kenya is truly a "white-man's country" is a matter for debate'. She thought that question 'primarily biological, and which cannot therefore, be settled for several generations'. The question was settled, in fact, in a quarter of a century, and the answer had nothing to do with biology. Delamere Avenue, once graced by a statue of the pioneer, has for long been Kenyatta Avenue. The statue has gone, though descendants remain.
3. In 1954 coffee accounted for less than 4 per cent of the value of sales of produce from small farms.
4. See L.D. Smith, Ch. 4, in J. Heyer, J.K. Maitha, and W.M. Senga, eds., *Agricultural Development in Kenya: An Economic Assessment*, Oxford University Press, Nairobi, 1976.
5. G.N. Kitching, 'Economic and Social Inequality in Rural East Africa: the Present as a Clue to the Past', Centre for Development Studies, University College of Swansea, March 1977, quoting research by M. Cowan.
6. *Survey of Industrial Production*, 1957.

7. Though not those of the Asian population, particularly of Asians who did not acquire Kenya citizenship.

CHAPTER 3

1. In both 1964 and 1977 stock changes were small, so that the percentage of resources devoted to fixed capital formation is the same as that for gross investment in those two years. In some years they have differed significantly because of changes in stocks. The figures show a large build-up of stocks in 1974 and a run-down in 1975, but the estimates of stock changes are subject to large revisions, so figures must be used with caution.
2. *Economic Survey*, 1978, p. 62.
3. See Tony Killick, 'Understanding Kenya's Inflation', *Weekly Review*, 3 Mar. 1975.
4. *Economic Survey*, 1978, p. 48.
5. *Economic Survey*, 1977, p. 40.
6. *Economic Survey*, 1978, p. 48.
7. International Labour Office, *Employment, Incomes and Equality: A Strategy for Increasing Productive Employment in Kenya*, Geneva, 1972. References below to ILO or ILO Report are to this important document.
8. *Economic Survey*, 1977, p. 41.
9. Loc. cit.
10. See Chapter 4.
11. World Bank, *Kenya: Into the Second Decade*, Baltimore and London, 1975. References below to World Bank or World Bank Report, without qualification, are to this work.
12. See ILO, op. cit.
13. Compare the rate of growth between 1960 and 1970 of GDP in USA of 4.3 per cent and in UK of 2.9 per cent. For that period the Kenya rate is quoted in fact as 7.1 per cent. World Bank, *World Development Report*, 1978 Table 2.
14. *Economic Survey*, 1976, p. 1.
15. The three groups defined in terms of per capita annual income in constant 1971 US dollars are: up to $US 300; $US 300–750; above $US 750. See H. Chenery *et al., Redistribution with Growth*, OUP, London, 1974, pp. 8–9.
16. World Bank, *World Development Report*, 1978, Table 1.
17. I.B. Kravis and others, *A System of International Comparisons of Gross Product and Purchasing Power*, The Johns Hopkins University Press, Baltimore and London, 1975, Table 1.3.

CHAPTER 4

1. This chapter does not pretend to deal comprehensively with the enormous range and complexity of issues in the agricultural economy of Kenya. For example, irrigation, ranching, and the Special Rural Development Programme are not discussed. The first two of these topics have chapters devoted to them in Heyer, Maitha, and Senga, eds., *Agricultural Development in Kenya: An Economic Assessment,* OUP, Nairobi, 1976. One SRDP project is examined in G. Holtham and A. Hazlewood, *Aid and Inequality in Kenya*, Croom Helm, London, 1976.
2. See Heyer *et al*., p. 255.
3. The figures in Table 4.2 are out of date, being derived from the 1969 census of population. The population of the different Provinces has increased at different rates, but not by enough to affect the general picture shown in Table 4.2.

4. *Crop Forecast . . . 1978*, p. 2.
5. Subtraction of the 0.6 m. hectares transferred to smallholder settlement (see Table 4.4) from the 3.1 m. ha. of large farms before land transfer began, gives a remaining large farm area of 2.5 m. ha. compared with a recorded area of 2.7 m. ha. (*Statistical Abstract*, 1977, Table 95). The difference is explained by the fact that land transferred to settlement farms operated as compact units under co-operative management are included in the 2.7 m. ha. In the light of the discussion in the text, it cannot be presumed that all the land of these farms is in fact being operated in large units.
6. Agricultural Census of Large Farms, *A Brief Review of Farming Activities*, CBS, March 1978, p. 1.
7. The figure for the small-farm area is taken from the 1974–5 Integrated Rural Survey which covered only the predominant small-holder areas. 'Thus although all districts in Central, Nyanza and Western Provinces were included in the sample, some of the districts in Eastern, Coast and Rift Valley Provinces were only partially covered . . . The partial coverage of smallholders is particularly apparent in data pertaining to Rift Valley Province.' The sampling frame did not include households with holdings over 20 hectares. 'The traditional pastoral areas, urban areas and all the former scheduled areas (except those which had by then been subdivided into settlement schemes) were excluded from the sample.' See *Integrated Rural Survey, 1974–75*, March 1977, pp. 8 and 10.
8. The contrast between high- and low-density was a feature of the original, pre-Independence settlement schemes.
9. See the discussion of small farms below, and references stated there.
10. It was noted above that part of the land transferred to small-scale settlement is being cultivated co-operatively in unified holdings, and this area is included in the large farms statistics. Hence the stated area under large farms is greater than the area of the Scheduled Areas minus the areas shown in Table 4.4 (a).
11. In 1975 some 40 per cent of the coffee estates, accounting for some 60 per cent of the area under coffee estates, remained in non-African hands. 'The African ownership of Estates by the end of the season stood at 389 estates out of 669 (58.2%). This represents 11,992 ha. out of 29,641 ha. (or 41.9%). Out of the lot owned by Africans, 48 farms (2,220 ha.) are owned by Co-operatives', Coffee Board of Kenya, *Annual Report* for the year ended 30 Sept. 1975.
12. This estimate for the total registrable land can be derived from *Economic Survey*, 1978, Table 8.19 and *Statistical Abstract*, 1977, Table 5. Earlier sources imply a much smaller total area of registrable land, based on the recommendations of the Lawrence Mission (*Report* of the Mission on Land Consolidation and Registration in Kenya, 1965–6) for the registration of high and medium potential land, but later the definition of registrable was extended to include a considerable proportion of the marginal land. The *Statistical Abstract* gives a smaller area of land actually registered than the *Economic Survey* because it excludes ranches, particularly in West Pokot, Narok, and Kajiado Districts of Rift Valley Province.
13. *A Plan to Intensify the Development of African Agriculture in Kenya*, Government Printer, Nairobi, 1955.
14. D. Brokensha and E.H.N. Njeru, 'Some consequences of land adjudication in Mbere Division, Embu', IDS Working Paper, No. 320, September 1977. The reference is to the title of a novel by Chinua Achebe about Nigeria.
15. See Chapter 2.

16. See Tony Killick, 'Strengthening Kenya's Development Strategy: Opportunities and Constraints', Institute for Development Studies, University of Nairobi, Discussion Paper No. 239, October 1976.
17. 'No sooner does the Government give the poor some land than the grabbers offer to purchase it with sums of money the poor settled people have never even heard of.' Joe Kadhi, *Sunday Nation*, 24 Sept. 78. The Eastern Provincial Commissioner warned people who will be settled on Mwea Trust Land 'not to sell their tract of land as that would defeat the Government's policy of settling the landless'. *Sunday Nation*, 24 Sept. 78.
18. '. . . officials in local government and settlement schemes owning many plots registered in different names of members of the same family . . .', Joe Kadhi, loc. cit.

    The MP for a Masai constituency deplored the 'systematic grabbing of land in his constituency by a few greedy people . . . where land adjudication . . . had not been fairly done . . . a few educated people . . . take advantage of illiterate or ignorant Masai . . .' *Nairobi Times*, 24 Sept. 78.

    'What has produced problems in allocation of land has not been the system but those who are charged with making it work . . . If the Land Boards and all the officials in the office of the commissioner of lands operated strictly according to the laid down regulations [and] people in high places . . . abstained from applying undue pressure upon the various civil servants charged with . . . allocating government land, there would be not much complaint from the public.' *Weekly Review*, 22 Sept. 78.

    The same situation has arisen in the allocation of urban plots. 'For several years now the allocation of business and residential plots . . . has not been a straight affair . . . MPs have often charged that civil servants with inside information know . . . when plots are to be allocated [and] many of the choice plots have already been earmarked for a number of civil servants . . . There are reportedly a number of senior civil servants who have had plots allocated to them in the names of their own children who are still minors.' *Weekly Review*, 22 Sept. 78. It is to be noted that the criticism comes from 'MPs who feel at a disadvantage when looking for government plots to acquire'!
19. This is still true, though less so than in the past now that special statistical inquiries have become more common.
20. It is now realized that the determinants of the amount of maize marketed are complex. It is not a simple sale of what is surplus to household needs: during a year households both buy and sell.
21. Heyer *et al.*, p.324.
22. *Development Plan, 1974-1978*, p.233.
23. It may be deduced from the IRS that small-holders sold 596,000 tons in 1974–5. Marketing Board purchases from large farms as well as smallholders totalled 365,000 tons in 1974 and 488,000 tons in 1975.
24. Sales to MPB 1977 424,000 tons (*Economic Survey*, 1978, p.104). Assume none of this from small farms ('Small farmers sold very little to Maize Board agents in 1977'. *Crop Forecast . . . 1978*, p.3) so that it is total output from other farms, any small amounts from small farms balancing own-consumed output of large farms. Small-farm output 1977 14 m. bags of 90kg = 1,260,000 tons (*Crop Forecast*). Total production = 424,000 + 1,260,000 = 1,684,000 tons. If value of 424,000 tons is K£18.8 m. (*Economic Survey*, 1978, p.96), then value of 1,260,000 tons is £74.7 m. Coffee sales 1977 K£192.2 m., Tea sales K£92.7 m. (*Economic Survey*, 1978, Table 8.3).

25. *Integrated Rural Survey, 1974–75*, Table 10.3. *Economic Survey*, 1978, Table 8.16.
26. Namely, wheat, barley, temporary industrial crops, permanent crops, wool, hides and skins. There is no doubt some own-consumption of these items, as there are some products not deducted which are not own-consumed, but the value must be small on both sides.
27. *Integrated Rural Survey, 1974–75*, Table 8.12. Average value per holding of total consumption of own-produce multiplied by number of holdings.
28. IRS–1 used a sample frame which allowed for a farm to be counted as a single holding when it was, in fact, being operated as more than one holding; the sample frame for IRS–2 allowed such subdivision to be identified. IRS–2 included squatters on large farms who were excluded from IRS–1, but not co-operatively run large farms. IRS–2 also had a larger geographical coverage in Rift Valley Province.
29. See below in this chapter.
30. Proportion of holdings below 1 ha: 2–3 member families, 44 per cent; 8–10 member families, 28 per cent; 11–15 member familes, 24 per cent. IRS–1, Table 7.3.
31. Areas under various crops by Province are given in *Integrated Rural Survey, 1974–75*, Table 9.1.
32. Only a third of Nyanza farmers grow hybrid maize, but it is said that Nyanza farmers have been obtaining yields of local maize comparable to those obtained from hybrid maize in Rift Valley and Western Provinces (*Integrated Rural Survey, 1974–75*, p.77).
33. *Integrated Rural Survey, 1974–75*, Tables 9.9–9.13.
34. Forty-four per cent compared with an average of 50 per cent.
35. The source of these figures is L.D. Smith, op.cit., Tables 13 and 16.
36. For the history see Heyer *et al.*, op.cit., p.116 (Smith) and p.193 (Heyer and Waweru).
37. *Economic Survey*, 1978, p.106.
38. This paragraph is based on Heyer and Waweru, op.cit., p.193.
39. Not so much undesirable because of disease dangers and other reasons, as with coffee.
40. There had been small quantities grown and simply processed without a factory in Murang'a District, then Fort Hall, from the middle 1940s.
41. See G. Holtham and A. Hazlewood, op.cit., Ch. 5, Part two, for a detailed examination of Mumias. The statement in Heyer *et al.*, p.335, that there is no nucleus estate at Mumias is mistaken.
42. See *Economic Survey*, 1976, Table 8.2, 1978, Table 8.4.
43. p.240.
44. 'Cane worth millions being left to rot . . .' was a headline (*Sunday Nation*, 10 Sept. 78) reporting an allegation by a Nyanza MP. It was denied by the chairman of the Kenya Sugar Authority, but nevertheless the President was emphasizing in speeches the need to expand factory capacity so as not to frustrate the growers. It should be noted that 1977 and 1978 were very good years for cane, and drier weather could appreciably reduce yields.
45. *Economic Survey*, 1978, p.105.
46. L.D. Smith, op.cit., Table 23.
47. See J.L. Lijoodi and Hans Ruthenberg, 'Income Distribution in Kenya's Agriculture', *Zeitschrift für ausländische Landwirtschaft*, April–June 1978.
48. See K. Griffin, 'Increasing Poverty and Changing Ideas about Development Strategies', *Development and Change*, 1977, p.502.

49. These figures are calculated from the tables in Agricultural Census of Large Farms, 1975 and 1976, *A Brief Review of Farming Activities*, 1978.
50. *Development Plan, 1966–70*, p.154.
51. It was announced in the newspapers in such terms as 'Huge loan for "problem farms" ', *Nation*, 19 Aug. 1975.
52. See Heyer *et al.*, p.242.
53. Op.cit., pp.246–7.
54. *Development Plan, 1974–1978*, p.199.
55. There are small-scale sugar-processing methods, but it is not clear that the product is acceptable to Kenyan tastes.
56. This section draws heavily on Chapter 10, 'The Marketing System', in Heyer *et al.*, and on L.D. Smith, op.cit.
57. Heyer *et al.*, p.359.
58. Any movement of more than two bags of maize between districts or of ten bags within a district legally requires a permit from the Maize and Produce Board.
59. See L.D. Smith, op.cit.
60. In one year American yellow maize was imported at high cost which was very much not to the Kenyan taste and there were strong objections from consumers. (See pp. 84–5 on the highly developed tastes of poor people.)

CHAPTER 5

1. Frances Stewart, 'Kenya: Strategies for Development' in *Development Paths in Africa and China*, ed. U.G. Damachi *et al.*, Macmillan, London, 1976, pp.88–9.
2. In 1970 some 30 per cent of output was of this kind. Figure calculated from Table 3(K), *Statistical Analysis of Industrial Production in East Africa (1963–1970)*, EAC, 1974.
3. The most interesting statistic on the growth of manufacturing would be of manufacturing capacity, but data are available only on production, that is, on the use made of capacity.
4. *Census of Industrial Production, 1972*, and *Statistical Abstract*, 1977, Table 130. 'Employment' means 'number engaged' and includes self-employed as well as employees. Censuses of Industrial Production have been carried out at five-year intervals. The 1967 Census covered firms with five and more employees, and the 1972 Census included a sample of smaller firms. In other than Census years data were collected only for large firms, though summary data for all firms and establishments have been published for 1973–5 (see *Statistical Abstract*, 1977, Table 134).
5. To provide some comparison the following table gives figures for Kenya (1972) and the UK (1973). The similarity is perhaps surprising. What the table does not reveal is the extent to which a firm with 100 engaged is in fact small. In the UK 42 per cent of all employment is in establishments of 1,000 and over, and nearly 10 per cent in establishments of 10,000 and over.

	Employment per Establishment					
	Less than 50		50–99		100 and over	
	Kenya	UK	Kenya	UK	Kenya	UK
Percentage of total engaged	18	11	11	7	71	82
Percentage of total establishments	78	80	10	8	12	12
Average number engaged per establishment	14	11	69	70	371	533

6. There is also local participation in ownership. In 1977 the Kenya Government through ICDC and with Kenya private investors through the ICDC Investment Company (see Chapter 8, pp. 159–60, for a discussion of these institutions), acquired a further major shareholding in East African Industries, bringing the total to over 45 per cent.
7. The differences in coverage and response rate make it unlikely that the difference in the recorded percentage of foreign ownership between 1967 and 1972 is significant.
8. The 1972 Census of Production showed non-citizen ownership accounting for 59 per cent of gross domestic product from all firms in manufacturing, but for only 46 per cent from firms with between five and nineteen persons engaged.
9. The division between locally owned and foreign owned (Citizen and non-Citizen ownership) can only be approximate because many firms have both local and foreign participation: the 1972 data are for 'wholly or mainly owned' by non-citizens or citizens. Local ownership is not, of course, the same thing as Kenya African ownership, but includes ownership by Kenya citizens of Asian and European origin as well as public enterprises.
10. A bizarre example is the following: 'In a major sales drive, Coca Cola are conducting a talent spotting contest in the African locations of Nairobi, offering a total of Shs. 4,000 in prize money. During the contest . . . the Crown Corks of Coca Cola bottles will be printed black on red instead of the usual white on red. These special crown corks will be exchangeable for a series of figurines featuring Walt Disney characters' (*East African Trade and Industry*, June 1958). I am indebted to Mr R. Eglin for this quotation, and for some of the other facts in this section.
11. World Bank, p.309.
12. Furfural, a chemical product produced from maize cobs.
13. ILO, p.446.
14. ILO, p.447.
15. ILO, p.148.
16. ILO, p.379.
17. See ILO Report, pp.140 and 438–9.
18. World Bank, p.278.
19. ILO Report, p.134.
20. This issue is discussed on pp. 84–5. Quotation from ILO Report, p. 134.
21. The definitions are: 'Output is the value of sales or work done, plus resales, plus change in stocks of semi-finished and finished goods, plus rents received on non-residential buildings, plus self-produced capital assets, minus cost of goods sold in same condition as purchased, minus excise duty'; 'Gross Product is the aggregate difference between Output and Input. It includes labour costs, interest payments, depreciation charges, and net profit before tax'; 'Input includes industrial costs plus all other overhead costs like rents, rates, water, stationery, advertising expenses, transport, head office costs, insurance, audit fees, legal expenses etc.' See *Statistical Abstract*.
22. Input–Output Tables which would provide the data for such an exercise are available for 1967 and 1971, but these years are too near to each other for the tables to reveal any changes over the period with which we are concerned.
23. *Input-Output Tables for Kenya, 1971*, Central Bureau of Statistics, Ministry of Finance and Planning, August 1976.
24. Gross output, £95,755 m.; net output £36,984 m. UK Census of Production 1975.

25. In manufacturing as a whole, excluding chemicals and petroleum, the percentage was actually higher in 1973 than in 1963, and only just over two points lower in 1975. It is these two points which are largely explained, it is suggested, by the indirect effect of the rise in world oil prices. The percentage for All manufacturing is just over six percentage points lower in 1975 than in 1963 and 1973, but the percentage is only two points lower when chemicals and petroleum are excluded. It is the four points difference which is the direct result of the rise in world oil prices.
26. If 1973 = 100, the following are the 1975 values: Gross Product = 141; Input = 514; Output = 431; average value crude-petroleum imports = 480; average value petroleum-products exports = 400. It is to be noted that the ratio of the index value of petroleum-products exports and crude imports (400/480) is the same as the ratio of the index value of Output to Input (431/514). Source: *Statistical Abstract*, 1977, Table 133, Basic industrial chemicals and petroleum, and Tables 59 and 67 for exports and imports.
27. Nor is it necessarily the case that 'low vertical integration leads to the phenomenon of import dependence' (World Bank, *Kenya: Into the Second Decade*, p.280). With vertical integration the value added in the integrated enterprise would be greater, but not necessarily the total value added in manufacturing, than with disintegrated production. And, of course, low value added does not necessarily imply dependence on *imported* inputs. The extent of vertical integration seems, in fact, to be an irrelevancy.
28. It should be noted that the element of payment to domestic factors is boosted by protection and would be smaller at 'world prices'.
29.

	1976	1977
Exports to Tanzania (K£ m.)	33.4	9.8
Exports to Uganda (K£ m.)	33.2	52.0

30. World Bank, p.265.
31. *Economic Survey*, 1977, p.125.
32. Total exports, 1977, K£480.3 m., Primary exports K£317.3 m., therefore Processed exports K£163 m. Exports of processed fuels K£83 m. *Economic Survey*, 1978, Table 7.7.
33. *Development Plan, 1970–1974*, pp.304–5.
34. World Bank, p.94.
35. World Bank, p.6.
36. This conclusion is directed at the argument that import substitution itself increases reliance on imports. It does not affect the seriousness for the balance of payments of the fact that, because of price increases unrelated to the import substitution process, the value of imports as a proportion of GDP has increased. Although the argument about import dependence is most relevant to monetary GDP, it is worth noting that the same conclusion, that dependence has not increased, applies to total GDP, monetary and non- or semi-monetary. At constant prices, imports amounted to 32 per cent of total GDP in 1964 and to 24 per cent in 1976.
37. If rate of import substitution is defined as the rate at which self-sufficiency increases, i.e. the percentage increase between the two years in $(1 - m)$, where m is the proportion of imports in total supply, the rate is as follows: consumer goods 14.9; intermediate goods 21.3; capital goods 22.0.
38. ILO, p.438.
39. See below, Chapter 8, for a discussion of these two organizations.
40. Budget Speech, 17 June 1976.
41. Op.cit.

42. See later in this chapter and Chapter 7.
43. World Bank, op.cit., p.xi.
44. J.K. Maitha, Tony Killick, and G.K. Ikiara, 'The Balance of Payments Adjustment Process: Kenya', A Report to UNDP/UNCTAD, March 1978.
45. 'The increase of 15 per cent in the volume of output in 1977 would have been higher but for the fact that many manufacturing firms had difficulties in obtaining import licences for raw material requirements . . .', *Economic Survey*, 1978, p.132.
46. '. . . controls have exacerbated the effects of the tariff system, and have not worked against the system to any great extent', World Bank, op.cit., p.294.
47. ILO Report, p.286.
48. The World Bank refers to 'the very dubious practice of giving "infant industry" protection to subsidiaries of powerful foreign companies', op.cit., p.310.
49. It is worth noting that the procedure has often been to provide protection on application from a particular actual or prospective investor, rather than setting up a barrier to encourage investment in a particular industry. In other words, protection has been given on the initiative of the investor rather than investment being the response to protection. The former procedure seems inherently more likely to lead to an *ad hoc*, unplanned structure of protection.
50. *Economic Survey*, 1976, p.52.
51. See e.g., Colin Leys, *Underdevelopment in Kenya: the Political Economy of Neo-Colonialism*, Heinemann, London, 1975, Ann Seidman, *Comparative Development Strategies in East Africa*, East African Publishing House, Nairobi, 1972, and Frances Stewart, op.cit.
52. 'An extreme example in Kenya [of import reproduction] is the substitution for imported blackcurrent juice, of domestically produced blackcurrent juice which involved imported blackcurrents . . . Import substitution would allow . . . substitution of pineapple or orange juice . . .' F. Stewart, op.cit., n.28. Of course, pineapple juice and juices of other locally grown fruits are exactly what all but an infinitesimal proportion of Kenya fruit juice production is devoted to.
53. Figures from *Statistical Abstract*, 1977, Tables 117, 121, 106, 134(b). Money income calculated as difference between total income, Shs. 3652/– (Table 121), and consumption of own produce. Shs. 1297 (Table 117), equals Shs. 2355, or K£117.75. Total expenditure is calculated as the difference between total consumption, Shs. 3450/–, Table 117, and consumption of own produce, equals Shs. 2153/– or K£107.65.
54. See K. King, *The African Artisan: Education and the Informal Sector in Kenya*, Heinemann, London, 1977.
55. *Development Plan, 1974-1978*, Part I, p.280.
56. ILO, p.6.
57. K. King, op.cit., p.60.
58. The following discussion is based on the most interesting study of Kenneth King, op.cit.
59. It is to be noted that the bicycle has major use as a goods vehicle as well as a passenger vehicle, so that a sturdy carrier is an important producer's good.
60. King, p.57.
61. King, op.cit., pp.44–5.
62. Leys, op.cit., p.267.
63. 'What the "informal sector" does is to provide the "formal sector" with goods and services at a very low price, which makes possible the high profits of the "formal sector" ', ibid.

CHAPTER 6

1. *Development Plan, 1966-1970*, p.269.
2. Op. cit., p.267.
3. Loc. cit.
4. Op.cit., p.270. In recording this perfectly understandable desire for Africanisation, however, it would be wrong not to acknowledge the enormous contribution made to the development of Kenya by Asians in commerce.
5. Op.cit., pp.268-9.
6. *Development Plan, 1966-1970*, p.269.
7. *Development Plan, 1974-1978*, Ch. 2.
8. 'Window-dressing' directors or 'rubber stamp' traders they are sometimes called. See, for example, *Daily Nation* 6 Oct. 1978.
9. *Development Plan, 1974-1978*, pp.41-2.
10. See below, Chapter 8, for a discussion of the ICDC.
11. See below, Chapter 8, for a discussion of KNTC.
12. ILO Report, p.207.
13. See below, Chapter 8.
14. See *Sessional Paper on Employment*, No. 10 of 1973, para. 170.
15. *Development Plan, 1974-1978*, p.11.
16. See A. Hazlewood, *Economic Integration: The East African Experience*, Heinemann, London, 1975.
17. One example of the clash of interest occurred in 1918 when a surcharge was imposed on traffic to assist the finances of the Kenya Government. There were also objections by Uganda to the railway tariff, which it was argued protected Kenya's industry at Uganda's expense and favoured Kenya's exports. The validity of these arguments is not the point; valid or not it was the belief that Kenya was getting the benefits of the joint arrangements that was important.
18. The abandonment of the common currency in 1966 made it easier to avoid transferring funds to the Corporation's headquarters.
19. International Bank for Reconstruction and Development (IBRD), *The Economic Development of Kenya*, 1963, p.184. Elsewhere the mission remarks that 'Some people in Kenya would like to have a modern highway from Nairobi to Mombasa, but we do not think that the likely economic costs and benefits have been sufficiently considered. We ourselves do not believe that any possible benefits to be gained from this project in the near future justify it to the exclusion of many other projects of greater urgency and potential' (p.50).
20. Op.cit., p.181.
21. *Development Plan, 1966-1970*, p.279.
22. *Development Plan, 1970-1974*, p.381.
23. *Development Plan, 1974-1978*, p.345.
24. Statement reported in *East African Standard*, 17 Dec. 1954.
25. *Development Plan, 1974-1978*, p.344.
26. Op.cit., p.345.
27. See A. Hazlewood, *Rail and Road in East Africa: Transport Co-ordination in Under-Developed Countries*, Basil Blackwell, Oxford, 1964.
28. *Development Plan, 1974-1978*, p.350. It must be added that there were times when the railway was unable to handle all the petroleum traffic it was offered.
29. See *Development Plan, 1970-1974*, pp.377, 381, 407-8.
30. See *Development Plan, 1974-1978*, p.350.

31. The original proposal was for a pipeline from Mombasa to Kampala, but it was shown to be viable only to Nairobi. Most oil for Western Kenya is now carried by rail, and it is unlikely that many of the existing long-distance road tankers will be replaced when they reach the end of their life.
32. See *Development Plan, 1970-1974*, pp.377–81.
33. Op.cit., p.381.
34. *Development Plan, 1975-1978*, pp.345–6.
35. ILO, p.491.
36. There is a proposal to require third-party insurance for *matatus*. There is a good deal of comment about the dangerous condition of some vehicles, dangerous driving and dangerous overloading.
37. In one almost unbelievable incident, an Italian tourist paid for an aircraft to be refuelled so that he could complete his journey.
38. The story of the end of East African Airways and the establishment of Kenya Airways is told in the following issues of the *Weekly Review* of 1977: 24 Jan., 31 Jan., 7 Feb., 21 Feb.
39. *Economic Survey*, 1978, p.164.
40. The statistics measure departures by country of residence.
41. This drop in the number of visitors from Tanzania and Uganda has not caused a corresponding drop in hotel bednights by East African residents, to which reference has earlier been made, because that statistic includes Kenyans.
42. See Chapter 8.
43. An example is the Shs. 10.45 m. in the Nairobi Intercontinental, equal to a 33.8 per cent shareholding. Minister of Tourism, reported in *Standard Chartered Review*, May 1978.
44. Frank Mitchell, 'The Value of Tourism in East Africa', *Eastern Africa Economic Review*, June 1970.
45. See Mitchell, op.cit. *Development Plan 1970–1974*, p.436, suggests that employment in 1970 was 20,000 and would increase to 40,000 by 1974.
46. Which are comprehensible to, if not shared by, an author resident in a city as awash with tourists as Oxford.
47. *Development Plan, 1974-1978*, p.380.
48. *Weekly Review*, 17 Nov. 1975, p.24.
49. *Weekly Review*, loc.cit., p.25.
50. See the *Weekly Review*, 17 May 1976, pp.17–18, and 15 Nov., pp.20–8.
51. Though concentration, with isolation from the population, would presumably be preferred by those who emphasize 'the moral price of tourism' (*Weekly Review*, 17 Nov. 1975).
52. It was estimated that 85 per cent of the commercial tour vehicles entering the Northern Tanzanian game parks were registered in Kenya. See Mitchell, op.cit., pp.21–2, n.39.
53. See the *Weekly Review*, 21 Feb. 1977, pp.18–21, for an eloquent statement of the argument summarized here.

CHAPTER 7

1. Note that these are percentages of monetary GDP at market prices whereas those in Table 5.12 are of monetary GDP at factor cost.
2. Index on base 1972 = 100 linked to Index on base 1971 = 100. See *Economic Survey*, 1976 and 1978.
3. World Bank, p.266.
4. See A. Hazlewood, *Economic Integration: The East African Experience*, Tables 8.8 and 8.16.

5. See A. Hazlewood, op.cit., Ch. 3.
6. See above, Chapter 6(b), Transport.
7. World Bank, p.280.
8. Op.cit., pp.299-300.
9. p.280.
10. World Bank, p.287.
11. See the discussion earlier in this chapter of the changes in the total value of exports and imports.
12. Sixteen times, if the comparison is made between 1964 and 1977.
13. These figures are for all flows, public as well as private. If the accounts were adjusted to show the 'true' outflow there would be no difference in the out-turn of the balance of payments, because the larger outflow of investment income would be matched by smaller payments for goods and other services. Of course, if the concealed profits were taxed the outflow would be reduced.
14. Colin Leys, op.cit., pp.126-7 and 137-8.
15. It is perhaps truer to say that the words become the slogan on a political banner instead of an instrument of exposition and analysis.
16. Entering excessive prices for imports from an overseas branch of the same company so as to shift part of the profits abroad.
17. ILO Report, pp.453-7. Leys says, after reference to the ILO's discussion of another means of minimizing tax liability, 'The ILO mission thought it fair to conclude from this that foreign manufacturing companies must also be assumed to be exporting capital by "transfer pricing".' The ILO Report neither makes this statement nor provides any justification for it. Leys also (p.138) conflates the question of foreign investment with the quite different issue of the incentive for residents – he refers to the Asian community – to export capital.
18. World Bank, p.43.
19. World Bank, p.310.
20. For a fuller treatment of the issues treated summarily here see G. Holtham and A. Hazlewood, *Aid and Inequality in Kenya*, 1976.
21. OECD, *Development Cooperation, 1977 Review*, Table D.3.
22. OECD, op.cit., Table D4.
23. G. Holtham and A. Hazlewood, op.cit., Table 3.
24. UNDP *Compendium*, Nairobi.
25. Sessional Paper No.10 of 1965, *On African Socialism and its Application to Planning in Kenya*, para.103.
26. Holtham and Hazlewood, op.cit., Ch.5, Pt.1.
27. UNDP, op.cit.
28. World Bank, p.267.
29. J.H. Power, 'The Role of Protection in Industrialization Policy with Particular Reference to Kenya', *Eastern Africa Economic Review*, June 1972, p.19.
30. H.G. Johnson, *Aspects of the Theory of Tariffs*, George Allen & Unwin, London, 1971, p.348.
31. World Bank, op.cit., p.325.
32. World Bank, op.cit., p.322.
33. In both cases assuming there is no 'water' in the tariff and the price is set as high as the tariff permits.
34. See, e.g., in World Bank, op.cit., p.320.
35. See Power, op.cit., for advocacy of such a policy.
36. e.g. World Bank, op.cit., p.325.

37. A similar objection is raised to quantitative controls on intermediate goods (p.298) even though it is acknowledged, in a somewhat confusing phrase, that 'this offsets to some extent the low effective protection apparently given to intermediates by the tariff'.
38. This is to make no criticism of the competence of the calculators of effective protection rates (which an author who was tutor to one of them would not wish to do!). It is a complex business and involves a struggle with many data deficiences.
39. The most-quoted calculations for Kenya are M.G. Phelps and B. Wasow, 'Measuring Protection and its Effects in Kenya', Working Paper No. 37, Institute for Development Studies, University of Nairobi, April 1972.
40. Power, op.cit., p.18.
41. World Bank, p.268.
42. See A. Hazlewood, *Economic Integration, the East African Experience*, for the story down to March 1975, when as it turned out the East African Community had less than two years to go before it finally lost is hold on life.
43. See below, Chapter 8(c), for a discussion of these two institutions.
44. See Central Bank of Kenya, *Annual Report*, 1968, p.13.
45. See *Economic Survey*, 1972, p. 22.
46. See *Economic Survey*, 1976, p. 29.
47. See Central Bank of Kenya, *Annual Report*, 1976, p.7.
48. World Bank, p.32.
49. Ministry of Commerce and Industry, *A Guide to Industrial Investment in Kenya*, 2nd edn., 1972, p.3.
50. Budget speech, 12 June 1975.
51. World Bank, p.309.
52. Op.cit., p.310.
53. See above, § (c) of this chapter.
54. See ILO, pp.191, 453–5, and World Bank, 302, for a more detailed discussion, including the arithmetic, of surplus transfer through over-invoicing.
55. See *Economic Survey*, 1977, p.39.
56. 'Perhaps the most important policy we have adopted here in Kenya is that all major new industries will have substantial government and local shareholding' (Minister of Finance and Planning reported in DFCK, *Industry in Kenya*, June 1977). 'Preference . . . is . . . given to foreign investors who are interested in equity participation with the government through its parastatal bodies such as ICDC and/or local investors' (ICDC, *Kenyan Partner in Progress*, p.8).
57. See also Chapter 8 on ICDC.

CHAPTER 8

1. The fiscal year runs from 1 July. This increase is at current prices so that the increase in 'real' terms was smaller.
2. Export taxes on coffee and tea were reintroduced in the 1977 budget.
3. For the 1973 income year, companies accounted for 55 per cent and persons for 45 per cent of the tax assessed. See *Statistical Abstract* 1977, Table 238(b).
4. J.R. Nellis, 'Who Pays Tax in Kenya', Research Report No. 11, The Scandinavian Institute of African Studies, Uppsala, 1972, p.6.
5. M. Westlake, 'Kenya's Extraneous and Irrational System of Personal Income Taxation', Institute for Development Studies, University of Nairobi, Staff Paper No. 101, June 1971.
6. World Bank, pp.188–9.
7. See *Economic Survey*, 1978, Table 6.3.

8. An increase in the sugar excise in 1976 did not raise prices but effected a transfer to the Exchequer from the Sugar Equalization Fund. See Budget Speech, June 1976.
9. ILO Report, pp.271–2.
10. World Bank, p.191.
11. *African Socialism and its Application to Planning in Kenya*, Sessional Paper No. 10, 1965, p.35. The role of fiscal policy was reiterated in the *Development Plan, 1974-1978*, which declared that 'the better-off members of the community will contribute proportionately more to Government revenue through taxation.' (Part I, p.3.)
12. *African Socialism* pointed out that 'Some of these allowances were designed during colonial times to serve expatriate civil servants and settlers who looked overseas for security, vacations, and education for their children' (p.35).
13. See Tony Killick, Discussion Paper No. 239, 1976, p.36.
14. World Bank Report, p.16.
15. *Economic Survey*, 1976, p.51.
16. See *Economic Survey*, 1975, p.176, and 1978, p.173. The elimination of tuition fees was extended to Standard 5 in 1978 and it is planned further to extend it to Standard 6 in 1979 and to Standard 7 in 1980. See *Economic Survey*, 1978, p.170.
17. Compare 'In Kenya, education is the outstanding example of a service which has claimed an ever increasing proportion of the recurrent budget, and which now appears to absorb a disproportionate share of national resources.' World Bank, p.171. The figures quoted above have been for total expenditure, not recurrent expenditure. Education takes a larger share of the latter than the former, because it has large expenditures on salaries as compared with capital formation. But there is no different conclusion reached from the recurrent expenditure alone. In 1971/2 the proportion of expenditure on education in all recurrent expenditure was 24 per cent; in 1976/7 the figure was 26.6 per cent. The provisional figure for 1977/8 amounts to under 21 per cent, though the figure budgeted for 1978/9 amounts to 27 per cent. The increase hardly qualifies for alarm at 'an ever increasing proportion', though it is large by any standards, it is a matter of judgement whether it amounts to 'a disproportionate share of national resources'. There had earlier indeed been a sharp rise in the proportion of recurrent expenditure devoted to education, just as there had been in the proportion of total expenditure, recurrent and development, at the time of the transfer of responsibility from the County Councils. The World Bank figures, Table 17, pp.226–7, which are remarkably constant between 1964/5 and 1968/9, show a jump from 12 per cent in the latter year to 18.1 per cent in 1969/70 and to 25.8 per cent in 1970/1 (the World Bank percentages are higher than those given above, because they have made some deductions from total recurrent expenditure, but the argument is unaffected). The relative constancy of the percentage reappears in the subsequent years. It looks as if the World Bank seized on the illusion rather than the reality by ignoring the effect on the figures of the transfer of responsibility for primary education from the County Councils.
18. See *Economic Survey*, 1972, p.171.
19. See *Economic Survey*, 1978, p.170.
20. This, we must hasten to add, is a purely hypothetical statement, and should not be taken as a hint that there is or ever has been any intention to do so. It has been estimated that in 1976 private expenditure on education, including fees and other charges at government schools, totalled K£37.9 m. Of the total

K£15.0 m. was on 'self-help' *Harambee* education. See *Economic Survey*, 1978, p.171.

21. World Bank, p.171. Elsewhere in the Report, however the authors diminish the force of this alarming prophecy by acknowledging that 'the share of recurrent expenditure going to education in the 1973/4 budget has declined slightly over the last year.' See p.201.
22. World Bank, p.171n.
23. World Bank, p.171.
24. World Bank, p.37.
25. This is suggested by the remarks in World Bank, p.177.
26. World Bank, p.271.
27. ILO Report, p.70.
28. ILO Report, p.67.
29. *Economic Survey*, 1968, p.118.
30. *Economic Survey*, 1978, p.71.
31. *Economic Survey*, 1977, p.57.
32. This is the proportion using the classification adopted in the *Economic Survey*. The *Statistical Abstract* puts expenditure on roads and water works in a separate class of Community Services, which reduces the total of Economic Services to less than that of Social Services.
33. For most of the points made in this paragraph see *Economic Survey*, 1968, pp.121-2.
34. There are some statistical difficulties as a new classification was introduced in the 1978 *Economic Survey*, and there seems to be some incompatibility with the previous issue.
35. *Economic Survey*, 1978, p.57.
36. Loc.cit.
37. See *Economic Survey*, 1978, Table 6.12.
38. See *Economic Survey*, 1977, Table 6.15. These figures do not, of course, include service charges on debt contracted after the beginning of 1976.
39. *Economic Survey*, 1978, pp.74–5.
40. See World Bank, pp.181–2.
41. *Economic Survey*, 1978, p.66.
42. Funded and the internal Unfunded Debt. Source of figures: *Economic Survey*, 1978, Tables 6.9 and 6.10.
43. See, e.g., A. Hazlewood, 'The Economics of Colonial Monetary Arrangements', *Social and Economic Studies*, 1954.
44. See W. T. Newlyn, *Money in an African Context*, Nairobi, 1967, and E.L. Furness, *Money and Credit in Developing Africa*, London, 1975.
45. Newlyn, op.cit., p.34.
46. See A. Hazlewood, *African Integration and Disintegration*, Oxford University Press, London, 1967, pp.102–5.
47. See W.T. Newlyn, op.cit., pp.42–9.
48. Newlyn, op.cit., p.146.
49. The information on which the discussion is based is taken mainly from the *Annual Reports* of the Central Bank of Kenya.
50. The following account relies heavily on J.R. King, 'Financial Policy in Kenya: The Background to the Reserve Crisis of 1971', Discussion Paper No. 186, IDS, University of Nairobi, November 1973. See also J.R. King, *Stabilization Policy in an African Setting: Kenya 1963-1973*, Heinemann, London, 1979.
51. See J.R. King, op.cit.
52. See *Economic Survey*, 1972, p.28n, and Central Bank of Kenya, *Annual Report*, 1972, p.12.

53. *Economic Survey*, 1972, p.29.
54. Net Government indebtedness to the Banking System: June 1971 to June 1972, + K£17.4 m.; June 1972 to June 1973, + K£3.7 m. Source: Central Bank of Kenya, *Annual Report*, p.17.
55. Central Bank of Kenya, *Annual Report*, 1972, p.22.
56. Central Bank of Kenya, *Annual Report*, 1975, p.17.
57. Central Bank of Kenya, op.cit., p.16.
58. Loc.cit.
59. Central Bank, *Annual Report*, 1978, p.17.
60. See Central Bank of Kenya, *Economic and Financial Review*, March 1969, p.15.
61. Central Bank of Kenya, *Annual Report*, 1977, p.16.
62. Central Bank of Kenya, *Annual Report*, 1976, p.7.
63. Central Bank of Kenya, op.cit., p.15.
64. Central Bank of Kenya, *Annual Report*, 1977, pp.13–14 and 17.
65. Central Bank of Kenya, *Annual Report*, 1978, p.14.
66. *Development Plan, 1974-1978*, pp.179–182. See also pp.28–31.
67. See Central Bank of Kenya, *Annual Report*, 1976, pp.12, 15–16, and 20.
68. Central Bank of Kenya, *Economic and Financial Review*, March 1969, p.15.
69. D.H. Robertson, *Money*, 1937 edn., p.179.
70. International Bank for Reconstruction and Development, *The Economic Development of Kenya*, 1963, p.108.
71. Though not the European Settlement Board! The 1963 IBRD report said 'It is easy to see in the present boards' structure the system of organization which divided farming in Kenya into geographic areas on racial lines, with commercial production being undertaken almost entirely in the scheduled areas by expatriate farmers.' (p.109.).
72. *African Socialism . . . in Kenya*, paras. 83, 84, 91, 114, 120, 123.
73. P.Marris and A.Somerset, *African Businessmen: A Study of Entrepreneurship and Development in Kenya*, Routledge & Kegan Paul, London, 1971.
74. The ICDC Investment Company was established in 1967 to promote African participation, and ICDC is off-loading its shares by sales to citizens. Some three-quarters of its capital was held by local investors at the beginning of 1978. See ICDC, *Kenyan Partner in Progress* (1978).
75. ICDC News, December 1977.
76. See ICDC, Report and Accounts, 1976/7.
77. Kenya Industrial Estates Ltd. *Annual Report*, 1976–7.
78. See ILO, p.194.
79. *Industry in Kenya*, DFCK Newsletter, August 1976.
80. See Marris and Somerset, op.cit., pp.169–70.
81. Bruce Dinwiddy, *Promoting African Enterprise*, Croom Helm and Overseas Development Institute, London, 1974.
82. International Monetary Fund, *Surveys of African Economies*, vol. 2, Washington, D.C., 1969, p.161.
83. For a highly critical examination of DFCK see V. Vinnai, 'The Role of the Development Finance Company of Kenya in the Industrialization Process', Discussion Paper No. 180, IDS, University of Nairobi, November 1973.
84. DFCK, *Annual Report*, 1977, p.7.
85. ILO, p.205n.
86. ILO, p.207.
87. Leys, pp.152–3.
88. *Development Plan, 1974-1978*, p.377.

89. The full list is: (a) Cereals and Sugar Finance Corporation; Agricultural Finance Corporation. (b) Agricultural Development Corporation; Kenya Tea Development Authority; National Irrigation Board; Sugar Authority; Pineapple Authority. (c) Kenya Meat Commission; Coffee Board of Kenya; Pyrethrum Marketing Board; Maize and Produce Board; Cotton Lint and Seed Marketing Board. (d) Kenya Sisal Board; Kenya Dairy Board; Pyrethrum Board; Pig Industry Board; Tea Board of Kenya; Wheat Board; Horticultural Cooperative Development Authority. See W.M. Senga in Heyer *et al.*, p.100.
90. See Heyer *et al.*, op.cit., p.324.
91. *Development Plan 1974-1978*, p.212.
92. *Economic Survey*, 1978, p.103.
93. *Development Plan, 1974-1978*, p.214.
94. *Development Plan, 1974-1978*, p.214.
95. Heyer, *et al.*, pp.355–6.
96. See Heyer *et al.*, pp.344–6.
97. See *Economic Survey*, 1976, p.90.
98. IBRD, *The Economic Development of Kenya*, p.128.
99. See Heyer *et al.*, pp.328–30 and references given there.
100. See Heyer *et al.*, pp.330–4.
101. *Development Plan, 1966-1970*, p.80.
102. B. Van Arkadie, *East Africa J.*, August 1970.
103. *African Socialism . . . in Kenya.*
104. p.36.
105. E.O. Edwards, *East African Economic Review*, December 1968.
106. *Development Plan 1966-1970*, pp.81–8.
107. Judith Heyer, 'Kenya's Cautious Development Plan', *East Africa Journal*, August 1966.
108. Judith Heyer, op.cit.
109. *Development Plan, 1966-1970*, pp.66–7.
110. D.P. Ghai, 'How Good is Kenya's Plan?' *East Africa Journal*, July 1964.
111. *Development Plan 1966-1970*, p.60.
112. Colin Leys, *East Africa Journal*, March 1970, which also contains comments on the Plan by D.P. Ghai, Emil Rado, Frank Mitchell, Peter Hopcraft, and L.D. Smith.
113. Sessional Paper No.10 of 1973, *Employment*, May 1973.
114. *Development Plan 1974-1978*, p.148.
115. This discussion of the Plan draws heavily on Tony Killick, op.cit.
116. Plan, p.207.
117. See Plan, p.199.
118. Plan, p.8.
119. Loc.cit.
120. See Chapters 5 and 7. See Plan, pp.169–70 and elsewhere.
121. *Development Plan 1974-1978*, p.iii.

CHAPTER 9

1. Annual mean 1967-75, North Eastern Province, Garissa, Central Province, Kiambu.
2. The Provincial comparison is to a significant degree a tribal comparison. Other tribal comparisons can also be made, as in John R. Nellis, 'The Ethnic Composition of Leading Kenyan Government Positions', Research Report No. 24, The Scandinavian Institute of African Studies, Uppsala, 1974.
3. 19.4 – 17.2 = 2.2.

4. The figures may also be affected, as may entries in other Rows of the Table, by the fact that the population figures are from the 1969 Census whereas the figures for the other items are for the middle or late 1970s. This cannot be avoided with the available data, and probably very little distortion is introduced in any case.
5. *Integrated Rural Survey, 1974–75*, pp.50–1.
6. The figures show dissaving in Central and Western Provinces and savings of 35 per cent and 25 per cent of income in Nyanza and Rift Valley Provinces respectively. Op.cit., Table 8.4.
7. See Lijoodi and Ruthenberg, op.cit.
8. Eric Crawford and Erik Thorbecke, 'Employment, Income Distribution, Poverty Alleviation and Basic Needs in Kenya', Report of an ILO Consulting Mission, Cornell University, April 1978.
9. There is also a 'modern rural' population which receives 23 per cent of income according to the analysis.
10. Crawford and Thorbecke take urban prices as 1.54 of rural prices. An earlier study (M.FG. Scott, J.D. MacArthur, D.M.G. Newbery, *Project Appraisal in Practice*, Heinemann, London, 1976, p.173) put the ratio as between 1.6 and 1.8.
11. e.g. a higher dependency ratio in rural than in urban households works in one direction and the remission of funds from urban to rural areas in the other.
12. *Economic Survey*, 1978, p.101.
13. Op.cit., p.58.
14. World Bank, p.283.
15. The *Integrated Rural Survey, 1974–75*, Tables 8.8 and 8.12, shows own-produced items (excluding housing) to be valued at 38 per cent of total consumption, and remittances and gifts to account for 11 per cent of household income over all, and for as much as 29 per cent in Coast Province. A Nairobi survey showed that 21 per cent of the urban wage bill was remitted (ILO Report, p.48.)
16. See ILO Report, p.46.
17. ILO Report, p.45.
18. Andrew Hake, *African Metropolis: Nairobi's Self-Help City*, Sussex University Press, 1977, p.173.
19. Hake, op.cit., p.54.
20. *Daily Nation*, 11 Oct. 1975.
21. *Sunday Nation*, 25 Sept. 1977.
22. *Standard*, 5 July 1977.
23. Hake, op.cit.
24. Hake, op.cit., p.161.
25. Hake, loc.cit.
26. Hake, loc.cit.
27. Sessional Paper on Employment, No. 10 of 1973.
28. See above, Chapter 6.
29. Hake, op.cit., p.168.
30. Hake, op.cit., p.170. It was reported (*Standard*, 4 Apr. 1978) that plots were to be allocated to shanty dwellers with security of tenure and assistance for self-help.
31. G.N. Kitching, op.cit., p.50.
32. A detailed and dispassionate collection of data on women is to be found in *Women in Kenya*, Central Bureau of Statistics, July 1978.

33. Nancy Owano, *Sunday Nation*, 2 Oct. 1977.
34. In only 7 per cent of households is water collected by adult males. One-quarter of households are more than 1 km from a supply of water; in Eastern Province the proportion is 35 per cent and in Coast Province 60 per cent. In more than half of all households water is collected three or more times daily. *Women in Kenya*, p.14, using data from 1975 Integrated Rural Survey.
35. See ILO Report, p.47.
36. See ILO Report, pp.358–9, for a vivid description of one example.
37. *Women in Kenya*, p.42.
38. Op.cit., p.45. Data from Labour Enumeration Survey.
39. Op.cit., p.18.
40. Op.cit., p.52.
41. Op.cit., p.62.
42. A side-light is thrown on attitudes by the remark of a magistrate in sentencing a prostitute for theft from a client, a District Officer, that she had 'abused the privilege accorded to her'. *Daily Nation*, 1 May 1976.
43. The debate was conducted, I recall from the newspaper reports at the time, with some jocularity and humour on the part of the male legislators.
44. S.B.O. Gutto, 'The Status of Women in Kenya', Discussion Paper No. 235. IDS, University of Nairobi, April 1976.
45. p.21.
46. Mrs. Mondlane, reported in *Sunday Nation*, 10 Sept. 1978.
47. See ILO, p.86.
48. See Chapter 6(a).
49. That the entrepreneurial spirit nevertheless survives is indicated, for instance by the 'window dressing' that goes on. An example is a report that in a country area where two Asians had been refused premise licences for a motor spares business, 'the council was surprised to find [them] later operating the business in different premises in protection of an influential African', *Standard*, 19 Aug. 1978.
50. ILO, p.88.
51. p.220.
52. ILO Report, p.96.
53. ILO Report, p.254.
54. Michael Hodd, 'Income Distribution in Kenya (1963–72)', *Journal of Development Studies*, April 1976.
55. *Economic Survey*, 1978, p.16.
56. By H. Chenery and others, World Bank, 1974.
57. By S. Jain, World Bank, 1975.
58. ILO Report, p.73n.
59. Dan Usher, *The Price Mechanism and the Meaning of National Income Statistics*, Clarendon Press Oxford, 1968, p.xi.
60. Usher, op.cit., p.53.
61. B. Disraeli, *Sybil Or the Two Nations*, 1845.
62. To this extent the argument used by I.B. Kravis *et al.*, op.cit., p.18, about the revealed preference of peasants for the consumption patterns of 'middle-income urban dwellers' is entirely valid. See below for further discussion of this point.
63. e.g. 'In Kenya, wage earners, especially in the urban formal sector, represent a privileged minority of the labor force' (*Kenya: Into the Second Decade*, p.100.) 'Persons with incomes between £200 and £600 may be labelled the middle-income group: this group would include a significant proportion of the employees in the non-agricultural formal sector' (ILO Report, p.75).

64. However, the Integrated Rural Survey shows more than one-third of those covered by the survey, which includes the poorer sections of the population, to be in this income group. Whereas the ILO figures show that 63 per cent of households have an annual income of below £60, that percentage of the IRS households have incomes below £200, which implies a very different degree of poverty.
65. Figures from ILO Report, pp.254–5.
66. The ILO Report contains an annex entitled 'The Anatomy of Low Income' in which there are brief case studies of how the poor survive. More understanding is to be gained from these few pages than from all the statistics on income distribution. What is needed, in addition to further research into poverty, are corresponding studies of 'The Anatomy of "High" Income'. Such documentation of the life of wage earners in the towns and of successful small farmers would begin to make it possible to give some meaning to the figures of income distribution.
67. I.B. Kravis *et al.*, op.cit.
68. The *Integrated Rural Survey Report* has figures for transfers and gifts.
69. This is the assumption made by Kravis and his co-authors.
70. The welfare loss in moving back to the old way of life would therefore be greater than the original gain from moving out of it.
71. It may also show that, given the incentive, the poor may have the ability to raise their attainments.
72. The point is succinctly made in the play *The Prisoner of 2nd Avenue*. The husband and wife are discussing their financial problems. She says, 'Well, we don't have to live in New York. We can move to Spain. People live on 1500 dollars a year in Spain.' He says, 'Spanish people'.
73. In the 1977 Budget Speech he said: 'It is difficult to avoid the conclusion that . . . there is now a significant body of persons in this country who are not paying the taxes they are legally required to pay. Deliberate tax evasion is now a serious problem.'
74. Reported in *Daily Nation*, 12 Sept. 1978.
75. Table 25 of the ILO Report, the figures of which are reproduced in Table 9.4 above, includes in its second highest income category, £600–£1,000 per household, 'big farmers', admittedly the 'less prosperous', but even so, how small can be big? The third-highest income group includes 'prosperous' smallholders, who get at least £200, and perhaps as much as £600 a year per household. It clearly does not require a very high income to be among the 'rich'.
76. F. Stewart in U.G. Damachi *et al.*, op.cit., pp.85, 97.
77. Even though that poverty is not measurable in terms of US cents 3 per head per day!
78. E. Crawford and E. Thorbecke, op.cit.
79. Households are not nuclear families and there is a very wide range of household sizes.
80. See *Integrated Rural Survey, 1974–75*, Table 6.10
81. Loc.cit., Tables 9.2–9.7. nor is it easy to reconcile the conclusion with the 35 per cent saving ratio in Nyanza. See above, p.179 and n.6.
82. Traditional and hybrid maize, beans, sorghum, and finger millet.
83. The study uses figures of consumption as a proxy for income because of problems they found with the IRS income figures.
84. For a discussion of the difficulties in a more general context see Colin Clark, *Population Growth and Land Use*, Macmillan, London, 1967, pp.123–30.

85. The 1979 population census may push forward knowledge of what is happening. It may show that fertility rates have fallen sharply, and if so it may be that poverty is the reason, but there cannot be much evidence at the moment.
86. See summary reports on the survey in *Social Perspectives*, September 1977, and *Economic Survey*, 1978, pp.186–7.
87. Although there have been surpluses for some years, a turn in the weather could bring a general scarcity and widespread hunger would be a possibility.
88. ILO Report, p.96n.
89. *Integrated Rural Survey*, Tables 7.1, 9.2, 9.3, 9.10.
90. *Economic Survey*, 1978, p.103.
91. ILO Report, p.405.
92. *Integrated Rural Survey, 1974–75*, Table 7.1. A rough calculation based on Table 7.1, using the mid-point of each size class except the largest open-ended class, indicates that 2,982,000 hectares, equal to 86 per cent of the total area of holdings (*Statistical Abstract*, 1977, Table 109), were in holdings of less than 8 hectares.
93. ILO Report, p.327.
94. There is much to be said, and much is being said, about the nature of education, its appropriateness to Kenya conditions, and its role in producing educated unemployed. The present author is disinclined to accept the fashionable view, in which reactionaries and progressives are kin, that an increase in education can be a bad thing, and that those who will end up as hewers of wood and drawers of water should be educated only for that role in life.
95. See Tony Killick, op.cit., for a thoughtful and balanced review of the question.
96. The following is an abbreviated version of Table 9.5 in which the labour force is divided by sex:

	(Thousands)			
	1976		1999	
	Men	Women	Men	Women
(i) Small-scale farming and other rural work	1,841	2,466	3,110	4,290
(ii) Modern sector, non-agricultural	623	110	2,290	1,184
(iii) All other economic activity	472	319	621	447
(iv) Residual: Unemployment	114	331	122	589
(v) Table (i)–(iv)	3,050	3,226	6,143	6,510

Source: As for Table 9.5.

97. See above, Chapter 4.
98. ILO Report, p.328.
99. See Killick, op.cit.
100. *Economic Survey*, 1978, p.188.

READING LIST

Official Periodical Publications

Central Bank of Kenya, *Annual Report.*

Central Bank of Kenya, *Economic and Financial Review* (Quarterly).

Central Bureau of Statistics, Ministry of Finance and Planning, *Economic Survey* (Annual).

Central Bureau of Statistics, Ministry of Finance and Planning, *Kenya Statistical Digest* (Quarterly).

Central Bureau of Statistics, Ministry of Finance and Planning, *Social Perspectives*, (Several issues a year since June 1976).

Central Bureau of Statistics, Ministry of Finance and Planning, *Statistical Abstract* (Annual).

History

History of East Africa, Vol. i edited by Roland Oliver and Gervase Mathew, 1963, Vol. ii edited by Vincent Harlow and E.M. Chilver, assisted by Alison Smith, 1965, Vol. iii edited by D.A. Low and Alison Smith, 1976, Clarendon Press, Oxford.

Sorrenson, M.P.K., *Origins of European Settlement in Kenya*, Oxford University Press, Nairobi, 1968.

Zwanenburg, Roger van, *The Agricultural History of Kenya to 1939*, East African Publishing House, Nairobi, 1972.

Wolff, Richard D., *The Economics of Colonialism: Britain and Kenya, 1870–1930*, Yale University Press, New Haven and London, 1974.

The Economy

Christian Council of Kenya, *Who Controls Industry in Kenya*? Report of a Working Party, East African Publishing House, Nairobi, 1968.

Clayton, Anthony and Savage, Donald C., *Government and Labour in Kenya, 1895–1963*, Frank Cass, London, 1974.

Cliffe, Lionel, 'Underdevelopment or Socialism? A Comparative Analysis of Kenya and Tanzania', in Richard Harris, ed., *The Political Economy of Africa*, John Wiley & Sons, New York, 1975.

Court, David, and Ghai, Dharam P., eds., *Education, Society and Development: New Perspectives from Kenya*, Oxford University Press, Nairobi, 1974.

Hake, Andrew, *African Metropolis: Nairobi's Self-Help City*, Chatto & Windus for Sussex University Press, London, 1977.

Hazlewood, Arthur, *Rail and Road in East Africa*, Basil Blackwell, Oxford, 1964.

—— *Economic Integration: The East African Experience*, Heinemann, London, 1975.

Heyer, Judith, Maitha, J.K., and Senga, W.M., eds., *Agricultural Development in Kenya: An Economic Assessment*, Oxford University Press, Nairobi, 1976.

Holtham, Gerald, and Hazlewood, Arthur, *Aid and Inequality in Kenya: British Development Assistance to Kenya*, Croom Helm and Overseas Development Institute, London, 1975.

International Bank for Reconstructions and Development, *The Economic Development of Kenya*, The John Hopkins Press, Baltimore, 1963.

International Labour Office, *Employment, Incomes and Equality: A Strategy for Increasing Productive Employment in Kenya*, ILO, Geneva, 1972.

Kaplinsky, Raphael, ed., *Readings on the Multinational Corporations in Kenya*, Oxford University Press, Nairobi, 1978.

King, J.R., *Stabilization Policy in an African Setting: Kenya 1963–1973*, Heinemann, London, 1979.

King, Kenneth, *The African Artisan: Education and the Informal Sector in Kenya,* Heinemann, London, 1977.

Leys, Colin, *Underdevelopment in Kenya: The Political Economy of Neo-Colonialism*, Heinemann, London, 1975.

Marris, Peter, and Somerset, Anthony, *African Businessmen: A Study of Entrepreneurship and Development in Kenya*, Routledge & Kegan Paul, London, 1971.

Nyangira, Nicholas, *Relative Modernization and Public Resource Allocation in Kenya*, East African Literature Bureau, Nairobi, 1975.

Ogendo, R.B., *Industrial Geography of Kenya*, East African Publishing House, Nairobi, 1972.

Rempel, Henry, and House, William J., *The Kenya Employment Problem*, Oxford University Press, Nairobi, 1978.

Sandbrook, Richard, *Proletarians and African Capitalism: The Kenyan Case, 1960–1972*, Cambridge University Press, London, 1975.

Sheffield, James R., ed., *Education, Employment and Rural Development*, The proceedings of a Conference held at Kericho, Kenya, in September 1966, East African Publishing House, Nairobi, 1967.

Sorrenson, M.P.K., *Land Reform in the Kikuyu Country: A Study in Government Policy*, Oxford University Press, Nairobi, 1967.

Ominde, Simeon, *The Population of Kenya, Tanzania and Uganda*, Heinemann, Nairobi, 1975.

Soja, Edward W., *The Geography of Modernization in Kenya: A Spatial Analysis of Social, Economic, and Political Change*, Syracuse University Press, Syracuse, N.Y., 1968.

Stewart, Frances, 'Kenya: Strategies for Development' in *Development Paths in Africa and China*, ed. U.G. Damachi *et al.*, Macmillan, London, 1976.

World Bank, *Kenya: Into the Second Decade*, The John Hopkins University Press, Baltimore and London, 1975.

INDEX